THE TRIUMPH OF INJUSTICE

THE TRIUMPH OF INJUSTICE

How the Rich Dodge Taxes and How to Make Them Pay

EMMANUEL SAEZ
AND **GABRIEL ZUCMAN**

W. W. NORTON & COMPANY
Independent Publishers Since 1923

Web addresses appearing in this book reflect existing links as of the date of first publication. No endorsement of, or affiliation with, any third-party website should be inferred. W. W. Norton & Co., Inc., is not responsible for third-party content (website, blog, information page, or otherwise).

For information about permission to reproduce selections
from this book, write to Permissions, W. W. Norton & Company, Inc.,
500 Fifth Avenue, New York, NY 10110

For information about special discounts for bulk purchases,
please contact W. W. Norton Special Sales at
specialsales@wwnorton.com or 800-233-4830

Manufacturing by Lake Book Manufacturing
Book design by Lovedog Studio
Production manager: Beth Steidle

ISBN 978-1-324-00272-7

W. W. Norton & Company, Inc.
500 Fifth Avenue, New York, N.Y. 10110
www.wwnorton.com

W. W. Norton & Company Ltd.
15 Carlisle Street, London W1D 3BS

1 2 3 4 5 6 7 8 9 0

CONTENTS

Introduction

REINVENTING FISCAL DEMOCRACY

The evening of September 26, 2016, was off to a good start for Hillary Clinton. The former secretary of state had the upper hand in her first election debate against Donald Trump, the reality-show celebrity who had won the Republican primary. Nervous and aggressive, the GOP candidate kept interrupting his opponent. The Democratic candidate, well prepared and relaxed, kept scoring points—when suddenly the debate turned to taxes.

Breaking with a tradition dating back to the early 1970s, Trump had refused to release his tax returns, claiming he was prevented by an ongoing audit from the Internal Revenue Service. Clinton baited the billionaire real estate developer into talking about how little he had paid over the years: "The only tax returns that anybody's seen was when he was trying to get a casino license, and they showed he didn't pay any federal income tax." Trump proudly admitted to it: "That makes me smart." Clinton did not snap back. A dispassionate exposition of the well-crafted, carefully weighted, thoughtful technocratic fixes she had envisioned for the nation's tax code would not have carried the day.

Politically, "That makes me smart" was a shrewd line. That one of the country's wealthiest men could, by his own admission, pay no tax at all was so absurd that it reinforced the central narrative of the Trump campaign: The Washington, DC, establishment had failed the country. The tax code, like everything else, was rigged. In Trump's answer there was an echo of President Ronald Reagan himself, who famously compared the tax code to "daily mugging." In both Trump's and Reagan's views, the relentless pursuit of self-interest supports the prosperity of all. Capitalism harnesses human greed for the greater good. Taxes are a hindrance and avoiding them is the right thing to do.

At the same time, "That makes me smart" exposed the paradox of this ideology. Relentless self-interest destroys the norms of trust and cooperation at the heart of any prosperous society. Trump himself would be nothing without the infrastructure that connects his skyscrapers to the rest of the world, the sewer system that carries their waste, the teachers who taught his lawyers how to read, the doctors and the public research that keep him healthy, let alone the laws and courts that protect his property. What makes communities thrive is not any unfettered free-for-all, it is cooperation and collective action. Without taxes there is no cooperation, no prosperity, no common destiny—there is not even a nation in need of a president.

Trump's boast revealed a failure of American society. It had become so natural that the affluent do not contribute to the public coffers that a candidate for the presidency would openly admit to it while his opponent offered no clear solution in response. The country's tax system—the most important institution of any democratic society—had failed.

We wrote this book with two objectives in mind: the first, to understand how exactly the United States got into this mess; the second, to help fix it.

THE TRIUMPH OF INJUSTICE

Candidate Trump's admission was only anecdotal evidence of a new injustice in America. Even as their incomes boomed, as they reaped the rewards from globalization, and their wealth skyrocketed to previously unseen heights, the most fortunate Americans have seen their tax rates fall. Meanwhile, for the working class, wages stagnated, work conditions deteriorated, debts ballooned, and taxes rose. Since 1980 the tax system has enriched the winners in the market economy and impoverished those who realized few rewards from economic growth.

Any democracy must debate the proper size of government and the ideal degree of tax progressivity. Informed by history and international experience, by statistics and abstract reasoning, it is natural for individuals and countries alike to sometimes change views. But have the tax policy changes of the last decades been the result of such an informed deliberation? Has the collapse in taxes for the ultra-rich reflected what Americans as a society wanted?

We doubt it. Some of these changes were the result of conscious choices. But many more have been borne passively: the outbreak of a tax-avoidance industry that obscures income and wealth; the emergence, with globalization, of new loopholes exploited by multinational companies; the spiral of international tax competition that has led countries to slash their tax rates one after another. Most of the changes in taxation are due not to a sudden popular appetite for exempting the wealthy, but to forces that have prevailed without input from voters. Whether or not tax cuts can have positive economic effects, the upheavals of the last decades are not, by and large, the product of rational choices deliberated on and made by an informed citizenry. The triumph of tax injustice is, above all, a denial of democracy.

The first contribution of this book is to tell the story of this great transformation. Our story is not one of Left versus Right. It is not about the triumph of small-government conservatives over spread-the-wealth liberals. It is the story of how the tax system established by the New Deal was undermined. At each step of its demise, we find the same pattern. It starts with an outburst of tax avoidance. It continues with policymakers letting this tax avoidance fester, paralyzed by supposedly invincible foes—tax shelters, globalization, tax havens, financial opacity. And it ends with governments slashing the tax rates of the wealthy under the pretense that taxing the richest among us had become impossible.

To understand this injustice, and which choices (and non-choices) have contributed to its triumph, we have undertaken an in-depth economic investigation. Drawing on a century of statistics, we have estimated how much each social group, from the poorest up to billionaires, has paid in tax since 1913 in the United States. Our data series include all taxes paid to the federal, state, and local governments: the federal income tax, of course, but also state income taxes, myriad sales and excise taxes, the corporate income tax, business and residential property taxes, and payroll taxes. The distinction between "taxes paid by households" and "taxes paid by businesses" is meaningless: all taxes are paid by people, and our work allocates all taxes to existing individuals over more than a century.

Our approach is systematic. President Trump may brag that he does not pay much tax, but what about other rich people? Is Trump an anomaly or an example of a broader phenomenon? Individual cases can raise awareness, but however eyepopping they cannot allow us to understand what's happening in society at large. To study the changes in taxation and their implications, we have methodically combined the available evidence in a consistent framework: tabulations of income tax returns; results from tax audits; household survey data; reports on the profits booked by US multinationals in their offshore subsidiaries; macroeconomic balance sheets; and national and international accounts. Economic statistics are never perfect—ours have their limitations, which we will note in due course. But taken together, this combination of data unveils which choices, laws, and policies have fueled tax injustice.

This comprehensive perspective—the fruit of years of research on the US economy—allows us to study long-run changes in the progressivity of the US tax system in its entirety, which no government agency or research institution had been able to do so far. The data reveal the scale of the changes that have occurred over recent decades including, for the first time, the consequences of Donald Trump's presidency.

Let's take a look: In 1970, the richest Americans paid, all taxes included, more than 50% of their income in taxes, twice as much as working-class individuals. In 2018, following the Trump tax reform, and for the first time in the last hundred years, billionaires have paid less than steel workers, schoolteachers, and retirees. The wealthy have seen their taxes rolled back to levels last seen in the 1910s, when the government was only a quarter of the size it is today. It is as if a century of fiscal history has been erased.

GLOBAL TAX JUSTICE NOW

Beyond America, our story is more fundamentally about the future of globalization and the future of democracy. For although the changes in taxation have been extreme on this side of the Atlantic, the triumph of tax injustice is not specific to the United States. Most countries have, to a varying extent, seen inequality rise and tax progressivity fall in a context of rising tax avoidance and unfettered tax competition. The same questions bubble up throughout the world, with the same urgency: If the taxes enacted by our elected officials keep boosting the income of a privileged minority, who will keep faith in democratic institutions? If globalization means ever-lower taxes for its main winners and ever-higher taxes for those it leaves out, who will keep faith in globalization? There is no time to lose: We must invent the new fiscal institutions and the new forms of cooperation that will help democracy and international openness flourish into the twenty-first century.

The good news is that we can fix tax injustice, right now. There is nothing inherent in globalization that destroys our ability to tax big companies and the wealthy. The choice is ours. We can let multinationals pick the country where they declare their profits, or we can pick for them. We can tolerate financial opacity and the countless possibilities of tax abuse that come with it, or we can choose to measure, record, and tax wealth. We can countenance a sprawling industry that helps the affluent dodge taxation, or we can choose to regulate it and weed out the supply of tax dodges. It is possible to make globalization and progressive taxation compatible. The second contribution of this book is to demonstrate how.

Many on both Left and Right are convinced that taxing multinational corporations is now nearly impossible. Try to tax them and they will relocate to Ireland, Singapore, or perhaps, tomorrow, China. Their capital is intangible, it can move to Bermuda in a nanosecond. Other countries have low tax rates? We must have low rates. Other countries are giving up on taxing multinational companies and high earners? We must give up too. Tax coordination among countries is a utopia and the only future is a race to the bottom.

No matter how sincerely held they may be, no matter how widely shared, these beliefs are incorrect. Instead of engaging in a giant fiscal free-for-all, we can coordinate our policies, as we've successfully done in many other areas of international relations. Rest assured, we know that some countries and social groups derive large benefits from globalization in its current form—but other forms are possible.

We will study, in the pages that follow, the arithmetic of tax competition and the central role it has played in the prosperity of a few. But we'll also see how a handful of countries acting together could whistle the end of this game. We will see how defensive measures could be taken against tax havens, and how today's race to the bottom can be replaced by a race to the top.

The notion that external or technical constraints—"international competition," "tax avoidance," "loopholes"—make tax justice idle fantasy does not withstand scrutiny. When it comes to the future of taxation, everything is possible. From the disappearance of the income tax—a plausible outcome if the trend of the last four decades is sustained—to levels of progressivity never seen before, there is an infinity of possible futures ahead of us.

DEMOCRACY

Should billionaires pay 23% of their income in taxes, as they do in today's America, or closer to 50%, as they did around 1970? Should corporate profits be taxed at 52% as in 1960 or at 21% as they have been since the 2018 tax reform? These questions will never be settled by data or science, and quite fortunately! They are not questions for economists. They are questions for all people, who should decide on them through democratic deliberation and the vote. Where economists can help is by assembling the information vital to a government of the people, by the people, and for the people. It is by showing the multiplicity of possible paths, and by describing these paths and their implications—how different distributions of taxes would affect each of us, and how the choices we make today will shape the growth of income for various social groups tomorrow.

The third contribution of this book is to create a new tool that does just that. *Taxjusticenow.org* is a simulation website that allows policymakers, activists, and all people—whatever their political stripe, school of thought, or knowledge about economics—to estimate the effect of tax policy changes on the distribution of taxes, the income and wealth of each social group, and the dynamics of inequality. The website allows anyone to assess how modifications of the parameters of the current tax system—as well as bolder reforms—would affect society. Would increasing the top marginal income tax rate to 70% suffice to make billionaires contribute more to the public coffers—all taxes included—than working-class Americans? What if we increased the corporate tax rate to 30% or created a new wealth tax on the super-wealthy? By how much could taxes on the middle class be cut, or the deficit reduced?

These questions will always play an important role in the political debate, yet there is currently no way for the public to obtain precise answers to them. Tax simulators exist within the US Treasury, the Congressional Budget Office, and some think tanks, such as the Tax Policy Center and the Institute on Taxation and Economic Policy, but they are out of reach to journalists, candidates, and the broader electorate.

In that context, most discussions about taxes end up quite vague. On the Left it's common to assert that the 1% owns so much wealth that sizable sums could be collected by taxing them more. This is true, but the assertion needs precision: How much revenue, exactly, could we expect to raise from increasing taxes on the affluent? Would it be enough to fund free public college education and health insurance for all? Among centrists, many lament existing tax loopholes in a steady drumbeat; if only we could plug these, no more changes would be necessary. Closing loopholes is important, but are we sure that it would make a real difference to the distribution of tax payments? On the right, orthodoxy dictates that, combining all taxes, one can see that top marginal tax rates are already high. Adding additional levies would be punitive or hurt economic growth; instead, the United States should introduce a consumption tax. Why not—but wouldn't such a tax system be even more regressive than today's?

Taxjusticenow.org provides factual answers to these questions, based on a new economic approach. Our simulator includes all taxes at all levels of government—not only the income tax or federal taxes. It makes it possible to simulate fundamental innovations, such as introducing a progressive tax on wealth or a broad-based tax to fund health care for all. And while existing policy tools focus on the effect of tax changes on government revenues, ours shows their implications for a parameter that's too often missing from tax policy debates: inequality.

We've all seen the headlines about the rise of income and wealth concentration in America: the surge at the top and the slow growth for the rest. It is real: the share of US national income earned by the 1% has increased from 10% in 1980 to about 20% today. Will this trend continue? So much depends on what policies future governments will choose to implement, and especially on which tax policy will prevail.

Under business as usual, income concentration is likely to keep rising in the medium run thanks to a snowball effect: the wealthy save a higher fraction of their income than the rest of the population, which allows them to accumulate more wealth, which in turn generates additional income. For most of the twentieth century, progressive taxation—and especially high tax rates on capital (as opposed to labor)—had kept this spiral under control. But the tax changes of the last two decades have dismantled this safeguard.

To prevent inequality from reaching extreme levels, we will need to create a new tax system for the twenty-first century. Later in the book we offer a slate of original and practical proposals to realize this transformation, from the taxation of extreme wealth to collecting from multinational companies; from the funding of health care to the reinvention of the progressive income tax. Our solutions are not perfect, nor are they the only possible answers. But they are precise (they are carefully scored, and we have thought hard about their implementation), transparent (anybody can simulate their effect on the distribution of taxes and the dynamics of income and wealth for each social group), and supported by evidence and theory from modern research.

Are these ideas for taming inequality realistic, politically? It is easy to lose hope—dark money in politics and self-serving ideologies are powerful foes. These problems are real, but we should not despair. Before injustice triumphed, the United States was a beacon of tax justice. It was the democracy with perhaps the most steeply progressive system of taxation on the planet. In the 1930s, US policymakers invented—and then for almost half a century applied—top marginal income tax rates of 90% on the highest income earners. Corporate profits were taxed at 50%; large estates at close to 80%. With the revenue generated, the United States built the schools that made its people productive and prosperous, funding public universities that are still, to this day, the envy of the world.

The history of taxation, as we'll see shortly, is full of U-turns. If it is any guide, "smart" billionaires who do not pay much tax today will not fool us forever.

THE TRIUMPH OF INJUSTICE

Chapter 1

INCOME AND TAXES IN AMERICA

How redistributive is America's tax system? For some observers there's no doubt, taxes in the United States are highly progressive—you owe more, as a fraction of your income, as you earn more. European countries rely a lot on value-added taxes— a levy on consumption which, since the rich save more, disproportionately hits the poor. But there is no value-added tax in America: low-earners, as the argument goes, thus must pay relatively little. At the top of the pyramid, the federal government has no qualms about making the rich pay the country's bills through its progressive income tax, according to this view.

For many on the other side of the debate about tax progressivity, the truth is the opposite. The wealthy get off almost scot-free, by way of myriad loopholes in the tax laws and other legislated, special-interest breaks.

Who's right? Before we can have a serene debate about policy, we must establish some basic facts about who really pays what. Unfortunately, government agencies such as the Congressional Budget Office—in charge of informing Congress about budget and economic issues—do not provide the answer to that question, at least not fully. They publish information about the distribution of federal taxes, but disregard state and local taxes, which account for a third of all taxes paid by Americans and are much less progressive than federal levies. Their statistics do not provide specific information on the ultra-wealthy, so it's not possible to tell whether Donald Trump is an exception or an instance of a broader phenomenon among billionaires.

Let's try to lift the fog.

THE AVERAGE INCOME OF AMERICANS: $75,000

Our investigation begins with a simple question: What is the average income of Americans today? To answer it, we must introduce a concept that will play a critical role in this book: national income. By definition, national income measures all the income that accrues to the residents of a given country in a given year, whatever legal form this income takes. It's the broadest possible concept of income. It's a figure larger, in particular, than the income reported on tax returns or recorded in household surveys. For instance, it includes all the profits made by corporations, whether or not those profits are distributed to shareholders. Like dividends, undistributed profits are a form of income for shareholders—the only difference being that this income is fully saved the year it is earned and reinvested in the firm. National income also includes all the fringe benefits—such as contributions to private health insurance—that workers get through their employers.

National income is closely related to the more familiar concept of "gross domestic product" avidly scrutinized in the media. GDP, as it is called, measures the value of all the goods and services that are produced in a given year. It's a concept that first emerged in the aftermath of the Great Depression and became popular in the 1950s and 1960s. Before that, the notion of national income prevailed.

Today, however, the growth statistics that presidents and pundits like to comment upon always refer to the growth of GDP. In the United States, GDP per adult reached close to $90,000 in 2019.[1] That is, the average adult produced goods and services worth $90,000.

To get from GDP to national income requires two adjustments. First, you subtract capital depreciation—the loss in the value of the buildings, machines, and equipment used during production—that is an integral component of GDP (the reason why domestic product is "gross"). Depreciation does not correspond to any income for anybody: Before paying their workers, distributing dividends, and investing in new machines, businesses must first replace their worn-out equipment and other capital assets. Tractors get old and break down, windows must be fixed, and so on. Depreciation as measured in the national accounts is large, about 16% of GDP. In fact, depreciation is even larger than the national accounts measurement because production often is accompanied by the depletion of natural resources and the degradation of ecosystems. These forms of depreciation logically should be subtracted from GDP but currently aren't, although there are ongoing efforts to fix this flaw in economic statistics.[2]

The second adjustment to move from GDP to national income involves adding the income that the United States receives from abroad and subtracting what it pays to the rest of the world. In the 1950s and 1960s, when international capital markets were shut down, these international flows were negligible. Today, cross-border payments of interest and dividends are sizable. The United States pays 3.5% of its GDP to foreign countries—in the form of interest and dividends—and receives the equivalent of 5% of it from the rest of the world. On net it receives more than it pays.

After removing depreciation and adding the net flows of foreign income, US national income reaches about $18.5 trillion in 2019, or $75,000 on average among the 245 million adults (aged twenty and above) who live in the United States. This $75,000 is the same whether one looks at income before taxes and before government transfers—such as Social Security benefits and publicly funded health care spending—or at income after taxes and transfers. Whatever the government takes in taxes, it ultimately redistributes to flesh-and-blood individuals, whether in cash (such as in the case of Social Security benefits), in kind (such as when it pays for your health care), or by paying the wages of police officers, soldiers, and other public-sector employees. The government, quite fortunately, does not destroy any income. Nor does it create any, for that matter.

THE AVERAGE INCOME OF WORKING-CLASS AMERICANS: $18,500

Most Americans earn less than $75,000; some earn much more. To study income distribution in more detail, it is useful to divide the population into four groups: the working class (people in the lower half of the distribution), the middle class (the next 40%), the upper middle class (the next 9%), and the rich (the top 1%). While these groups are not homogenous, this simple act of division already reveals stark inequalities.

Let's start with the working class, the 122 million adults in the lower half of the income pyramid. For them, the average income is $18,500 before taxes and transfers in 2019. Yes, you are reading this correctly: half of the US adult population lives on an annual income of $18,500. Pause for a second and consider the top line of your paycheck, before any income tax deduction. We expect many readers will immediately realize the gulf that separates them from half of their fellow Americans. For 122 million adults, what the market brings is a grand total of $18,500 a year, about a quarter of the average income of $75,000 in the entire population. This figure is the most comprehensive estimate possible; it is obtained by starting with the broadest possible measure of income—national income—and distributing this total across the entire adult population, leaving nothing out. That $18,500 includes, for instance, dollars immediately paid by workers to the government (in the form of payroll taxes, to take one example) or by their employers to private insurance companies.

Further up the income pyramid, the next 40% (the "middle class") earns $75,000 on average before taxes and transfers, coincidentally also the average income in the entire population. This group, comprising almost 100 million adults, in that sense can be seen as representative of the country. Though we've all heard doomsday stories about the demise of the American middle class, the reality is more nuanced. With an average income of $75,000, the US middle class is still among the most prosperous on earth. Moreover, middle-class income has grown 1.1% a year since 1980, which, although nothing spectacular, is not negligible. At a rate of 1.1%, income doubles every seventy years: newer generations earn twice as much as their grandparents. The striking fact about the American economy is not that the middle class is vanishing. It's how little income the working class makes.

What about the people making more than the middle class? When one looks at the top of the income pyramid, it's important to distinguish the upper middle class (the top 10% excluding the top 1%) from the rich (the top 1%), because these two groups are in entirely different leagues. The upper middle class (22 million adults) are certainly not to be pitied. With an average income of $220,000 and everything that goes with it—spacious suburban houses, expensive private schools for their children, well-funded pensions, and good health insurance—they are not struggling. But as a group they do not have much in common with the 1% (the 2.4 million richest Americans), whose members make $1.5 million in income a year on average.

THE GAINS OF THE 1%: AS LARGE AS THE LOSSES OF THE BOTTOM 50%

Since the emergence of the slogan "We are the 99%," the public has become familiar with the divergence between the fortunes of the rich and those of the rest of society. But the idea bears repeating, because it reflects a fundamental truth about the American economy: over the last few decades, income has skyrocketed for those at the very top of the income distribution, and nowhere else. Some believe that successful, well-off professionals (the top 20%, say) have pulled away from the rest of the country.[3] In reality, what the data show is that the main fault line in the American society is higher up the pyramid: it is between the 1% and everybody else.

Perhaps nothing summarizes more succinctly the metamorphosis of the US economy than this simple illustration. In 1980, the top 1% earned a bit more than 10% of the nation's income, before government taxes and transfers, while the bottom 50% share was around 20%. Today, it's almost the opposite: the top 1% captures more than 20% of national income and the working class barely 12%. In other words, the 1% earns almost twice as much income as the entire working-class population, a group fifty times larger demographically. And the increase in the share of the pie going to 2.4 million adults has been similar in magnitude to the loss suffered by more than 100 million Americans.

The United States is unique, among advanced economies, to have witnessed such a radical change in fortunes. Rising income inequality is undoubtedly a global phenomenon, but the speed at which income concentration has been rising over the last four decades depends markedly on which countries you are looking at. Compare, for instance, the United States with Western Europe. In 1980, the

1.1 THE RISE OF INEQUALITY IN THE UNITED STATES, 1978-2018

(Share of national income earned by the top 1% vs. bottom 50%)

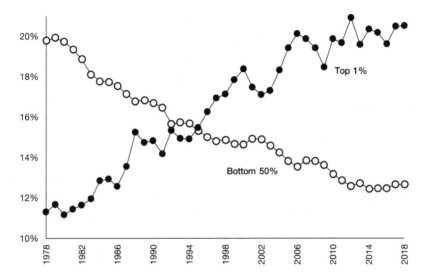

Notes: The figure depicts the share of pre-tax national income earned by the bottom 50% income earners and the top 1% earners since 1978. The unit is the individual adult with income equally split within married couples. The figure shows that the top 1% income share almost doubled from about 10% in 1980 to about 20% today. Conversely, the bottom 50% income share collapsed from around 20% in 1980 to about 12% today. Complete details at *taxjusticenow.org.*

top 1% share of national income was the same across the Atlantic, around 10%. In the ensuing years, however, the dynamic of inequality has looked very different. In Western Europe the top 1% income share has increased by two percentage points (instead of ten points as in America), to reach 12% today. The bottom 50% income share has declined two percentage points, from 24% to 22%.[4] Looking more broadly, there is no country among high-income democracies where inequality has increased as much as in America.

EVERYBODY PAYS TAXES

Now that we have a good view of how income is distributed in the United States, we can turn to taxes. In 2019, US residents paid the equivalent of a bit more than 28% of US national income in taxes to local, state, and federal governments combined. This corresponds on average to around $20,000 per adult. Of course, some pay more than $20,000 and others less. But nobody pays zero. Popular though it may be, the notion that 47% of the population does not contribute to the public coffers—the so-called "takers" lambasted by presidential candidate Mitt Romney in 2012—makes no sense. As a country, the United States has chosen to pool close to a third of its resources through its various forms of government. Every adult contributes to this effort. Romney was alluding only to the federal income tax, but there are many other taxes to consider when we ask, "Who pays?"

Broadly speaking, taxes in the United States—like in most other developed countries—can be grouped into four buckets: individual income taxes, payroll taxes, capital taxes, and consumption taxes. Each of these has a fascinating history and plays an important economic role.

The federal individual income tax, created in 1913, is the most well-known and largest tax in the United States, collecting about a third of all revenues (around 9% of national income out of 28%). Although the federal income tax is supposed to draw on all income, whether it derives from working (wages) or from owning capital (interest, dividends, capital gains, etc.), the income subject to taxation is less than the total amount of national income. Tax evasion contributes to this gap: since statisticians try to approximate the true income of Americans, they include estimates of the sums hidden from the taxman (based on random audits conducted by the IRS) to form an estimate of national income. But the main reason why income subject to taxation is less than national income is that many forms of income—especially of capital income—are legally tax-free.

Dividends and interest earned on retirement accounts? Tax-free. Undistributed corporate profits? Tax-free. Health insurance premiums paid through employers? Tax-free. The implicit rents that homeowners pay to themselves? The same. Today, income subject to the individual income tax (gross of any deduction) amounts to only 63% of US national income. Most of the rest of national income is legally exempted. Although politicians on both Left and Right generally insist that it's better to have a broad base—that is, the largest possible pool of money to draw taxes from—the base of the individual income tax has shrunk over the last decades. In 1980, 71% of national income was included in income subject to tax. The unceasing invocations of "base broadening" notwithstanding, Uncle Sam is taxing a smaller and smaller fraction of the pie.

The rates applied to this base ranged from 0% for the first $12,200 of income to 37% for incomes above $510,300 ($612,350 for married couples) in 2019. This makes the federal income tax a progressive tax. The opposite of a progressive tax is a regressive tax—one where the more you earn, the lower the fraction of your income you must pay. (And in between is the flat tax: a tax where everybody pays the same rate no matter his or her income.) Though it is progressive, today's income tax is much less so than it has been historically. Since the creation of the federal income tax in 1913, the top marginal income tax rate (the rate that applies to dollars earned in the top tax bracket, above $510,300 in 2019) has averaged 57%, twenty points more than the current top rate of 37%.

Besides the federal income tax, all states except seven[*] impose their own income taxes. States generally use the same definition of

---

[*] Alaska, Florida, Nevada, South Dakota, Texas, Washington, and Wyoming.

what constitutes taxable income as the federal government; they then apply their own rate schedule, with top marginal tax rates of up to 13% in California. A few cities (including New York) have their own income tax, too. Altogether, these state and local income taxes collect about 2.5% of national income in revenues, making total individual income tax revenues add up to 11.5% of US national income. With the corresponding tax base, as we have seen, at 63% of national income, the average income tax rate in the United States is a bit more than 18% (11.5% divided by 63%).

The second largest source of tax revenue is Social Security payroll taxes (8% of national income). These taxes are levied on labor earnings and come out of wage earners' paychecks—from the very first dollar earned—at a rate of 12.4%. They are capped at $132,900 a year in 2019, a figure that roughly corresponds to the threshold for being among the top 5% highest wage earners. Any earnings above that cap are exempt from taxation, making Social Security taxes deeply regressive. A separate tax is collected to fund Medicare—the government health insurance program for the elderly—at a rate of 2.9% on all earnings. Altogether these payroll taxes, which were small fifty years ago, have grown to become almost as large as the federal income tax itself. As we will see, this development has significantly contributed to eroding the progressivity of the American tax system.

The third largest source of tax revenue is consumption taxes: sales taxes levied by states and local governments, and excises (on gasoline, diesel fuel, alcohol, tobacco, etc.) levied by both the federal and sub-federal governments. License taxes (such as motor vehicle licenses and levies on the extraction of natural resources) also fall into this category, as well as trade tariffs—which are nothing other than sales taxes on imported goods. Altogether, consumption taxes total $3,500 per adult on average. That's equivalent to an average tax of 6% on personal consumption expenditure. Sales taxes represent about half of this total and excises and licenses the other half.

In spite of a sharp increase under President Trump, import duties still represent small sums, about a tenth of total consumption taxes in 2019.[5]

The last—and smallest—source of tax revenue is capital taxes. We include under this category the corporate income tax, residential and business property taxes, and the estate tax. Some tax capital income flows (the corporate income tax, which taxes corporate profits); others tax capital assets (either annually, as in the case of property taxes, or at the time of death or when gifts are made, as in the case of the estate and gift tax). Capital taxes add up to a bit more than 4% of national income. Since the total flow of capital income represents about 30% of national income in the United States, capital taxes are equivalent to an average tax of about 13% (4% divided by 30%) on capital income.

ONLY PEOPLE PAY TAXES

Regardless of which bucket they fall into, all taxes are paid by people. It would be great if "big corporations" or "robots" could pay taxes for us, but alas this is impossible. Just as all national income ultimately accrues to flesh-and-blood individuals, so too are all taxes ultimately borne by real persons. For example, in the same way that undistributed profits of corporations constitute income for shareholders (income that's saved and immediately reinvested by companies), corporate taxes are also taxes paid by shareholders: they reduce the profits of companies, which reduces how much dividends shareholders can receive or how much profits they can reinvest.

Although only people pay taxes, some of the people who pay them may live elsewhere. In that sense, it's possible to make foreign countries pay, or at least try to make them pay. However, except for some very specific situations—such as small oil-producing nations—no country has ever succeeded in making foreigners contribute a large fraction of its tax revenues. In the case of the United States, some of its property and corporate taxes are paid by foreigners; for instance, Chinese residents who own real estate in Los Angeles pay property taxes to the state of California. Similarly, close to 20% of the shares of US corporations are owned by foreigners,[6] so the US corporate income tax is, to some extent, a tax on foreign owners. But the overall amount of US taxes paid by non-US persons is small, of the order of 1% of national income. And it works both ways. Americans own shares of foreign corporations and real estate in London and in Spain, so they pay corporate and property taxes abroad too—about as much as foreigners pay to the United States. In the end, US governments collect 28% of national income in taxes, and Americans pay 28% of their income in taxes.

Figuring out how tax payments are distributed among individuals—that is, which social group pays what—involves a bit of detective work. In the 1970s and 1980s, Joseph Pechman at the Brookings Institution produced pioneering estimates of the distribution of all taxes in the United States, but oddly enough nobody attempted to emulate him, and the last estimates that exist are for the year 1985, when inequality was much lower than today and the structure of taxation quite different too.[7]

The main hurdle to figuring out who pays what is that although in the end only people pay taxes, the entity that legally remits the check to the IRS is not necessarily the person who pays the tax. For instance, employers remit half of federal payroll taxes and employees pay the other half. But the distinction is meaningless: in the end, all payroll taxes are based on the labor income of workers. That these taxes are administratively split into two parts—one remitted by employers, the other by employees—is a legal fiction that has no economic implications. As a general rule, taxes on labor (such as payroll taxes) are paid by workers, taxes on capital (such as corporate taxes and property taxes) are paid by the owners of the corresponding capital assets, and taxes on consumption are paid by consumers. Once one realizes this, allocating taxes to who actually pays them, although it requires marshaling a lot of information, is in concept a simple task.

The question of who pays the taxes collected by governments today is different from the question of how the economy would look if specific taxes were lower or higher tomorrow—what economists call, quite confusingly, "tax incidence." For example, what would happen if the corporate tax rate were cut? In principle, many things could change: firms could boost shareholder income with higher dividend payments or share buybacks; they could increase the wages of their employees; they could slash the price of the products they sell; they could expand investment in factories or in research and development.

We will discuss questions of tax incidence later in the book, in the context of potential reforms. In the meantime, the critical thing to understand is that determining who pays existing taxes is a different project from imagining how the world would look if those taxes were changed. Regardless of what firms might do if the corporate tax rate were cut tomorrow, today's corporate taxes are paid by shareholders and nobody else.[8]

IS THE US TAX SYSTEM PROGRESSIVE?

We can now attempt an answer to the key question: Once we account for all taxes and all forms of income that contribute to national income, does America really make the rich contribute more than the poor?

To address this question, we compute how effective tax rates varied across the income distribution in 2018, the year following President Trump's tax reform. We divide the population into fifteen groups: the bottom 10% (that is, the 24 million adults with the lowest pre-tax income), the next 10%, and so on, until we reach the top 10%, which we decompose into smaller and smaller groups, until we reach the 400 wealthiest Americans. (This focus on the top of the pyramid is necessary because the rich, although few in number, earn a large fraction of total income and thus account for a large share of potential tax revenue.) We compute the amount of taxes paid by each group and divide that figure by each group's pre-tax income.[9] By construction, all the groups combined pay on average 28% of their income in taxes—the macroeconomic rate of taxation in the United States in 2018. The interesting question is how the effective tax rate varies across the distribution. Do the ultra-rich, for example, contribute more—relative to their ability to pay—than minimum wage workers?

The short answer is: "No." Today, each social group funnels between 25% and 30% of its income in taxes into the public coffers, except the ultra-wealthy who barely pay 20%. The US tax system is a giant flat tax—except at the top, where it's regressive. The view that America, even if it may not collect as much taxes as European countries, at least does so in a progressive way, is wrong.

More precisely, the working class—the five bottom deciles of the income distribution, who earn on average $18,500 a year—pays around 25% of its income in taxes. This rate slightly increases for the middle class—the next four deciles—and stabilizes at around 28% for the upper middle class. Taxes then rise a bit for the rich but never substantially exceed the average rate of 28%. Finally, they fall to 23% for the 400 richest Americans. As a group, and although their individual situations are not all the same, the Trumps, the Zuckerbergs, and the Buffetts of this world pay lower tax rates than teachers and secretaries. How can a tax system that many view as progressive be, in fact, so regressive?

1.2 THE US TAX SYSTEM: A GIANT FLAT TAX THAT BECOMES REGRESSIVE AT THE TOP

(Average tax rates by income group, 2018)

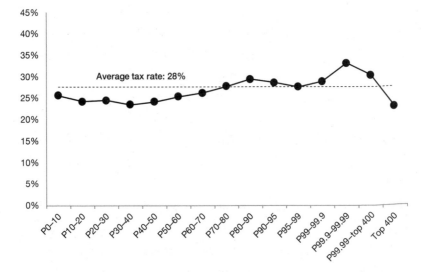

Notes: The figure depicts the average tax rate by income groups in 2018. All federal, state, and local taxes are included. Taxes are expressed as a fraction of pre-tax income. P0–10 denotes the bottom 10% of the income distribution, P10–20 the next 10%, etc. Taking all taxes together, the US tax system looks like a giant flat tax with similar tax rates across income groups but with lower tax rates at the very top. Complete details at *taxjusticenow.org*.

WHY THE POOR PAY A LOT

Let's start with the bottom of the income ladder. The heavy tax burden imposed on the least fortunate Americans has two culprits.

The first is payroll taxes. Every worker in the bottom deciles, no matter how small her wage, sees her paycheck immediately reduced by 15.3%: 12.4% for Social Security contributions and 2.9% for Medicare. Meanwhile, the minimum wage has collapsed: a work

employed full time at the federal minimum wage makes barely $15,000 a year in 2019, only a fifth of the average national income per adult. In 1950, that same minimum-wage worker earned the equivalent of more than half of the average income.[10] Alongside this dramatic reduction in their pre-tax income, minimum-wage workers have seen their payroll taxes rise, from 3% of income in 1950 to more than 15% today.

Other countries have followed the opposite route: increasing the minimum wage while cutting payroll taxes at the bottom of the wage distribution. In France, the minimum wage has grown faster than inflation, to reach 10 euros in 2019, the equivalent of $11.50 (against $7.25 in America). Meanwhile, payroll taxes for minimum-wage workers—which fund an extensive welfare state, including universal health insurance—have been cut from more than 50% in the 1990s to less than 20% today.[11]

The second and primary culprit for the high tax rates paid by working-class Americans is consumption taxes. The United States may not have a value-added tax, but it has a proliferation of sales and excise taxes that, like a VAT, make prices higher. And there's a twist: in contrast to regular value-added taxes, US levies exempt most services, which the affluent consume at high rates as a percentage of their overall spending. This twist means that the consumption of the poor (goods) is taxed, while that of the rich (services) is largely exempted. The United States does not have a VAT; it has a poor man's VAT.

Do you enjoy going to the opera? No sales tax. Have a country club membership? No sales tax. Need a lawyer? No sales tax. But if you drive, dress, or buy appliances, sales taxes apply all the way. Admittedly, most states have reduced rates for grocery purchases, which account for about 15% of consumption for the poorest people. But this generosity is largely offset by the extreme regressivity of excise taxes on fuel, alcohol, and tobacco. Excise taxes—in contrast to sales taxes—do not depend on the price of the product pur-

1.3 THE US FLAT TAX: COMPOSITION BY TYPE OF TAX

(Average tax rates by income group, 2018)

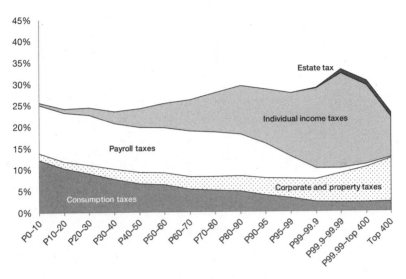

Notes: The figure depicts the average tax rate by income group and its composition by type of tax in 2018. All federal, state, and local taxes are included. Tax rates are expressed as a fraction of pre-tax income. The working class pays almost as much as the middle class and the rich because of regressive consumption taxes and payroll taxes. The super-rich pay less than other groups because most of their income is not subject to taxation. Complete details at *taxjusticenow.org.*

chased but only on the quantities consumed (liters of wine or ounces of beer). High-end wines and beers thus end up being taxed more lightly relative to their price than common beverages.

The best available estimates show that sales and excise taxes, when combined, are extremely regressive in the United States. They absorb more than 10% of income in the bottom deciles compared to barely 1% or 2% at the top.[12] Much of this regressivity flows from the fact that the poor consume all their income, while the rich save part of theirs (and the ultra-rich almost all of theirs: try spending a billion dollars a year). But the exemption of services also plays a major role. Conservative critics of a European-style VAT contend that if implemented in the United States, the tax would become an uncontrollable money machine that would transform America into a "socialist" nation. But there's a less well known reason for their displeasure: unlike current archaic consumption taxes, an American VAT would hit the wallets of the wealthy.

Although sales taxes are local—not federal—there's no tax haven for the poor: their burdens do not change much from one state to the other. Some states have lower consumption taxes or larger reductions for groceries, but overall they have overwhelmingly regressive tax systems. It's indeed a general rule that taxation at the sub-federal level tends to be regressive. It's much easier to implement progressive taxes at the federal level, both for practical reasons (federal agencies have access to more information and more resources) and because of tax competition (the wealthy can more easily move across state lines than across national borders). Ignoring state and local taxes in the analysis of the distribution of tax burdens, as most commentators do, gives a misleading picture.

WHY THE RICH PAY LESS

Since their inception, progressive taxes have had a core purpose: to offset the regressivity of consumption taxes, thereby making taxation socially acceptable. In the United States, as we'll see in the next chapter, the first justification for the federal income tax introduced in 1913 was to offset the regressive impact of tariffs that, at the time, had been the only source of federal tax revenue. The other justification was to dampen the upsurge of inequality observed during the Gilded Age.

Unfortunately, today's income tax largely fails to achieve these goals, for three key reasons.

The first problem, and the essential reason why billionaires pay low rates, is that most of their income is not subject to the personal income tax. As we have seen, only 63% of national income is included in the base of the income tax—many forms of income are legally exempt. A significant portion of taxpayers benefit from these exemptions, but the truly wealthy benefit even more. For many of them, virtually all of their income is exempt. Think about it: what's the true economic income of Mark Zuckerberg? He owns about 20% of Facebook, a company that made $20 billion in profits in 2018. So his income that year was 20% of 20 billion, $4 billion. However, Facebook did not pay any dividend, so none of these $4 billion were subject to individual income taxation. Like many other billionaires, Zuckerberg's effective individual income tax rate is close to 0% today, and it will remain close to 0% for as long as he does not sell his stocks.

The only sizable tax Zuckerberg pays is his share of Facebook's corporate tax. But now the second problem comes into view: the corporate tax has almost disappeared. Facebook has never excelled at paying its dues: by shifting its profits to the Cayman Islands, it has dodged billions in corporate taxes over the years, and as we will see in more detail in Chapter 4, Facebook is far from the only multinational to do so. On top of that tax avoidance, in 2018, the US corporate tax rate was slashed from 35% to 21%. The consequence? Federal corporate tax revenues have fallen by almost half from 2017 to 2018.[13] We'll return at length to this development, but it's worth recording here its most direct implication: low corporate taxes mean the ultra-rich, whose income mostly derives from owning shares in corporations, now really can get off almost scot-free.

The third reason why the wealthy pay low taxes is the recent transformation of the federal individual income tax. In less than two decades, the federal income tax has morphed from a comprehensive tax—taxing labor and capital equally—to one that favors capital over labor income explicitly. Since 2003, dividends have benefited from reduced rates of 20% at the maximum. This change means that even when corporations—like Microsoft—pay dividends, their owners—like Bill Gates—pay at most 20% in income taxes on those dividends. Since 2018 business income—income earned by doctors, lawyers, consultants, venture capitalists, etc.—has enjoyed a 20% deduction, so that the top marginal tax rate for business income is 29.6% instead of 37% as for wages. This is one of the key changes introduced by the Trump tax reform, and one of its most controversial aspects (indeed, all economists seem to oppose it, a rare feat). The deduction is limited for the self-employed, for instance for a successful consultant working solo. But it is unlimited for income generated by businesses that employ many employees or own a large enough capital stock. For instance, quite conveniently, someone in the business of owning and renting skyscrapers in New York City.[14]

The only category of income that does not benefit from any exemption, deduction, reduced rate, or any other favor is wages. At any income level, wage earners are thus more heavily taxed than people who derive income from property. More broadly, people with identical incomes can have wildly different tax bills depending on the legal (and often arbitrary) classification of their income. The tax changes of the last twenty years have done away with a core principle of tax justice: the notion that people with the same income ought to pay the same amount of tax. It's no longer the case.

The explosive cocktail that is undermining America's system of taxation is simple: capital income, in varying degrees, is becoming tax-free. This process is not uniform: some capital taxes are disappearing faster than others. The profits of big multinational companies bear less tax than those of domestic businesses. Dividends bear less tax than interest income. Depending on the nature of their wealth, rich people thus benefit in varying degrees. The ultra-wealthy, whose income mostly derives from owning shares in big companies, have so far been the primary winners.

PLUTOCRACY

Is it really a problem if the tax system is a giant flat tax with preferential treatment for the ultra-wealthy? Why should we care? There are several ways to answer this question.

Let's first mention that we've done nothing to exaggerate our numbers, quite the contrary. If anything, our estimate of the extent to which American taxation has become regressive at the top is likely to be conservative. We've assigned the same effective corporate tax rate to every firm, although it's possible, perhaps even likely, that those controlled by the rich avoid more taxes—for instance by shifting a higher fraction of their profits to offshore tax havens. Should this be true, we would overestimate the taxes paid by billionaires.

We should also make clear that the United States is not the only democracy where the overall tax system is much less progressive than it may appear at first sight. Conducting rigorous international comparisons is difficult, for reasons we'll return to in Chapter 5, but the best evidence suggests that the United States is in good company: the tax system of France, for example, appears to be no more progressive than America's.[15]

In our view, the lack of progressivity in US taxation is a problem for three reasons.

First, for basic budgetary considerations. Even if one only looks at the very top end of the income ladder, where taxes become regressive, the stakes are large. The top 0.001% currently pay 25% of their income in taxes. Doubling their rate to 50% would generate more than $100 billion in revenue each year, everything else being equal. That's enough money to increase the after-tax income of each working-class adult by $800 a year, for instance by reducing their payroll taxes. The extreme concentration of income on the top end means that, for the United States, the tax bills paid by the super-rich matter a lot for the government's overall finances.

The second reason is, quite simply, fairness. The taxes the wealthy don't pay, the rest of us must cover. It's always possible to argue that everybody receives the market income they deserve; that the rich, who were unfairly treated in the 1960s and 1970s, are now getting their just deserts from ever more unfettered and global markets. We don't agree with this ideology—sometimes known as market fundamentalism—but at least it's a consistent world view. However, what argument can justify that billionaires should pay less than each of us, and pay less and less as they get wealthier and wealthier? What principle could justify such an obviously perverse situation?

But probably the most fundamental reason to oppose America's current tax regime is the inequality spiral that it feeds. As we've seen, the income share of the top 1% has ballooned while that of the working class has collapsed. And yet, instead of tamping it down, the tax system has reinforced this trend. The wealthy used to pay a lot; they now pay less. The poor used to pay relatively little; their duties have increased. In 2018, for the first time in the last hundred years, the top 400 richest Americans have paid lower tax rates than the working class.

This looks like the tax system of a plutocracy. With tax rates of barely 20% at the top, wealth will keep accumulating with hardly any barrier. And with that, so too will the power of the wealthy accumulate, including their ability to shape policymaking and government for their own benefit.

It's always possible to shrug off the risk of an entrenched plutocracy. To believe that whether a few super-rich own a large fraction

1.4 US BILLIONAIRES NOW PAY LOWER TAX RATES THAN THE WORKING CLASS

(Average tax rates: bottom 50% income earners
vs. 400 richest Americans)

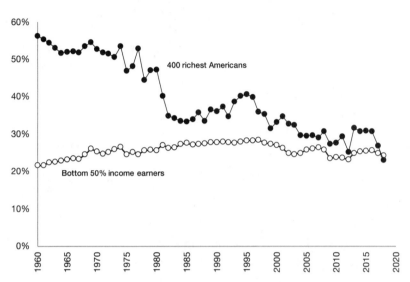

Notes: The figure depicts the average tax rate for the 50% of adults with the lowest incomes and for the top 400 highest earners since 1960. Tax rates are expressed as a fraction of pre-tax income. Before the 1980s, the very top paid much more than the bottom 50%. In 2018, for the first time, the bottom 50% has paid more than the top 400. Complete details at *taxjusticenow.org.*

of the country's wealth is irrelevant. That America's institutions are so strong that they cannot be captured by special interests. That from Boston to Los Angeles, democracy will always and forever beat plutocracy. And certainly, democracy has overcome plutocracy in the past. It triumphed over the slaveholding plutocracy of the South. It beat back the nascent industrialist plutocracy of the Gilded Age.

In one case it took a war; in the other a tax revolution.

Chapter 2

FROM BOSTON TO RICHMOND

The history of taxation in the United States is anything but linear. It's a story of dramatic reversals, of sudden ideological and political changes, of groundbreaking innovations and radical U-turns.

From 1930 to 1980, the top marginal income tax rate in the United States averaged 78%. This top rate reached as much as 91% from 1951 to 1963.[1] Large bequests were taxed at quasi-confiscatory rates during the middle of the twentieth century, with rates nearing 80% from 1941 to 1976 for the wealthiest Americans.

Some commentators look at this history and dismiss the idea that high marginal rates were ever successful as policy. In practice, they maintain, hardly anybody paid the full rate and loopholes were plentiful. America, according to this view, may have appeared to tax the rich, but never genuinely did so.

So, did America's ultra-wealthy ever contribute to the public coffers a large fraction of their income? And if they did, was this only in the context of world wars, or did progressive taxation extend beyond the wars and reflect broader choices about justice and inequality that may still have a bearing on today's tax debates? To address these questions, we must consider the comprehensive, long-run evidence on the evolution of the effective tax rates imposed on the various groups of the population. By extending the computations presented in the previous chapter over more than a century, we'll see how progressive exactly the US tax system used to be. We'll see also how America pioneered some of the key progressive fiscal innovations in world history, often paving the way for other countries.

Of course, there is no such thing as an "American way" of taxing—not any more than there is "a French way" or a "Japanese way." There are specific national trajectories, experiments, institutional tinkering, breakthroughs, and retreats. Like that of other countries, America's fiscal history is deeply linked with the dynamic of inequality, the transformation of beliefs about private property, and the progress of democracy. Understanding this history offers a window onto understanding the conditions for change today.

THE INVENTION OF WEALTH TAXATION . . . IN THE SEVENTEENTH CENTURY

Ever since they arrived in the New World, the settlers of the Northern colonies—from New Hampshire to Pennsylvania—cared about making sure the affluent contributed to paying the common bills. In the seventeenth century, they developed incredibly modern tax systems for their time. The key innovation? Taxing wealth. Not only real estate and land, as England already did at the time. But all other assets too, from financial assets (stocks, bonds, loan instruments) to livestock, inventories, ships, and jewelry.

As far back as 1640, the colony of Massachusetts taxed all forms of property.[2] Although valuation methods differed over time and across states, the general principle held that prevailing market prices were to be used to assess the taxable value of each asset. When market values were not readily available, they were estimated by elected local assessors or computed by applying multiples to the income flow generated by the assets. A house that could be rented for £15 annually, for example, was deemed to be worth £90 (six years of income) and taxed as such in Massachusetts in 1700.

The colonies' tax systems, to be sure, were not perfect or even fair by today's standards. Their wealth taxes had serious limitations. Their rates were low and they were not progressive. Wealth taxes were supplemented by levies that disproportionately hit the poor, such as import duties and poll taxes—flat, per-person levies. Some colonies, such as New York, relied more on regressive consumption taxes than on property taxes to fund public expenditures.

But overall the tax systems of Northern colonies were unusually progressive for the time. They were far more advanced and democratic than anything that existed in Europe. Take France, the most populous country of the Old World. While Massachusetts made a serious attempt at taxing the rich, French kings pampered the affluent and bludgeoned the populace. France had an income tax (*taille*), whose main claim to fame was that it exempted almost all privileged groups: the aristocracy, the clergy, judges, professors, doctors, the residents of big cities, including Paris, and, of course, the tax collectors themselves—known as the *fermiers généraux* (tax farmers). The most destitute members of society, at the same time, were heavily hit by salt duties—the dreaded *gabelle*—and sprawling levies (*entrées* and *octrois*) on the commodities entering the cities, including food, beverages, and building materials. Since everybody needed food and salt (this was before refrigeration) the levies on consumption that formed the backbone of tax collection in the Old World were much less progressive than New England's property taxes.[3]

THE TWO FACES OF THE NEW WORLD

Taxation in the Northern colonies was also far more progressive than anything that existed in the South. Up to the outbreak of the

Civil War, the tax system of Virginia—the largest Southern colony—consisted essentially of a poll tax and myriad levies on necessities. While Massachusetts had developed an elaborate system to assign values to every form of wealth, Virginia made no effort to put any value on anything. The main source of revenue? Levies on pounds of tobacco, cows, and horses, the number of wheels in carriages, billiard tables—and poll taxes.[4] During the eighteenth century, the taxes in Thomas Jefferson's home state were even more archaic than in Louis XVI's France. Income taxation was nonexistent; property taxation restricted to land.

As in the North, there were variations in tax policy among various states, but in general taxes in the South were more regressive. In her masterly book *American Taxation, American Slavery*, historian Robin Einhorn shows the deep link between this backwardness and slavery. A fear haunted the slaveholders of the South: that non-slaveholding majorities would use taxation to undermine—and eventually abolish—the "peculiar institution." They particularly feared wealth taxation: at a time when 40% of the population in Southern states was considered property, property taxes were an existential threat for slaveholding planters. They fought such taxes tirelessly, and for two centuries wielded their power to keep taxes and public institutions archaic. How? By stifling democracy.

In lieu of elected local governments, seventeenth- and eighteenth-century Virginia operated with a system of self-perpetuating local oligarchies. Offices carried life tenures and were transmitted from one generation of plantation owner to the next; county court members were appointed on recommendation of the incumbents. When Virginia's planters did not appoint themselves as tax collectors, they bribed whoever had the job. When property taxation eventually emerged, landowners self-assessed the value of their land. Unsurprisingly, they used ridiculously low values. Virginia's voters would wait until 1851 to elect their governor for the first time.

"Americans hate taxes! It's in their DNA!" You've heard this anti-tax rhetoric many times. It has a few recurring clichés: That one of the key founding political acts of the United States, the Boston Tea Party of 1773, was a tax revolt. That Americans, contrary to Europeans, believe in personal responsibility, in upward mobility, in the notion that everyone, through hard work and ingenuity, can make it to the top. That the poor, in the United States, see themselves as temporarily embarrassed millionaires.[5] America, so this logic goes, hates taxes and is only true to itself when it is "starving the beast."

To find the wellspring of this rhetoric, Einhorn teaches us, do not look to Boston, Massachusetts. Look to Richmond, Virginia. Look not at the common men longing for liberty; look at the slaveholders who fought to defend their immense but precarious wealth. Perhaps more than any other social group, they are the artisans of the anti-government belief system that, in various forms, suffuses American history. They embraced the supreme primacy of private property— even when that property consisted of human beings. They railed against the evil of "inquisitorial" income and wealth taxes that allow tax collectors to "invade" private homes. They invoked a looming "tyranny of the majority" that sought to impose "spoliation" upon a small group of wealthy citizens. While the sources of anti-government sentiment in America are complex, over the last centuries, few have done more to perfect the anti-tax narrative than Southern slaveholders.

After the outbreak of the Civil War, this long-standing antipathy toward taxes and democratic governments severely handicapped the Confederate states. Because they mostly relied on tariffs, revenues collapsed when the Union blocked Southern ports. With little experience collecting taxes on income and wealth, the Confederacy was unable to recoup the lost revenue; it had to rely on debt to fund the war against the Union. As the Confederate government issued more and more bonds, inflation skyrocketed.

The Union, by contrast, built upon an existing tradition of direct taxation to fund the war effort. The Revenue Act of 1862 created the Internal Revenue Bureau. In the same year, the first federal income tax was levied with a rate of 3% on income above $600 and 5% above $5,000.[6] The $600 exemption threshold was equal to about four times the average income in the country, or the equivalent of $250,000 today.[7] So the tax, albeit with small rates, was progressive. The Revenue Act of 1864 increased the rates to 5% on income over $600, 7.5% over $5,000, and 10% on income over $10,000—the equivalent of more than $3 million today. The law mandated a public disclosure of income tax payments, and in 1865 the front page of the *New York Times* listed the income of New York's moneyed elite: William B. Astor declared an income of $1.3 million (5,200 times the average income of the time, the equivalent of $400 million today); Cornelius Vanderbilt, $576,551 (the equivalent of $170 million today), and so on.[8] The Union also borrowed heavily to fund the war and inflation increased a result, but much less than in the South.[9]

WHEN THE INCOME TAX WAS UNCONSTITUTIONAL

After the abolition of slavery in 1865, wealthy industrialists piggybacked on the slaveholders' rhetoric to fight the income tax created during the Civil war. They recycled and updated the Southern oligarchs' well-oiled argument against the evils of interference with private property. In 1871, the Anti-Income Tax Association was created in New York. It brought together some of the great fortunes of the time: William B. Astor, Samuel Sloan, and John Pierpont Morgan Sr., among others.[10] And the association's efforts were successful: the income tax, whose rates had already been reduced by Congress after the war, was repealed in 1872. It would remain in limbo until 1913 despite many efforts by reformers to reinstate it during the Reconstruction era and the Gilded Age that followed.

The efforts to reintroduce progressive taxation during the late nineteenth century had two main justifications. The first was blatant unfairness in the federal tax system. From 1817 until the cataclysm of the Civil War, Congress had levied only one tax: the federal tariff on imported goods. On top of the progressive income tax introduced in 1861, the Civil War had seen the proliferation of excise taxes on just about everything: luxury goods, alcohol, billiard tables, playing cards, but also corporations, newspaper advertisements, legal documents, manufacturing goods, and so on. Some of the newly created internal taxes—as these levies on domestic consumption were called, in opposition to the tariff, an "external tax"—were repealed after the defeat of the Confederacy, but others remained. In 1880, internal revenues accounted for a third of federal government tax receipts; the import tariff for the remaining two-thirds.[11] In both cases, the burden of federal taxes heavily fell on the shoulders of the poor. After they succeeded in abolishing the federal income tax, the great fortunes of the Gilded Age barely paid any federal tax; virtually all federal government revenue originated from consumers.

The second—and novel—development that catalyzed reform efforts was the upsurge of inequality. As rapid industrialization, urbanization, and cartelization took hold, it was impossible not to notice that fortunes were getting more and more concentrated. Economists made efforts to quantify inequality. In 1893, George K. Holmes, a statistician from the Department of Agriculture, used data from the 1890 Census and contemporaneous lists of millionaire families to estimate that the top 10% of households owned more than 71% of the nation's wealth.[12] Others obtained similar findings.[13] It was a large increase over antebellum levels of inequality, when the top 10% owned less than 60% of total wealth. Of course, the estimates of wealth concentration for the nineteenth century have their margin of error.[14] Absent any federal income or wealth tax, the primary material to estimate inequality was limited. Alongside rising inequality came a growing demand, in the upper echelons of society, for denying its rise. Economists were distorting the facts; their statistics were faulty. But to anybody who was paying attention, there was no doubt that a dramatic development was under way.

The case for progressive taxation grew. A number of economists—most prominently Edwin Seligman, a professor at Columbia University—explained why an income tax was a necessary step to "round out the existing tax system in the direction of greater justice."[15] Bills were introduced in Congress—usually following an economic crisis, such as the Panic of 1873 and that of 1893—to reinstate a progressive income tax. These legislative efforts were supported by an emerging progressive and Democratic coalition representing Southern whites and poor and middle-class white voters from the Northeast and the West. They were opposed by the new alliance between Southern elites and Northern industrialists. For the well-to-do, income taxation was "inquisitorial," "class legislation" to please "Western demagogues." It infringed on privacy. Perhaps worse, according to New York senator David Hill, it was "un-American," imported by "European professors."[16]

An income tax bill nonetheless passed Congress in 1894, with a rate of 2% for income in excess of $4,000—about twelve times the average per adult income of the time, or the equivalent of $900,000 today. The debate that followed revolved around the issue of whether a federal income tax was constitutional. According to the Constitution, direct taxes had to be apportioned among the states according to the population of each state. For example, if 10% of the US population lived in the state of New York, 10% of tax revenue had to come from there—even if a third of national income was earned in that state (which was roughly the case at the end of the nineteenth century), and even if most taxable individuals (those earning more than $4,000) lived there. Neither the 1894 income tax nor the one of 1862 were apportioned among the states, because apportioning them would have been nonsensical: it would have forced the government to tax the rich very little in the states where they were overrepresented (such as New York), defeating the whole purpose of progressive income taxation.

Though it mandated that direct taxes be apportioned, the Constitution did not define the term "direct tax." In a famous moment during the Philadelphia Convention, on August 20, 1787, Rufus King, a delegate for Massachusetts, asked, "What was the precise meaning of direct taxation?" No one answered. Was a federal income tax a direct tax? Or did the term only refer to poll taxes and levies on land? The Supreme Court took up the issue in 1895. Ruling in *Pollock v. Farmers' Loan and Trust Company*, the justices declared that the federal income tax was a "direct tax," and as such had to be apportioned among states according to their population. This decision meant that the 1894 income tax was unconstitutional, which led to its repeal. For the rest of the Gilded Age, all federal government revenue would originate from tariffs and excises on tobacco and alcohol.

AND PROGRESSIVE TAXATION WAS BORN . . .

After the Pollock decision, creating a progressive income tax was only possible if the Constitution changed. This hurdle was cleared in 1913, when three-quarters of the states ratified the Sixteenth Amendment following its adoption by two-thirds of both houses of Congress in 1909—the two steps required to amend the Constitution. "The Congress shall have power to lay and collect taxes on incomes, from whatever source derived, without apportionment among the several States," reads the amendment. A federal income tax was enacted that same year.

The United States did not pioneer progressive income taxation. The policy's rise in the late nineteenth century and early twentieth century was an international phenomenon. Germany, Sweden, and Japan were the first countries, between the 1870s and 1890s, to create progressive income taxes other than for emergency war funding purposes. The United Kingdom quickly followed suit. Where the United States innovated was in quickly making its income tax highly progressive. In 1913 the top marginal tax rate in the United States was 7%. As early as 1917 it reached 67%. At that point, no other country on the planet taxed the affluent so heavily.

The reasons for the sharp increase of tax progressivity are multifold.[17] There was a desire to prevent war profiteering during the First World War—the type of profiteering that had enriched so many during the Civil War. To prevent a "shoddy aristocracy" from emerging again, an excess profits tax was imposed during the conflict. At first it covered the munitions industry only; then after America entered the war in April 1917, the tax was extended to all firms. All profits made by corporations above and beyond an 8% rate of return on their tangible capital—buildings, plants, machines, etc.— were deemed abnormal. Abnormal profits were taxed at progressive rates of up to 80% in 1918.

Even though it played a role, it does not seem that the war context was the key impetus for the rise of tax progressivity in America. None of the countries involved in the war were keen on encouraging war profiteering; each belligerent imposed an excess profits tax on domestic business. But no country increased its top marginal income tax rate as drastically as the United States (though the United Kingdom came close). More than the mere product of exceptional wartime circumstances, the rise of progressive taxation in America stemmed from the intellectual and political changes that had begun in the 1880s and 1890s: the evolution of the Democratic party, brutally segregationist in the South, but eager to unite low-income whites in the North and the West against Republican financial elites by means of an egalitarian economic platform; the social mobilization in favor of more economic justice, in a context of surging inequality and industrial concentration. Simply put, a growing fraction of the population refused to see America become as unequal as Europe, which at the time was perceived as an oligarchic antimodel.[18] The economist Irving Fisher captured this mindset when he denounced the "undemocratic concentration of wealth" in his address to the American Economic Association in 1919.[19]

And so it was that, in peacetime, the United States pioneered two of the key fiscal innovations of the twentieth century.

The first of these innovations was the introduction of a sharply progressive tax on property. As we have seen, by the beginning of the century, US states already had a long history of property taxation behind them. But these property taxes had a major limitation: they were not progressive. The same rate applied to all property owners, regardless of their wealth. There had been efforts to make these taxes progressive over the course of the nineteenth century, but they had failed as states adopted "uniformity clauses" mandating that all assets—no matter their nature (real or financial, for instance) or the wealth of their owners—be taxed at the same rate.[20] In 1916, the federal government introduced its own progressive tax on property, in the form of a progressive tax on wealth upon death: the federal estate tax. Its rates were initially moderate: in 1916 the top estate tax rate reached 10% for the largest estates; it rose a bit during World War I before stabilizing at 20% in the late 1920s.

This changed between 1931 and 1935, when the rate applying to the top fortunes rose from 20% to 70%. It would hover in the 70%–80% range from 1935 to 1981. Over the course of the twentieth century, no continental European country ever taxed large successions in direct line (from parents to children) at more than 50%. The only exception? Allied-occupied Germany between 1946 and 1948, when tax policy was decided . . . by the Americans, who imposed a 60% rate.[21]

The second tax policy innovation was even more far-reaching.

2.1 WHEN THE UNITED STATES TAXED HIGH INCOMES AT MORE THAN 90%

(Statutory top marginal tax rates)

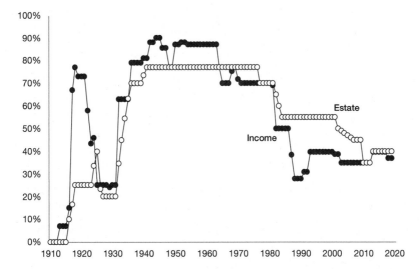

Notes: The figure depicts the top marginal tax rates for the federal individual income tax and the federal estate tax since 1913. From the 1930s to the 1970s, the United States had top marginal income and estate tax rates in excess of 70%, the highest among Western countries (along with the United Kingdom). Complete details at *taxjusticenow.org*.

From its creation through to the 1930s, the goal of the income tax had been to collect tax revenue. The tax compelled the rich to contribute to the public coffers in proportion to their ability to pay. After his election, President Franklin Delano Roosevelt added a new objective: Make sure nobody earns more than a certain amount of money. In short, confiscate excessive incomes. In 1936, he increased the top marginal income tax rate to 79%; in 1940 to 81%. During World War II, the top rate came close to 100%.

FDR's thinking is best reflected in his message to Congress on April 27, 1942: "Discrepancies between low personal incomes and very high personal incomes should be lessened; and I therefore believe that in time of this grave national danger, when all excess income should go to win the war, no American citizen ought to have a net income, after he has paid his taxes, of more than $25,000 a year." A 100% tax on net income above $25,000—equivalent to more than $1,000,000 today—was to be implemented, not only on salaries, but on all income sources, including interest from tax exempt securities. Congress found 100% to be slightly excessive and instead settled on a top marginal income tax rate of 94%. It also enacted a mechanism that limited the average tax rate, so that in practice taxes paid could not exceed 90% of income.

Seventy years prior, during a Civil War in which 620,000 soldiers died (about as many as all US deaths during the two world wars, the Korean, Vietnam, Iraq, and Afghanistan wars combined), the debate about how to tax the wealthy had involved rates between 0% and 10%. Now the question was whether 90% or 100% was more appropriate—proof if need be that the rise in tax progressivity had more to do with the political changes of the early twentieth century than with the necessities of war. From 1944 to 1981, the top marginal income tax rate would average 81%.

These quasi-confiscatory top tax rates applied to extraordinarily high incomes only, the equivalent of more than several million dollars today. In 1944, for example, the top marginal tax rate of 94% started biting above $200,000, the equivalent of ninety-two times the average national income per adult, or more than $6 million today. For incomes above $1.2 million in today's dollars, tax rates in a range of 72% to 94% still applied. But below that level, taxation was in line with what's typical nowadays. Incomes in the hundreds of thousands of today's dollars were taxed at marginal rates in a range of 25% to 50%.

Ever since the Civil War, the opponents of progressive taxation have found it an effective strategy to pretend that the middle class is hit by taxes that only concern the ultra-wealthy. But nobody except the ultra-rich was ever subjected to America's confiscatory top tax rate policy. The upper middle class certainly never was.

As Roosevelt's message to Congress expresses clearly, the quasi-confiscatory top marginal income tax rates championed by the United States were designed to reduce inequality, not to collect revenue. Why would anyone try to earn more than a million dollars if all of that extra income went to the IRS? No employment contract with a salary above a million would ever be signed. Nobody would amass enough wealth to receive more than a million in annual capital income. The rich would stop saving after they reached that point. They most likely would give their assets to heirs or charities once they surpassed the threshold. As such, the goal of Roosevelt's policy was obvious: reduce the inequality of *pre-tax* income. The United States, for almost half a century, came as close as any democratic country ever has to imposing a legal maximum income.

HIGH TOP TAX RATES, LOW INEQUALITY

The justification for continuing the FDR-era policy has always been that sky-high incomes are, for the most part, earned at the expense of the rest of society. This is obviously the case during wars, when arms dealers flourish as the masses fight. But it can be equally true in peacetime whenever income at the top of the pyramid derives from exploiting monopoly positions, natural resources rents, power imbalances, ignorance, political favors, or other zero-sum economic activities (we'll study one of these, the tax-dodging industry, in the next chapter). In such cases, confiscatory top marginal income tax rates do not reduce the size of the economic pie; they simply reduce the size of the slice that goes to the wealthy, increasing income for the rest of the community one for one.[22]

We can, of course, debate the merits and demerits of this view, and whether it might make sense to return to 90% top marginal income tax rates today, an idea we'll discuss in Chapter 8. But to start thinking about such a proposal, we must first address a basic question: Did FDR's tax policy work? Did it really reduce the concentration of pre-tax income?

There is one indication that it did: from the 1940s to the 1970s, very few taxpayers reported gigantic incomes to the IRS. Only a few hundred families showed up in the top tax brackets subject to the confiscatory rates. The inequality of fiscal income—that is, income as reported to the tax authority—collapsed. The share of fiscal income earned by the top 0.01% reached a historical nadir in the postwar decades. From the creation of the income tax in 1913 to FDR's inauguration in 1933, this group earned on average 2.6% of all fiscal income each year. From 1950 to 1980, that number fell to 0.6% on average.[23] Looking at tax data, there is no doubt that Roosevelt's policy achieved its goal.

But what if tax data are misleading? It is possible, after all, that the wealthy found ways to shelter income out of sight of the IRS. Maybe they used legal or illegal tricks to dodge the top marginal tax rates. If we push this line of thought to the extreme, it's possible to imagine that inequality never really fell in the United States, or at least not nearly as much as suggested by tax statistics. What if the massive swings in the share of fiscal income going to the top groups are an illusion caused by tax avoidance?

It would be a mistake to dismiss this argument out of hand. As a theory it has intuitive appeal: when top marginal tax rates are high, it seems plausible that the affluent will seek to hide income. If they were successful, then inequality might not have declined much. Important economic phenomena—like how much inequality there is—rarely reveal themselves effortlessly; they must be patiently and scientifically constructed, and no science is definitive. The best way to measure inequality involves tracking all forms of income, including income that does not have to be reported to the IRS, such as profits kept within firms, interest earned from tax-exempt bonds, and so on. In other words, we must distribute the totality of national income to the various groups of the distribution, as we did in the previous chapter for more recent years.

The picture that emerges from this exercise corroborates, for the most part, what fiscal income data suggest. The inequality of national income truly fell from the 1930s to the 1970s, during the period when exorbitant incomes where taxed at quasi-confiscatory rates. The decline is a bit less spectacular than what a simple reading of the income tax statistics would suggest, mostly because corporate retained earnings rose in the postwar decades, to reach about 6% of national income in the 1960s. When profits are not distributed, they do not show up on the individual income tax returns of shareholders, and can thus lead observers to underestimate how much inequality there really is. When they were subject to individual tax rates as high as 91%, some wealthy shareholders instructed their companies to reinvest their profits (free of individual income taxation) instead of paying dividends (which were subject to the individual income tax).

But even after accounting for retained earnings and all other forms of untaxed income, income concentration did fall dramatically from the 1930s to the 1970s.[24] The share of America's total pre-tax national income earned by the top 0.01% declined from more than 4% on the eve of the Great Depression to 1.3% in 1975, its lowest level ever recorded. Yes, some profits were kept tax-free within firms, but these sums were not as large as one might think. Retained earnings were sizable in the 1960s (6% of national income), but not incommensurate with what's been typical in the long run—for example, corporate retained earnings have amounted to 5% of national income since the turn of the twenty-first century. The reasons retained earnings were not much larger when dividend tax rates were higher are multifold. Dividend distribution policies are sticky: once a mature business starts to distribute dividends to shareholders it rarely reverses course, unless the business is close to bankruptcy. General Electric, DuPont, Exxon and other corporate behemoths did pay large dividends after World War II. Shareholders prefer earning cash to letting profits sit within big companies, because there is always a risk that corporate managers will dissipate undistributed profits with dubious investments. High undistributed profits also give ammunition to unions—which were powerful in the 1950s and 1960s—to ask for wage increases.

Overall, there is no indication that under the presidencies of Harry Truman and Dwight Eisenhower the wealthy were rich in ways that fiscal data massively underestimate. And indeed, to anybody alive in the 1950s, it was clear that the world, for the rich, had changed—and not in good a way. In 1955, *Fortune* magazine ran an article titled "How Top Executives Live."[25] It is a heartbreaking read. "The successful American executive gets up early—about 7:00 A.M.—eats a large breakfast, and rushes to his office by train or auto. . . . If he is a top executive he lives on an economic scale not too different from that of the man on the next-lower income rung." How come? "Twenty-five years have altered the executive way of life noticeably; in 1930 the average businessman had been buffeted by the economic storms but he had not yet been battered by the income tax. The executive still led a life ornamented by expensive adjuncts that other men could not begin to afford. . . . The executive's home today is likely to be unpretentious and relatively small—perhaps seven rooms and two and a half baths." Worse yet, "the large yacht has also foundered in the sea of progressive taxation. In 1930, Fred Fisher, Walter Briggs, and Alfred P. Sloan cruised around in vessels 235 feet long; J. P. Morgan had just built his fourth Corsair (343 feet). Today, seventy-five feet is considered a lot of yacht."

THE AVERAGE TAX RATE FOR THE RICH UNDER EISENHOWER: 55%

Not only did the wealthy see their incomes constrained, but on their reduced income they paid high effective tax rates.

Figure 2.2 shows the effective tax rate paid by the top 0.1% highest income earners since 1913, including all taxes paid at all levels of government. Today, as we have seen, America's tax system is mostly a giant flat tax: the most fortunate barely pay more than the middle class (and in fact pay less, the closer you get to the top). Half a century ago, things looked quite different. Working-class and middle-class Americans paid less than today, because payroll taxes were lower. The rich, on the other hand, paid much more. For forty years, from the 1930s to the 1970s, the wealthy paid more than 50% of their income in taxes, three times more than Americans in the bottom 90% of the income distribution. The average tax rate of the top 0.1% culminated at 60% in the early 1950s and remained around 55% during Eisenhower's two terms. Over this period the US tax system was undeniably progressive.

How were these high effective tax rates achieved?

First, by keeping tax avoidance in check. In the next chapter we'll explore how tax avoidance has changed over the last century. But what's important to realize already at this stage is that letting people or corporations dodge taxes is largely a choice that governments make. In the postwar decades, policymakers chose to fight avoidance and evasion; we'll soon see how.

But the more fundamental reason why the US tax system was so progressive is because of heavy taxes on corporate profits. In all capitalist societies, the richest people derive most of their income from shares, the ownership of corporations—the true economic and social

2.2 THE AVERAGE TAX RATE FOR THE RICH UNDER EISENHOWER? 55%

(Average tax rates: top 0.1% versus bottom 90% income earners)

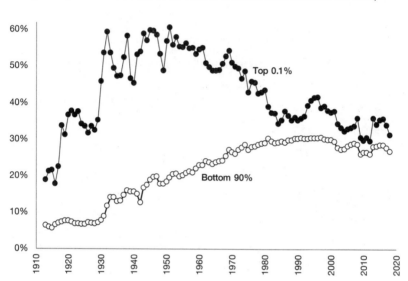

Notes: The figure depicts the average tax rate for the bottom 90% and for the top 0.1% income earners since 1913. Taxes include all taxes at all levels of government (federal, state, and local). Tax rates are expressed as a fraction of pre-tax income. Historically, the United States had a progressive tax system with the top 0.1% earners paying much more than the bottom 90%. In recent years, the bottom 90% has paid almost as much as the top 0.1%. Complete details at *taxjusticenow.org.*

power. When corporate profits are taxed stiffly, the affluent are made to contribute to the public coffers. That's true even when companies are instructed to limit their payments of dividends, because the corporate tax is on profits before reinvestment or dividend disbursements. In effect, the corporate tax serves as a minimum tax on the affluent.

From 1951 to 1978, the statutory rate of tax on corporate profits ranged from 48% to 52%. In contrast to the top-end individual income tax rates, these rates applied to all profits. They were not

2.3 THE KEY ROLE OF THE CORPORATE TAX FOR THE WEALTHY

(Average tax rate of the top 0.1% income earners)

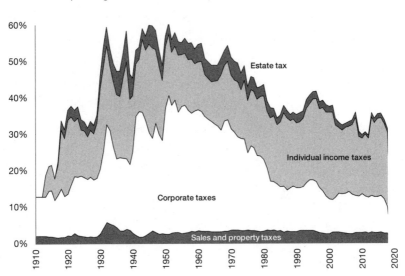

Notes: The figure depicts the average tax rate and its composition by type of tax for the top 0.1% income earners since 1910. All federal, state, and local taxes are included. Corporate taxes include business property taxes (while residential property taxes are lumped with sales taxes). The main driver of the top 0.1% tax rate has been the corporate income tax, which was very large from the 1930s to the mid-1970s and has eroded since then. Complete details at *taxjusticenow.org.*

marginal rates designed to deter rent-seeking and curb excessive incomes. They were flat rates meant to generate revenue. And generate revenue they did. In the 1950s and early 1960s, corporate profits were effectively taxed at rates approaching 50%. For any dollar of profit made in America, half went straight to government.

As we can see, it's through the corporate income tax—more than through the individual income tax—that the very rich contributed to the public coffers in the middle of the twentieth century. By design, few people were in the top individual income tax bracket where the top marginal tax rates of 90% applied. But essentially all shareholders faced 50% effective tax rates on their share of a firm's profits. In the postwar decades, the ownership of corporations was still highly concentrated in a few hands (this was before pension plans somewhat broadened equity ownership) and firms were highly profitable, so firm owners earned a lot of income. Companies paid half of their profits in tax straight to the IRS. On whatever remained after cutting that check, many firms paid dividends to their shareholders, and these dividends were taxed at rates as high as 90%.

Does that look like the policy of a country that doesn't care about taxing the rich?

Chapter 3

HOW INJUSTICE TRIUMPHS

The weather in Washington, DC, was beautiful; it was one of those Indian summer days with a crisp breeze and pale blue sky that makes October the most pleasant month in the country's capital. Orange and red leaves on the trees glowed against the white marble monuments on Pennsylvania Avenue. On the South Lawn at the White House, surrounded by about two dozen senators and representatives from both parties, Ronald Reagan was sitting by a little wooden table, a fountain pen in hand, elated.

The president had made overhauling taxation with dramatically lower tax rates the top domestic priority of his second term. On that 22nd of October 1986, about to sign into law the Tax Reform Act, he had reason to be joyful. Starting on January 1, 1988, the country that had pioneered the quasi-confiscatory taxation of high incomes would apply the lowest top marginal income tax rate in the industrial world: 28%. After three weeks of floor debates, the tax bill had passed ninety-seven to three in the Senate. Democrats Ted Kennedy, Al Gore, John Kerry, and Joe Biden all had enthusiastically voted "Yes."

The bill itself was not especially popular among the public,[1] but it is hard to overstate the fervor it garnered among the nation's political and intellectual elites. For them, it represented the triumph of reason, the victory of the common good against special interests, and the beginning of a new era of growth and prosperity. To this day, and although it is now widely recognized as one of the key contributors to the explosion of inequality,[2] the bill is still fondly remembered by all those involved in its crafting. For card-carrying economists working in American universities, it borders on professional duty to profess its virtues.[3]

How did the government of a country that for decades had taxed high incomes at 90% come to think, in the mid-1980s, that 28% would instead be preferable? This monumental reversal in part reflects dramatic changes in politics and ideology that had contributed to Reagan's victory six years earlier. Reactivating and modernizing the anti-tax rhetoric of the antebellum South, the Republican party had united high-income voters across the country with Southern whites. The small-government ideas championed by the Mont Pelerin Society from its creation in 1947, embodied by Barry Goldwater in his 1964 presidential run, and advanced by a network of conservative foundations in the 1970s, had finally spread into mainstream thought and prevailed politically.[4] In this ideology, the primary role of government is to defend property rights and the key engine of growth is the profit-maximizing business, minimizing taxes paid along the way. "There is no such thing as society, there are only individual men and women," according to this world view.[5] For the atomized individual, taxation is a dead loss; it amounts to legalized theft.

And indeed, speaking on the lawn of the White House, pen at the ready, Reagan denounced a tax system that had become "un-American"; its "steeply progressive nature struck at the heart of the economic life of the individual." The new bill, by contrast, was "the best job-creation program ever to come out of the Congress of the United States."

But on those terms alone, Reagan's tax reform would probably not have passed the Democrat-controlled Congress—let alone achieved such an overwhelming majority in the Senate. There was something else behind its triumph. According to both Reagan and the Democrats who championed the bill, lawmakers had had no choice. The income tax was a terrible mess and abuse was rampant. Given this state of affairs, all government could do was slash the rates while plugging loopholes to make up for the lost tax revenue.

The Tax Reform Act of 1986 illustrates how progressive taxation dies. It does not die democratically, struck down by the will of voters. Looking at most of the great retreats of progressive taxation, we find the same pattern: first, an outburst of tax dodging; then, governments lamenting that taxing the rich has become impossible and slashing their rates. Understanding this spiral—How does tax avoidance rise in the first place? Why don't governments stop it?—is key to understanding the history of taxes and the future of tax justice.

THE PRICE FOR A CIVILIZED SOCIETY

In the simplified world of economists, tax enforcement is straightforward: the threat of frequent audits, penalties for tax dodgers, and a simple, loophole-free tax system are all you need to ensure that people pay. And certainly these things are important and necessary. If tax evaders are likely to be detected and face large sanctions for their crime, fewer people will cheat. If the tax code is riddled with breaks for special interests, tax avoidance will proliferate.[6]

In the real world, however, what makes taxation work is more than a simple tax code and diligent auditors. It's a belief system: shared convictions in the benefits of collective action (the notion that we are more prosperous when we pool resources together instead of acting in isolation), in government's central role in organizing this collective action, and in the merits of democracy. When this belief system prevails, even the most progressive tax system can work. When this belief system founders, the forces of tax dodging, unleashed and legitimized, can overwhelm even the most sophisticated tax authority and overpower the best tax code.

This story—the embrace and abandonment of a belief in collective action—is the story of the tax system inherited from the New Deal, perhaps the most progressive in world history. As we saw, it successfully taxed the wealthy for more than three decades—not only on paper, but in actual fact. By design, few people paid the 80%–90% top marginal income tax rates that prevailed from the 1930s through to the 1970s. But, all taxes included, effective tax rates for the very affluent exceeded 50%. Tax dodging was kept in check.

Roosevelt had pioneered, in the 1930s, the enforcement strategy that would keep tax evasion and avoidance under control for the decades that followed. He gave the IRS the legal and budgetary resources to enforce the spirit of the tax code. But, and perhaps even more important, he also spent time explaining why taxes mattered, appealing to morality, and shunning tax dodgers. "Mr. Justice Holmes said, 'Taxes are what we pay for civilized society' [the words inscribed above the entrance to the headquarters of the Internal Revenue Service in Washington, DC]. Too many individuals, however, want the civilization at a discount." So said FDR in his message to Congress on June 1, 1937: Curbing tax avoidance was an issue on which civilization hinged. And through to the 1970s, social norms like this did limit the demand among taxpayers for dubious dodges. Laws and regulations expressing these norms prevented most Americans from exploiting loopholes in the internal revenue code.

The New Deal tax system was not perfect. The main loophole was that from the 1930s to 1986, capital gains were taxed less than other forms of income. Capital gains occur whenever an asset—such as corporate stock—is sold for more than it was purchased for. The resulting gains are included in taxable income but taxed at preferential rates in the United States. When the top marginal income tax rate exceeded 90%, capital gains were taxed at only 25%.[7] We can debate the merits and demerits of preferential rates on capital gains—a question we'll get back to in Chapter 7. But one obvious defect of such a policy is that it encourages the affluent to structure their affairs to earn income in the form of capital gains rather than dividends or wages. It creates opportunities for tax avoidance.

With high top marginal income tax rates in the postwar decades, you might guess that tax dodging was out of control. Surely the wealthy could not resist the temptation to transform—for tax purposes—their highly taxed wages and dividends into lightly taxed capital gains.

But let's look at the data. Since 1986, capital gains have represented 4.1% of national income on average each year. From 1930 to 1985, when the gap between the top tax rate on capital gains and on ordinary income was much larger—and hence the incentives to reclassify ordinary income as capital gains much bigger—the corresponding figure was 2.2%. Despite a massive tax advantage, capital gains were small in the postwar decades. Some affluent middle-of-the-century taxpayers certainly did reclassify ordinary income into capital gains, but it did not happen on a large scale.

Why? Because governments did not allow it to happen. There aren't so many ways to make ordinary income look like capital gains. The main strategy involves the use of share buybacks. When corporations buy back their own shares, this has, just like dividend payments, the effect of moving cash out of firms and into the pockets of shareholders. The main difference between the two forms of payouts is their tax implications: share buybacks generate capital gains for the shareholder who sells shares back to the company. Before 1982, share buybacks were illegal. The social norm, as enshrined in the law, was that dividends—subject to the progressive income tax—were how firms ought to distribute earnings to their owners.[8]

Another way that affluent people could avoid taxes was by earning income in the form of tax-exempt perks provided by their employers, such as company jets, lavish offices, gargantuan meals, company "seminars" in Cape Cod or Aspen, and so on. These things are harder to measure than capital gains. But there is no evidence, in any contemporary chronicles of how company executives lived in the 1940s, 1950s, and 1960s, that such perks were particularly common or large. Analyzing executive compensation shortly after World War II, the economist Challis Hall found that "company-paid-for expenses of the type which really reduce executives' buying costs and represent extra income are of negligible importance in large companies."[9] Today's CEOs do not seem to dine much more frugally than their peers from the 1960s, nor do they seem more economical in their use of company jets. Spending lavishly using corporate money was simply not the socially accepted way for company executives to behave before the 1980s.[10]

Schemes to avoid taxes did regularly pop up, but they were quickly prohibited. In 1935, the Revenue Act hiked the top marginal income tax to 79%, the highest rate to date. After its enactment, the wealthy looked for ways to shirk their new duties. In his 1937 message to Congress, Roosevelt attached a letter from the secretary of the treasury, Henry Morgenthau Jr., listing eight tax-avoidance devices that had blossomed and were to be outlawed immediately. First among these was "the device of evading taxes by setting up foreign personal holding corporations in the Bahamas, Panama, and Newfoundland, and other places where taxes are low and corporation laws lax." In 1936, dozens of wealthy Americans had created offshore shell companies, to which they had transferred the ownership of their stock and bond portfolios. The shell companies, instead of their flesh-and-blood owners, collected dividends and interest, thus escaping American taxation. The government was quick in changing the law to render this operation explicitly illegal.[11] From 1937 on, any income earned by foreign holding companies controlled by Americans would become immediately taxable in the United States. Instantly, owning foreign holding companies to avoid taxes became pointless.

In a similar vein, by the 1960s a growing number of rich Americans had started abusing the law by making tax-deductible charitable contributions to private foundations that they controlled. "Charitable," these contributions were not: the foundations provided grants to their own founders, their families, or friends; or they made politically motivated gifts. The Tax Reform Act of 1969 cracked down on this abusive self-dealing and the result was immediate: in a couple of years, from 1968 to 1970, the number of newly created private foundations plummeted by 80%. Following this reform, "charitable" giving by the rich fell durably by 30%.[12]

THE BIG BANG OF TAX DODGING

FDR's strategy worked as long as successive administrations upheld the New Deal–era belief system. That changed in the early 1980s. "Government is not the solution to our problem; government is the problem," Reagan famously said in his inaugural address of January 1981. If some people were tempted to eschew taxation, they were not to blame: high, "un-American" tax rates were. In the new ideology that swept through the United States in the early 1980s, dodging taxes became the patriotic thing to do. Since "taxation was theft," according to the revived libertarian creed, it was also the moral thing to do. Until the 1970s, successive administrations had fought the tax-avoidance industry. When Reagan entered the White House in 1981, the industry became government-approved. The tax-sheltering frenzy could start.

And *frenzy* doesn't begin to capture the scale of what happened. The industry mushroomed. A network of financial entrepreneurs, promoters, and advisers stormed the market. Some of these inventors required their staffers to come up with one new idea a week.[13] They brimmed with creativity and produced groundbreaking tax dodges.

Whenever the IRS shut down a particularly egregious scheme, several others would spawn. They'd be advertised in the *Wall Street Journal* and the financial sections of leading newspapers like toothpaste. The magic of the market economy operated in full swing; competition drove the price of these tax dodges down. Like any other product in a market economy, their invention enriched both producers and consumers. Financiers, promoters, and advisers pocketed commissions; tax avoiders rounded off their bottom line. A lot of surplus, as economists call these gains, was created. With a little twist: all of this surplus was generated, dollar for dollar, at the expense of the rest of society.

The iconic product of the Reagan era—the iPod of tax dodging, if you will—came to be known as the *tax shelter*. Here is how it worked. The income tax allowed taxpayers to deduct business losses against any form of income. So the tax-avoidance industry began selling investments in businesses whose sole charm was that they were making losses. These businesses were not regular corporations but partnerships, and as such not subject to corporate taxes. Instead, in a partnership profit is allocated each year to its investors (the partners), added (or subtracted, in the case of a loss) to the partners' own incomes, and subject to individual income taxes. Whoever invested in these loss-making partnerships—or tax shelters—could claim a share of the business's loss. For instance, a high-wage employee with a 10% stake in a partnership making a $1-million loss could deduct $100,000 from his earnings—and slash his income tax accordingly. Same thing for a wealthy individual living off interest or dividend income.

Some of these partnerships were sham companies with no economic activity whatsoever. Their raison d'être was to record fictitious paper losses that could be carried on to their owners' tax returns. Others were genuine businesses that were actually profitable but generated tax losses because of specific provisions of the tax code, such as lavish depreciation allowances in the oil, gas, and real estate sectors. The first tax law of the Reagan era, the Economic Recovery

Tax Act of 1981, allowed businesses to depreciate their assets more quickly, boosting the effectiveness of this type of tax shelter.

While the tax shelter industry was born a few years before Reagan entered the White House, it's only in the early 1980s that it truly boomed. Let's look at the numbers: In 1978, the amount of partnership losses declared on individual income tax returns represented the equivalent of 4% of the total pre-tax income of the top 1%. It rose first slowly, then exponentially, to reach the equivalent of 12% of the top 1%'s income in 1986—the highest level ever recorded in the history of the US income tax. From 1982 to 1986, fictitious losses reported by investors in tax shelters exceeded the total profits made by real partnerships throughout the country.[14] That's correct: the total amount of partnership net income—profits minus losses—reported on tax returns was negative, a truly unique phenomenon. Even during the Great Depression this had not been the case. Nineteen eighty-two was a recession year but from 1983 to 1986, the economy recovered and grew fast. Yet tax sheltering had reached such high levels that entire industries, from real estate to oil, looked like they were making losses—paper losses, that is, deductible from the personal income of their owners.

Income tax receipts collapsed. By the mid-1980s, federal income tax revenues—individual plus corporate—reached their lowest level as a fraction of national income since the recession of 1949, which had been one of the most severe downturns in modern US history. Meanwhile the federal government deficit rose to over 5% of national income between 1982 and 1986, the highest level on record since the Second World War.

This outburst of tax dodging ultimately strengthened Reagan's hand when negotiating the 1986 Tax Reform Act. At that point the deficit was so high that Democrats insisted any change to the law must not further deteriorate the fiscal balance. Reagan obliged: tax rates would be slashed, but the cut would be made revenue-neutral thanks to the abolition of tax shelters. Gone would be the days when a fictitious $100,000 paper loss could erase a real $100,000 salary. Business losses, from then on, would only be deductible against business gains.[15] Given the level that tax sheltering had reached in the mid-1980s, plugging this loophole was poised to bring in billions. And it did. After the enactment of the law, partnerships, as if by magic, stopped making paper losses. From 12% of the pre-tax income of the top 1%, the total amount of partnership losses fell to 5% in 1989 and 3% in 1992. By the early 1990s, the tax shelter had disappeared.

TAX AVOIDANCE VERSUS TAX EVASION: A FLAWED DEBATE

Markets are the most powerful institution invented so far to satisfy the infinity of human desires; the most efficient way to supply diverse products that address the changing needs of billions of individuals. But they are inherently devoid of any concern about the common good. The same markets that provide us with ever-speedier cellphones and more tasty breakfast cereal can without flinching supply services of no or negative social value: services that enrich one part of society but make another part just as poor, or even make us collectively poorer. The tax-avoidance market is an example of such a market. It does not create a dollar of value. It makes the rich richer at the expense of the government—that is, every one of us. Behind every epidemic of tax dodging lies not a sudden aversion for taxation among the population, but an outburst of creativity in the market for tax dodges.

To be sure, not all of the services provided by tax lawyers and tax consultancy firms are worthless from a social standpoint. Some help individuals and companies understand the tax law, clarify ambiguities, or more basically fill out tax forms on their behalf. These services are all legitimate. But manufacturing products that do nothing but slash taxes owed is not very different from selling burglary tools. At least that's how this activity was treated before 1980: the market for tax dodges was considered repellent and it was not allowed to prosper. No market exists in a vacuum: governments decide which can exist and which can't, or at the very least which are to be severely regulated. Tolerating tax avoidance is a choice that governments make.

Which brings us to a series of interesting questions. First, if it's pure theft, how does the tax-dodging industry manage to legitimize itself?

In America, the rhetoric that condones tax dodging can be traced back to the earliest days of progressive taxation. In 1933, the *New York Times* revealed that J. P. Morgan—a titan of American wealth—had paid no income tax for 1931 and 1932. The financier soon found himself under attack by the Senate banking committee and became increasingly unhappy with the Democrats' and FDR's shaming of tax dodgers.[16] Their sin, in Morgan's view? Lumping tax evasion and tax avoidance together. Tax evasion was breaking the law; everybody agreed it was bad. But tax avoidance wasn't: it was merely using loopholes in the tax code to keep more of one's income. There was no moral responsibility to shun loopholes, he insisted. The responsibility was the government's: if a loophole was there, policymakers had to fix it. In the meantime, those smart enough to exploit it were not to blame. No surprise, Morgan insisted he merely avoided taxes but never evaded.

This line of defense is still at the core of today's tax-dodging industry. But it was wrong when J. P. Morgan advanced it and it is wrong now. Why? Because the law of the United States—like that of most other countries—contains a set of provisions, known as the economic substance doctrine, that make illegal any transaction that has no other purpose than a reduction of tax liability. Everyone understands that the market for tax dodging will always be one step ahead of governments: it's impossible to anticipate the myriad ways in which highly paid and motivated tax accountants and consultants will try to circumvent the law. That's why the economic substance doctrine preemptively invalidates transactions that have no other purpose than avoiding taxes. Investing in sham partnerships to generate tax-deductible paper losses? Creating shell companies in Bermuda with the sole purpose of dodging taxes? Even if they are not explicitly prohibited by the law, these transactions violate the economic substance doctrine. As such, they are illegal.

Of course, it can be hard to know why individual taxpayers enter certain transactions. Sometimes, schemes that look like pure tax dodging also advance a legitimate economic goal. Governments also use the tax system to promote certain activities, for instance investing in local government bonds (whose interest payments are tax-exempt in the United States). Granting these incentives is often bad policy—because it reduces tax revenues for dubious reasons, often under the pressure of special interest groups—but exploiting them is not reprehensible. J. P. Morgan was correct about that. The problem is that a great deal of supposedly "perfectly legal" tax dodging—like the creation of shell companies in small tropical islands—evidently violates the economic substance doctrine, and as such breaks the law.[17]

POLITICS AND THE LIMITS OF ENFORCEMENT

Which brings us to the second fundamental question. If many transactions that cost billions in tax revenue really are illegal, why aren't they challenged in court? What prevents governments from enforcing the economic substance principle?

To understand this puzzle, we must start with the fact that tax authorities can't possibly investigate all suspicious transactions. There is, to start with, a basic information problem: learning about the universe of schemes that pop up takes time, and the tax-avoidance industry can easily overwhelm the examination capacities of the IRS. In 1980, the US Tax Court had 5,000 tax-sheltering cases pending; by 1982, as the tax-dodging frenzy was gaining steam, that number had tripled to 15,000.[18] In a few months, the court had to learn about and rule on thousands of different schemes that had spawned, an impossible task.

There's also a resource problem. The most tax-averse Americans collectively spend billions of dollars each year to craft their tax-optimization strategies, and they spend larger and larger sums. The human and monetary resources available at the IRS are smaller, and they are dwindling. This makes it harder not only to discover dubious schemes, but also to investigate, prosecute, and ultimately invalidate illegal transactions. Even when a fishy stratagem is identified, deep-pocketed taxpayers can hire the best lawyers to defend it (including former lawmakers), extending the legal battle for years and boosting their chances to prevail in court.

In an ideal world, the IRS would rely on self-regulation within the tax-planning industry. Tax lawyers and accountants would follow high ethical principles and see it as part of their professional duty to help enforce the spirit of the law; they would refrain from commercializing dodges that violate the economic substance doctrine. The problem, however, is that these lawyers and accountants are paid by the very promoters and consumers of tax dodges, and thus face a serious conflict of interest.

A good illustration of this issue is the business that has developed since the 1980s wherein aggressive tax dodges are sold along with written legal opinions affirming their plausible legality. These opinion letters, in effect, serve as fraud insurance, protecting tax avoiders against potential penalties in case the scheme they adopt is dubbed abusive by the IRS. Tax lawyers are bound by ethical guidelines (and their conscience) to provide a fair legal opinion. But opining on whether a grey-zone dodge is closer to the black than to the white involves a good deal of subjectivity, and when the monetary reward is high enough, the temptation to supply the "correct" opinion—meaning the one that will whitewash even the dirtiest scheme—can be overwhelming.

Finally, and perhaps most importantly, there can be a lack of political will to enforce taxes. The clearest case in point is the slow death of the estate tax. While estate and gift tax revenues amounted to 0.20% of household net wealth in the early 1970s, since 2010 they have barely reached 0.03%–0.04% annually—a reduction by a factor of more than five. Some of this fall owes to the rise in the exemption threshold and the decline in the top marginal tax rate (from 77% in 1976 down to 40% today), but the bulk of it stems from a collapse in enforcement. In 1975, the IRS audited 65% of the 29,000 largest estate tax returns filed in 1974. By 2018, only 8.6% of the 34,000 estate tax returns filed in 2017 were examined.[19] The capitulation has been so severe that if we take seriously the wealth reported on estate tax returns nowadays, it looks like rich people are either almost nonexistent in America or that they never die. If we believe the wealth reported on estate tax returns, wealth is more equally distributed in the United States today than in France, Denmark, and Sweden.[20] When people listed by *Forbes* as being among the 400 richest Americans die, the wealth reported in their estate is on average only half of the *Forbes* estimate of their true wealth.[21]

What happened? There has always been estate tax avoidance.[22] But successive administrations have addressed the problem with varying degrees of enthusiasm. Since the 1980s efforts have been, to say the least, minimal. Disparaged as a "death tax" by its opponents, the estate tax is the only federal tax on property. It's also the most progressive of all federal levies—having exempted since its inception more than 90% of the population.[23] As such, it has been one of the prime targets of the property-sacralizing, inegalitarian ideology that has shaped American politics since the 1980s. It is impossible to understand the success of today's estate tax planning industry—the proliferation of "charitable" trusts, the abuse of valuation discounts, not to mention well-documented cases of outright (and unprosecuted) fraud[24]—outside of this political context. Politics shapes enforcement priorities, most importantly the choice to implement the economic substance doctrine or to tolerate transactions that have the sole purpose of reducing one's tax bills.

Enforcement decisions are why, in contrast to what's commonly believed, tax compliance does not necessarily increase whenever tax rates are slashed—quite the contrary. When Reagan reduced the top income tax rate from 70% to 50% in 1981, tax sheltering escalated. Ever since top estate tax rates were cut in the early 1980s (from 70% in 1980 to 55% in 1984) and then again in the 2000s (from 55% in 2000 to 40% today) estate tax dodging has similarly gained steam. In both cases, changes in tax enforcement—changes that reflected the deeper political and ideological shifts driving the decline in statutory rates in the first place—trumped the supposed pro-compliance effects of lower top tax rates.[25]

"THE POOR EVADE, THE RICH AVOID" . . . OR VICE VERSA?

Who evades taxes today? Answering this question is difficult: measuring illegal activity and the underground economy is by definition fraught with uncertainties. However, we are not completely in the dark. There are two key sources to estimate the size and distribution of tax evasion. The first is random tax audits. In addition to its operational audits, which are targeted at people most likely to be cheating, the IRS examines the tax returns of a subset of randomly selected taxpayers each year. In so doing, the agency's goal is not to pursue likely tax dodgers but to estimate the size of the tax gap— how much taxes in total go uncollected—and learn more about who evades. That's why the audited returns are, for the purpose of this research program, selected at random.[26]

Random audits are a powerful tool that can uncover unreported self-employment income, abuses of tax credits, and more broadly all relatively simple forms of tax evasion. But they have one main limitation: they do not capture the tax evasion of the ultra-rich well. It is almost impossible in the context of a random audit to detect the use of off-shore bank accounts, exotic trusts, hidden shell corporations, and other sophisticated forms of tax evasion. Most of these forms of tax dodging occur via legal and financial intermediaries, many of which operate in countries with a great deal of financial opacity. To supplement random audits, one needs to use other sources of information that can capture these complex forms of tax evasion. These sources include leaks from offshore financial institutions—like the 2016 "Panama Papers," a leak of internal documents from the Panamanian firm Mossack Fonseca—and tax amnesties—government programs where tax evaders are encouraged to come clean in exchange for reduced penalties.

A famous saying among American tax lawyers is that "the poor evade but the rich avoid." Only boorish taxpayers violate black letter law; the wealthy use civilized and legal loopholes to slash their bills, according to this view. Once we combine random audits with leaked data and amnesty data, however, there is scant evidence that the saying conveys any truth. As shown in Figure 3.1, taking into account all taxes at all levels of government, all social groups in the United States evade part of their tax duties. But the rich seem to evade more than the rest of the population. The fraction of taxes owed but unpaid is stable across most of the income distribution,

3.1 THE RISE OF TAX EVASION AMONG THE WEALTHY

(Taxes evaded as percentage of taxes owed,
by pre-tax income groups)

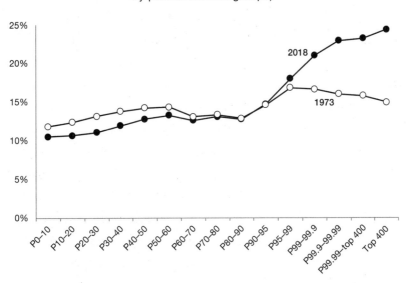

Notes: The figure depicts the amount of taxes evaded as a fraction of taxes owed, by groups of pre-tax income, in 1973 and 2018. All taxes at all levels of government are included. In 1973, the rate of tax evasion was fairly constant across income groups. In 2018, the rich evaded more (around 20% to 25%) than the working class and middle class (who evaded around 10% to 12% of their taxes). Complete details at *taxjusticenow.org.*

from the working class to the upper middle class, at a bit more than 10%—before rising to almost 25% for the ultra-rich.[27]

How can we explain this finding? First, the working class and the middle class are unable to evade much. Most of their income consists of wages, pensions, and investment income earned through domestic financial institutions. These income sources are automatically reported to the IRS, which makes tax evasion impossible. There is, of course, tax evasion at the bottom of the income pyramid—mostly evasion of consumption taxes (for instance through the use of cash transactions) and of payroll taxes (for instance, in the case of self-employed individuals), the two main taxes paid by working-class Americans. But tax dodging, for the vast majority of the population, is limited by the systematic reporting of information by employers, banks, and other third parties to the IRS.[28] As we move up the income pyramid, less and less income is third-party reported, making tax evasion possible.

The second and main reason why tax evasion rises with income is that, in contrast to the rest of society, the rich can count on the tax-dodging industry to help them shirk their duties. This industry has become more elitist over time: it targets wealthier taxpayers today than it did four decades ago. Back in the early 1980s, promoters of tax shelters advertised their creations in mainstream newspapers. On the plus side, they had hundreds of thousands of clients: doctors, lawyers, regular employees, and wealthy heirs alike. But the scams they created were highly visible and always at risk of being shut down by the IRS. The modern tax-planning industry targets the global economic elite through invitation-only events such as galas, golf tournaments, and art exhibition openings. As inequality rises the big wealth management banks—as well as the law firms and fiduciaries that create shell companies, trusts, and foundations—can earn large fees by courting a few extremely rich clients.[29]

That's how tax evasion, which back in 1973 (the first year the IRS random audits program was carried out) was roughly constant across the income spectrum, today rises as we move up the income distribution. With the deregulation of the financial industry and the rise of inequality, the tax-dodging industry has never been more extensive—and more concerned with servicing the ultra-rich. This evolution has been reinforced by two concurrent trends. The first is changes in enforcement—as we saw in the case of the estate tax. The second is globalization, which has opened new forms of tax dodging: the shifting of corporate profits to tax havens (which we will study thoroughly in the next chapter) and wealth concealment in secrecy jurisdictions.

3.2 "THE POOR EVADE, THE RICH AVOID" . . . OR VICE VERSA?

(Taxes evaded as percentage of total taxes owed,
by pre-tax income groups)

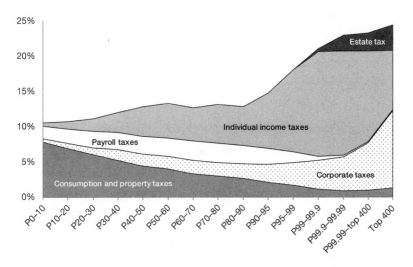

Notes: The figure depicts the amount of taxes evaded as a fraction of total taxes owed, by groups of pre-tax income, in 2018. The graph also displays the composition of tax evasion by type of tax. All taxes at all levels of government are included. In 2018, the rich evaded more than the working class and middle class due to weak estate tax enforcement, aggressive corporate tax dodging by multinationals, and offshore individual income tax evasion. Complete details at *taxjusticenow.org*.

THE GREAT ESCAPE: TAX EVASION ACROSS BORDERS

At the heart of today's tax dodging lies a powerful and versatile technology: the offshore shell company. Popularized in 2016 by the revelations in the Panama Papers, the offshore shell company is like a multi-tool. It can be used to avoid estate taxes, capital gains taxes, ordinary income taxes, wealth taxes, corporate income taxes, withholding taxes on cross-border payments of interest, dividends, and royalties. It also comes in handy if you want to defraud the IRS, ex-spouses, children, business partners, or creditors. It's not unhelpful if your goal is to practice insider trading, launder money, pocket illegal commissions, fund an electoral campaign under the table, or finance terrorist groups. As an emblem of the zero-sum economy, the offshore shell has no rivals.

The use of this technology has skyrocketed since the 1980s. In 1936, as we have seen, a number of wealthy Americans incorporated offshore shell companies to try to avoid income taxes, before Congress made it illegal to earn income abroad without paying tax in the United States. But it's only over the last three decades that the market for shell companies has taken off. Consider Mossack Fonseca, for which thanks to the Panama Papers leak comprehensive data are available. From its creation in 1977 to 1986, Mossack Fonseca incorporated a few hundred shell companies a year. From 1986 to 1999, thousands a year. From 2000 to 2010, more than ten thousand a year. After the financial crisis, the number of new company formations fell back to slightly less than 10,000 a year. At the time of the leak in 2016, Mossack Fonseca alone had created 210,000 companies in twenty-one offshore financial centers, most prominently the British Virgin Islands and Panama.[30] There are no reliable estimates of the total number of active shell companies globally, but it's likely to be in the hundreds of thousands, and possibly in the millions.

In the United States, shell companies have gained new notoriety thanks to the fraud of Paul Manafort. In August 2018, jurors in Virginia found that President Trump's former campaign chairman had forgotten to report on his tax returns millions paid by Ukrainian oligarchs to his bank accounts in Cyprus. Just like the vast majority of the offshore bank accounts used by tax evaders throughout the world, his Cypriot accounts belonged on paper to shell companies incorporated in zero-tax places. Why? Because shell companies disconnect bank accounts from their owners, creating financial opacity that makes it harder for tax authorities, investigators, and regulators to know who really owns what. In Switzerland, historically the global epicenter of offshore wealth management, more than 60% of the wealth held by foreigners is owned through shell companies, primarily incorporated in the British Virgin Islands and Panama.[31]

FIGHTING TAX EVASION: THE LESSON OF FATCA

For a long time, the notion that offshore tax evasion could be fought effectively was greeted with polite circumspection, to say the least. Isn't Switzerland, like all sovereign nations, entitled to its own laws? If it wants to enforce strict bank secrecy, forbidding financial institutions from sharing information about their clients, what on earth could make it change?

And yet change happened in 2010, when Congress passed and President Obama signed into law the Foreign Account Tax Compliance Act (FATCA), which imposes an automatic exchange of data between foreign banks and the IRS. Financial institutions throughout the world must identify who among their clients are American citizens and tell the IRS what each person holds in his or her accounts and the income earned on them. Failure to take part in this program carries stiff economic sanctions: a 30% tax on all dividends and interest income paid to the uncooperative financial institutions by the United States. Under that threat, almost all countries have agreed to apply this law. Emulating the United States, many other countries have secured similar agreements with tax havens and the automatic sharing of bank information has since 2017 become the global standard. The main tax havens, including Luxembourg, Singapore, and the Cayman Islands, participate in this new form of international cooperation.

Although it is still too soon to provide a quantitative assessment of this policy, it marks a major qualitative departure from earlier practices. Before the Great Recession, there was almost no exchange of data between banks in tax havens and other countries' tax authorities.[32] Hiding wealth abroad, in that context, was child's play. Doing so nowadays requires more sophistication and determination.

The new regime is imperfect. It would be naïve to think that the same bankers who, for decades, have been hiding their clients behind shell companies, smuggling diamonds in toothpaste tubes, and handing out bank statements concealed in sports magazines, are now all honestly cooperating with the world's tax agencies. Financial opacity is still extreme, and it's too easy for offshore bankers to pretend that they don't have American or French clients—but that they only manage accounts "belonging" to shell companies in Panama or the Bahamas—and thus send no information to the relevant authorities. Even so, it is important to realize the progress made since the mid-2000s, when secrecy and lack of cooperation prevailed.

Time and again, the key lesson emerges: What's been accepted yesterday can tomorrow be outlawed. New forms of international cooperation, deemed impossible by many, can materialize in relatively short periods of time. Tax evasion is not an unchangeable fate that condemns any project for greater tax justice to failure. Tolerating tax evasion is a choice we collectively make, and we can make other choices.

Chapter 4

WELCOME TO BERMULAND

I t was a cold winter day in Washington, DC, so the ceremony took place indoors. In the Oval Office President Donald Trump signed into law the Tax Cuts and Jobs Act—"the biggest tax cut, the biggest reform of all time"—on December 22, 2017. The key feature of the bill was a cut in the corporate income tax rate from 35% to 21%. According to its proponents, the bill was going to spur growth and create jobs. But even those who did not agree with this optimistic forecast recognized that reform was long overdue. The corporate tax was broken. Between 1995 and 2017, while the federal corporate tax rate had remained constant at 35% and profits had grown faster than the economy, corporate income tax revenue (as a share of national income) had fallen by 30%. Massive amounts of profits had been shifted to low tax places. American firms had accumulated more than three trillion dollars in Bermuda, Ireland, and other offshore tax havens.[1] The market for tax dodges was brimming with innovation; tax authorities were overpowered. Does this ring a bell?

For the majority of the nation's political, economic, and intellectual elites, slashing the corporate tax rate was the right thing to do. During his presidency, Barack Obama had advocated in favor of reducing it to 28%, with a lower rate of 25% for manufacturers. Trump's reform did not garner the same bipartisan fervor as Reagan's Tax Reform Act of 1986: Democratic lawmakers considered 21% too low a rate, objected to the changes the bill made to individual income taxes, and did not vote for it. But most lawmakers agreed that lower corporate tax rates were in order. In holding that opinion, they were in line with most policymakers in rich countries. As Trump's bill passed, French president Emmanuel Macron vowed to cut the corporate tax from 33% to 25% between 2018 and 2022. The United Kingdom was ahead of the curve: it had started slashing its rate under Labour prime minister Gordon Brown in 2008 and was aiming for 17% in 2020. On that issue, the Browns, Macrons, and Trumps of the world agree. The winners of global markets are mobile; we can't tax them too much. Other countries are cutting their rates? We must cut our rates too. Google has moved its intellectual property—and thus most of its profits—to Bermuda? We must give the company tax incentives to move its IP back to the United States.

There's a problem with this world view. If globalization means ever-lower taxes for its main winners—the owners of big multinational companies—and ever-higher taxes for those it leaves out—working-class families—then it probably has no future. Tax injustice and inequality will keep increasing. And to what end? There is a significant risk that more and more voters, falsely convinced that globalization and fairness are incompatible, will fall prey to protectionist and xenophobic politicians, eventually destroying globalization itself.

WHEN BIG CORPORATIONS PAID A LOT OF TAX

From the creation of the corporate income tax at the beginning of the twentieth century until the late 1970s, large companies did not avoid much tax. It was not for lack of opportunities—the laws that govern the taxation of multinational firms have not changed much since the beginning of the twentieth century. But two elements kept tax avoidance in check. First, as they did for individuals, Franklin Roosevelt and his successors limited corporate tax dodging with a proactive enforcement strategy, shaming tax dodgers, and appealing to morality.

But more importantly, corporate executives conceived of their role differently. In the United States today, conventional wisdom holds that the goal of CEOs must be to grow the stock price of their firms. Corporations, according to that world view, are nothing more than a conglomerate of investors pooling their resources together. Although some corporate leaders may lament being hamstrung by activist shareholders, they all consider it their duty to maximize shareholder value. And dodging taxes unquestionably enhances shareholder value. Less tax paid means more after-tax profits that can be distributed in dividends to shareholders or used to buy back shares.

But the shareholder-is-king doctrine is not universal, as evidenced by the diverse compositions of corporate boards across the world. In many countries, employee representatives make up a third of the members of corporate boards; in Germany the number is half in large companies.[2] Before the 1970s US corporations, although workers' representatives were not on their boards, were also widely considered responsible to a broad class of stakeholders beyond their owners: employees, customers, communities, and governments.[3] Which, for our purposes, has one implication: company executives did not consider it their duty to dodge taxes and did not have much of a tax-planning budget. Fifty years ago General Electric, though it was already a globe-spanning conglomerate, did not employ a thousand tax lawyers as it has recently.

Let's take a look: in the early 1950s, the federal corporate income tax collected 6% of national income, almost as much as the individual income tax! As we've seen in Chapter 2, up to the 1970s the cor-

4.1 THE SLOW AGONY OF THE CORPORATE TAX

(Federal corporate and individual income tax revenue,
percentage of national income)

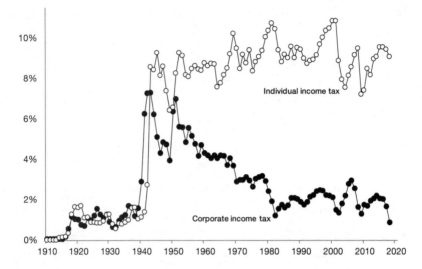

Notes: The figure depicts federal corporate tax revenue and federal individual income tax revenue as a share of national income since 1913. Both the corporate and individual income tax increased sharply during World War II. Individual income tax revenue has stayed about stable (around 10% of national income) after World War II while corporate income tax revenue has eroded. In 2018, federal corporate tax revenue was only about 1% of national income, the lowest since the Great Depression. Complete details at *taxjusticenow.org*.

porate tax accounted for the majority of the tax payments made by the wealthy, thus playing a key role in the progressivity of the overall US tax system.

We should be careful not to exaggerate the contribution of the corporate tax. The high corporate tax receipts of the early 1950s were in part the result of exceptional circumstances. During the Korean War, the US government reinstated an excess profit tax (a levy it had applied during the two world wars), at a rate of 30% on top of the

47% statutory tax rate in place; this surtax boosted revenue between 1950 and 1953. After it was repealed, corporate tax revenue stabilized to 4%–5% of national income in the late 1950s and 1960s.

What's important to realize, however, is that 4%–5% is still much more than today: in the aftermath of the Trump tax reform, the federal corporate tax now barely collects 1% of national income in revenue. It's been reduced by a factor of four over half a century. What happened?

THE BIRTH OF PROFIT SHIFTING

The first dent occurred in the late 1960s and early 1970s, in the context of rising inflation and declining corporate profits. In the 1950s and up to the late 1960s, with virtually no competition from Europe or Japan, US corporations were highly profitable. This started to change in 1969 and 1970, when the US economy entered a recession as the government increased taxes to close the budget deficits of the Vietnam War and the Federal Reserve tightened interest rates to fight inflation. The decline in profitability continued with the Oil Shock of 1973 which led to a severe recession and the large increase in interest rates during the 1970s. Because interest is tax deductible, high interest payments reduce the tax base and hence corporate tax revenue.

These macroeconomic effects were followed, in the late 1970s and in the first half of the 1980s, by the birth of the corporate tax-dodging industry—at the same time the tax-sheltering industry swelled, and in the same ideological context.

What was the equivalent, for corporations, of the sham partnership that was all the rage for high-earning individuals? The Netherlands Antilles finance company. A US firm would set up a subsidiary on the island of Aruba, Bonaire, or Curaçao. It would then have this affiliate borrow money from a European bank at the prevailing interest rate, around 3%, and lend it back to the US parent company at a much higher interest rate, around 8%.[4] The benefit of this maneuver was twofold. The offshore finance company would earn income from the five points of interest margin, and because there was no income tax in the Netherlands Antilles, this income would be tax-free. More important was the gain for the US parent: since interest paid is deductible from the corporate income tax base, the sums paid to Antilles affiliates reduced the amount of tax owed to Uncle Sam. Like sham partnerships, this was a gross tax dodge that authorities eventually shut down in the mid-1980s.

To see corporate tax avoidance in full flower, we must wait for the mid-1990s. Tax avoidance and evasion do not bloom spontaneously; as we've seen in the previous chapter, they're fueled largely by the peddlers of tax dodges. And the tax-avoidance industry does not function in a vacuum: the ideological, economic, and legal context in which it operates matters. In the 1990s, all the lights turned green. The Berlin Wall had just fallen; free-market ideas were triumphing. A new generation of executives, indoctrinated into the shareholder-is-king model in the 1980s, were taking up the reins of America's multinationals.

At the same time, globalization was opening new tax-saving opportunities. Up to the 1980s, US companies made less than 15% of their earnings abroad. When all your customers are in the United States, setting up shell companies in the British Virgin Islands can look suspicious in the eyes of the tax authorities. In the mid-1990s, however, the share of earnings made outside of the United States exploded, reaching about 30% in the first decade of the twenty-first century. The profit-shifting frenzy could start.

Here's how it unfolded.

WELCOME TO BERMULAND

Profit-shifting exploits frailties in the legal system that governs the taxation of multinational firms. This legal system was designed in the 1920s, quickly after the invention of the corporate tax, and has remained largely unchanged.[5] It embraces the notion that any subsidiaries of a multinational firm should be treated as separate entities. Apple Ireland must be considered for tax purposes as a firm of its own, distinct from Apple USA. Any profit made by Apple Ireland must be taxed in Ireland, and any profit made by Apple USA must be taxed in the United States.

The problem is simple: because the corporate tax rate in Ireland (12.5% according to the law, and in practice often much less) is lower than in the United States (21%, not including state corporate taxes), Apple is better off booking its profits in Ireland than in America, and the company has ample opportunities to do so. Of course, certain rules constrain the division of global profits across the subsidiaries of a given multinational group. In theory, firms must determine the location of their profits by exchanging goods, services, and assets internally—as if their various subsidiaries were independent entities. In each exchange, the subsidiaries must trade at the prevailing market price for the good, service, or asset—what is known as the arm's-length principle. In practice, however, multinationals are substantially free to decide for themselves what prices they use (and therefore where they book their profits) thanks to the tax-dodging industry.

In the 1990s, the industry began selling multinationals on internally exchanging assets and services that possessed one key virtue: no market price. Assets and services such as logos, trademarks, and management services have no observable market value, thus making the arm's-length principle impossible to enforce. What's the price of Apple's logo? It's impossible to know: this logo has never been sold in any market. What's the price of Nike's iconic "swoosh"? What's the price of Google's search and advertisement technology? Since these logos and trademarks and patents are never traded externally, firms can pick whatever price suits them.

The product peddled by the tax-dodging industry is all-in: a creative intragroup transaction, and a certified "correct" transfer price to be charged for that transaction. In practice, the transfer prices used are typically those that maximize tax savings for the multinational group. The accountants that propose and certify these transfer prices are paid by the multinationals themselves. The outcome of all of this? Thanks to the proliferation of intragroup transactions conducted at doctored prices, high profits end up being recorded in subsidiaries where tax rates are low, and low profits in places where they are high.

To see how this works in practice, it's worth considering a few examples.

In 2003, a year before it was listed as public company in August 2004, Google sold its search and advertisement technology to its own "Google Holdings," a subsidiary incorporated in Ireland, but for Irish tax purposes a tax resident of Bermuda, an island in the Atlantic where its "mind and management" are supposedly located. The price charged for this transfer is not public information. When the US corporate income tax was created in 1909, the law provided for firms' tax returns to be made public—with a view, precisely, to prevent tax evasion. But Congress repealed the mandatory public disclosure in 1910, and ever since the tax affairs of America's corporate giants have remained well-kept secrets.

Nonetheless, it's easy to conjecture that the price paid by Google Holdings to acquire Google's technology was modest. Why? Because if it had been high, Google would have paid a substantial tax in the

United States in 2003. But that year, according to the prospectus it filed in 2004 with the Securities and Exchange Commission, it paid $241 million globally.[6] Even if the company's entire tax bill resulted from the sale of Google's intangibles to its Bermuda subsidiary (which is unlikely, as Google probably paid taxes for other reasons), it would imply a sale price for the intangibles of less than $700 million. That's not much for an asset that has generated dozens of billions in revenue since then. In just one year, 2017 (the latest year available), Google Holdings in Bermuda made $22.7 billion in revenue. How so? Because it's the legal owner of some of Google's most valuable technologies. Google Holdings licenses the right to use its technology to Google's affiliates throughout Europe. (A similar scheme is used in Asia, with Singapore in lieu of Bermuda). Google's subsidiaries in Germany or France pay billions of dollars in royalties to Google Holdings for the right to use the so-called Bermudian technology, reducing the tax base in Germany and in France, and increasing it in Bermuda by the same amount.[7]

The corporate tax rate in Bermuda? Zero.

European firms do this too. In 2004, a few months after Google transferred its intellectual property to Bermuda, Skype—a company founded by a Swede and a Dane—moved most of its voice-over-IP technology to a subsidiary incorporated in Ireland. What's interesting in the case of Skype is that thanks to "LuxLeaks"—a trove of confidential documents leaked in 2014 from PricewaterhouseCoopers— we know the details of this transaction. According to PwC, how much was the groundbreaking technology that was going to disrupt the telecommunications market worth? A grand total of 25,000 euros.[8] In September 2005, a few months after this transaction, Skype was bought by eBay for $2.6 billion.

It's not a coincidence that Google and Skype sold their intellectual property at the same time to shell companies located somewhere between Ireland and Bermuda. Around 2003–2004, this was the dodge of choice for the tax-avoidance industry. Skype, like Google, was given the same advice: move fast, before being listed as public companies or bought back by another firm. Why? Because it's harder to pretend your core technology is nearly worthless when the market values you in the billions.

With these examples, we can see that corporate tax dodging, whatever may be said about it, is quite simple. At its core, it involves manipulating the price of intragroup transactions in goods (like iMacs), services (as when a US firm buys "management advice" from an affiliated party in Switzerland), assets (such as Google selling its search and advertisement technology to its Bermuda subsidiary), or loans (as happened during the Netherlands Antilles frenzy of the early 1980s). Variations on these schemes are made available throughout the world by the Big Four accounting firms, Deloitte, Ernst & Young, KPMG, and PricewaterhouseCoopers. And they all have the same consequence: paper profits end up being recorded in subsidiaries that are located in low-tax places, employ few workers, and use little capital.

FORTY PERCENT OF MULTINATIONAL PROFITS SHIFTED TO TAX HAVENS

Thanks to a sophisticated statistical system maintained by the US Bureau of Economic Analysis (BEA), we can track the evolution of the shifting of profits by US multinationals over the last half century. United States firms are asked to annually report detailed information about their operations to the BEA, in particular the profits they book and how much tax they pay in each of the world's countries.

Until the late 1970s, US multinationals, despite facing corporate income tax rates of 50%, barely used any offshore tax havens. Some of them did have offices in Switzerland or holding companies in small Caribbean islands, but overall the sums involved were negligible: around 95% of their foreign profits were booked in high-tax places, primarily Canada, the United Kingdom, and Japan.[9] Profit shifting picked up with the Netherlands Antilles epiphany of the late 1970s; in the early 1980s the fraction of foreign profits booked in tax havens by US companies shot up to 25%. At that time, however, US companies were still making the bulk of their profits in the United States. Even though they shifted a quarter of their foreign profits to tax havens, the sums involved were small when compared to their total (US plus foreign) earnings. In the end, the Netherlands Antilles craze had little impact on the global tax bill of America's corporate giants. It's only since the late 1990s that profit shifting has truly become significant.

Today, close to 60% of the—large and rising—amount of profits made by US multinationals abroad are booked in low-tax countries. Where exactly? Primarily in Ireland and Bermuda. A finer geolocation is unfortunately impossible: as we've seen with the case of Google (now Alphabet), the frontier between these two islands is not clear, and when studying the geography of profit shifting they are better considered as a single country somewhere in the Atlantic, a place that we will call Bermuland.

In 2016, US multinationals booked more profits in Bermuland alone than in the United Kingdom, Japan, France, and Mexico combined. Considerable sums are also booked in Puerto Rico, where they are taxed at a modest effective tax rate of 1.6%. The territory is not subject to the US corporate income tax and has long been a destination of choice for tax dodgers, from pharmaceutical giants such as Abbott to tech companies like Microsoft. Next come the Netherlands, Singapore, the Cayman Islands, and the Bahamas: in each of these territories, US multinationals book more profits than in China or Mexico. Last but not least, in what is perhaps the most grotesque aspect of this farce, US firms have in 2016 (the latest year available) booked more than 20% of their non-US profits in "state-less entities"—shell companies that are incorporated nowhere, and nowhere taxed.[10] In effect, they have found a way to make $100 billion in profits on what is essentially another planet.

United States multinationals are not the only ones to shift profit to low-tax locales: European and Asian firms do it too. The result of this giant free-for-all? All countries steal a bit of revenue from each other. American firms deprive European and Asian governments of tax revenues, while European and Asian firms return the favor to Uncle Sam. A recent study estimates that globally, 40% of all multinational profits—profits made by firms outside of the country where they are incorporated, such as the profits made by Apple outside of the United States, or those of Volkswagen outside of Germany—are booked in tax havens today.[11] This corresponds to around $800 billion in income earned in the United States, France, or Brazil that ends up being booked and taxed in the Cayman Islands, Luxembourg, or Singapore, usually at rates between 5% and 10%. In this war of all multinationals against all states, US multinationals appear to be the boldest: they shift not 40% (the world average) but 60% of their foreign profits to offshore tax havens each year.

Multinationals from all sectors of the economy practice this profit shifting. Because they have more intangible capital—which can more easily be moved abroad—there is a view that tech giants are primarily to blame (and therefore that finding a way to tax them is all we need to do). Certainly, Silicon Valley companies make extensive use of tax havens. But tax dodging is also widespread in the pharmaceutical industry (Pfizer), among financial firms (Citigroup), in manufacturing (Nike), in the automobile industry (Fiat), and in luxury (Kering).[12] Why? Because any company, properly advised by the Big Four accounting firms, can create its own intangibles (logos, know-how, patents) and sell them to itself at arbitrary prices. Any company can similarly buy nebulous services from its own subsidiaries in low-tax locales. These problems have solutions, as we will see in detail in the next chapter; but we have failed to implement them. They will require more comprehensive fixes than the taxes recently adopted in a number of European countries on the revenue of digital companies.

ARE PAPER PROFITS OR MACHINES MOVING TO TAX HAVENS?

To justify the enormous sums booked in tax havens, a frequent argument maintains that this is all an outcome of tax competition.[13] Firms, according to this view, are simply responding to differences in tax rates and relocating their activities where taxes are low. They have moved their factories to Ireland, their research and development teams to Singapore, and their bank offices to George Town, Grand Cayman. It's globalization at work.

The data, however, do not lend much support to this view. They show that by and large it's paper profits that have moved to low-tax locales over the last decades—not offices, workers, or factories. Some 95% of the 17 million workers employed outside of the United States by US multinationals work in countries with relatively high tax rates, primarily in the United Kingdom, Canada, Mexico, and China.* Some of them—a bit fewer than a million—do work in tax havens, mostly in Europe. One hundred twenty-five thousand, for example, are employed in Ireland. This is not negligible compared to the size of the Irish labor force—about 2.3 million individuals—and the multinationals' presence in Ireland generates real benefits for that country (above and beyond the tax revenue collected). But this population is almost fifteen times less than the number of peo-

---

* The same is true, in particular, for the workers employed in research and development: 95% of them are in high-tax countries.

ple that work for US companies in the neighboring United Kingdom, a country whose corporate tax rate has been two times higher than Ireland's on average since the turn of the twenty-first century.

Despite decades of tax competition, there is no evidence that production has moved to tax havens on any significant scale. Instead, US corporations have expanded their activity in emerging economies. More than a third of their overseas workers, or about 6 million people, are now employed in China, India, Mexico, and Brazil.

The conclusion is the same when we look at where firms own tangible assets including plants, equipment, and office buildings. The majority of these assets are located not where taxes are low, but where workers are. Only 18% of the stock of tangible capital owned by US firms outside of the United States is in low-tax places; the remaining 82% is in high-tax countries. Contrast that with our earlier finding that close to 60% of US companies' overseas earnings are booked in tax havens, and the conclusion is clear: what has migrated to tax havens is not production; it's paper profits.

No doubt taxes, along with many other factors, are considered when firms decide where to base their activity. There is even evidence that taxes may matter more today than they did a few decades ago. The capital stock situated in tax havens, as seen in Figure 4.2, is growing; it's even growing faster than the number of people employed by multinational firms in low-tax locales. This suggests that today big companies may be more willing to move plants and offices to save on taxes than in the past. It is also clear that in certain tax havens, such as Ireland, low taxes have been instrumental in getting companies to move not only paper profits, but also real activity.

Even so, there's one important conclusion to draw from the available data: from a global perspective, the relocation of capital to low-tax places has been much less widespread than commonly assumed. What has happened is not an upsurge of tax avoidance; it's an epidemic of tax evasion. Prominent havens, such as Bermuda, zero-tax Caribbean

4.2 PAPER PROFITS ARE MOVING TO TAX HAVENS; REAL ACTIVITY LESS SO

(Percentage of foreign profits, capital, and wages
of US multinationals in tax havens)

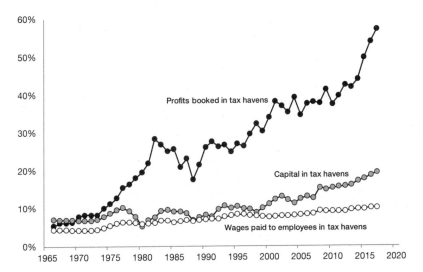

Notes: The figure depicts the evolution of the profits booked, tangible capital owned, and wages paid by US multinationals in tax havens since 1965, expressed as a fraction of the total foreign (i.e., non-US) profits, capital, and wages of US multinationals. The share of foreign profits booked in tax havens has surged from less than 5% in the 1960s to almost 60% today but workers and capital haven't moved to tax havens nearly as much. Complete details at *taxjusticenow.org.*

islands, or Malta, only lure paper profits—nothing of substance happens there. And the movement of capital toward places like Ireland is still small compared to the enormous swing of profits to treasure islands. Even the purchase of office space in Ireland by foreign multinationals might simply be a veneer of legitimacy meant to obscure the profits artificially shifted into the island—what looks like movements of tangible capital in the data may merely serve as cover up.

Today's corporate tax dodgers defend themselves with echoes of J. P. Morgan himself: this is all perfectly legal; corporations everywhere abide by the law; governments are to blame for maintaining an out-of-sync tax code. Apple pays a 1% effective tax rate in Ireland, and is ordered by the European Commission to pay back to Dublin the billions it has dodged? It's outrageous: "In Ireland and in every country where we operate, Apple follows the law and we pay all the taxes we owe."[14] Nike shifts billions in royalties to its tax-free Bermudian shell? Nothing to see here, "Nike fully complies with tax regulations." Besides, global policymakers are the ones at fault: "We encourage the OECD* to actually solve these issues," said Sundar Pichai, CEO of Google, in Davos when challenged about the tax dodging of the Mountain View, California, firm.[15]

It's a weak defense: nothing of substance happens in Bermuda, so it stands to reason that Google has booked $22.7 billion in revenue in that island to avoid taxes, in violation of the economic substance doctrine. This tax evasion persists because the political will to enforce the corporate tax has declined and the resources of multinational companies swamp those of the IRS. But that does not make the activity legitimate.

THE COMMERCIALIZATION OF STATE SOVEREIGNTY

Like the tax shelters of the early 1980s, the profit-shifting business enriches the suppliers of tax schemes and their clients while impoverishing the rest of the world. There is, however, a key difference between the tax-dodging market of the 1980s and the one that serves multinationals today. In addition to the suppliers of the dodges and their buyers, another party benefits from this commerce: the govern-

---

* Organisation for Economic Co-operation and Development.

ments of low-tax countries. These states sell a key ingredient, a vital input without which the scams peddled by the Big Four would be of little use: their own sovereignty.[16]

Since the 1980s, the governments of tax havens have engaged in a new sort of commerce. They've sold multinationals the right to decide for themselves their rate of taxation, regulatory constraints, and legal obligations. Everything is negotiable. Apple asks for a low tax rate to locate some of its companies in Ireland? Dublin obliges. Skype is worried that the taxman might one day contest the price at which it sold its intellectual property to its Irish subsidiary? Not to worry, the Grand Duchy sells insurance, in the form of what are known as advanced pricing agreements—contracts that rubber-stamp the transfer prices used by multinationals ahead of time. No profit shifting would be possible without the complicity of tax havens' governments, many of which boast high statutory tax rates, but in practice grant lower rates to the companies they court and provide them with an array of schemes to duck laws and regulations imposed elsewhere.

Why do they do this? Because the commercialization of state sovereignty is, itself, quite profitable. There are nonmonetary benefits: Luxembourg, for example, derives sizable influence within the European Union from its outsized role in the financial dealings of big companies. But most importantly there are cold, hard monetary rewards for countries that conduct this kind of commerce. By applying even tiny effective tax rates to the huge amount of paper profits they attract, tax havens generate large revenues. What country has the highest ratio of corporate income tax revenues to national income? The notorious tax haven of Malta. Number two? Luxembourg. Then come Hong Kong, Cyprus, and Ireland. At the bottom of the ranking, in 2017, we find the United States, Italy, and Germany, three countries with corporate income tax rates close to or above 30% that year.[17] The tax havens that impose low effective tax rates, between 5% and 10%, collect much more tax (relative to the size of their economy) than large countries that have rates in the 30s. The lower the rate, the higher the revenue!

We see here a striking illustration of "Laffer-curve" logic, named after the supply-side economist Arthur Laffer who popularized it in the 1970s. On this view, slashing tax rates boosts revenues. Even a rate of 0%, which on first blush may seem too low, can bring big bucks for small countries. The governments of the British Virgin Islands and Bermuda charge flat fees—and generate serious revenue—on the creation of the hundreds of thousands of shell companies they attract precisely because of their zero tax rate.

There is one small difference between the prosperity of tax havens and the one predicted by supply-side prophets. In Arthur Laffer's world, people work more, businesses invest more extensively, innovators innovate more relentlessly when taxes are low—and global GDP rises. In the real world, however, any dollar of revenue gained by Malta, Luxembourg, or Cyprus comes at the expense of other countries. It's a zero-sum transfer that does not make the world richer. When Bermuda supplies custom loopholes to big corporations, when Ireland gives sweet tax deals to Apple, when the tax office of Luxembourg works hand in hand with the Big Four, they steal the tax revenue of other nations, leaving global GDP constant. It is all zero-sum theft.

SAND IN THE WHEELS

Our intention is not to demonize this or that country, nor is it to pretend that all our problems would go away if some rogue states stopped their fiscal dumping. As globalization progresses, most countries have yielded to the temptation of selling part of their sovereignty in the hope of attracting some activity, a bit of tax revenue, whatever piece of the cake they can grab. Some—typically smaller countries, for which it's most profitable—have gone farther down that road than others. But as the world economy becomes more integrated and as new economic powerhouses emerge in the developing world, pretty much all countries are becoming small compared to the planet as a whole. The temptation to turn into a tax haven becomes overwhelming everywhere.

There have been attempts to curtail the commerce of sovereignty. The most ambitious effort to date is the OECD initiative called "inclusive framework on base erosion and profit shifting," or BEPS, that started in 2016. It is a coordinated effort to put sand in the wheels of the great tax-dodging machinery. It makes it harder for firms to manipulate transfer prices. It defines several harmful tax practices that countries are encouraged to abandon. It attempts to fix inconsistencies in the tax laws of various countries, and has compelled certain tax havens to abandon their most egregious schemes.

The data, however, suggest that BEPS and other efforts have been mostly unsuccessful. The share of US firms' profits booked in low-tax locales keeps growing year after year as depicted in Figure 4.2. The evidence is less comprehensive for non-US multinationals because the available data cover fewer years, but the trend seems to be the same. How can we explain this lack of success? The BEPS initiative does not attack the heart of the tax-dodging reactor. Firms are still supposed to exchange goods, services, and assets internally. The Big Four still manufacture transactions that have no market price. Transfer pricing accountants still have incentives to please their clients and certify as correct whatever arrangement will minimize their tax bill. In need of a Copernican revolution, we've been busy refining the Ptolemaic model of the heavens.

THE TRIUMPH OF TAX COMPETITION

The current attempts at international coordination eventually run up against a deeper limit: the lack of any serious attempt at harmonizing tax rates. Among policymakers today, there is agreement that profit shifting should be combatted, but that tax competition—as long as countries play by the books—is not reprehensible. According to that view, it is bad if a company produces patents in the United States and shifts them to tax-free Bermuda. But it is fine if the company produces them in Ireland and if Dublin taxes profits arising from patents at 6.25%, as it does today. It would still be fine if the tax rate were 1% tomorrow. Any rate is acceptable as long as the patents were made in Ireland, by local engineers working in Irish offices—BEPS allows countries to offer legal tax breaks for revenues derived from patents, what is called a "patent box." In addition to Ireland, the United Kingdom offers a rate of 10%, the United States 13.125% in the aftermath of the 2018 tax reform, to name a few.

International organizations such as the OECD are permitted to discuss ways to improve the definition of the tax base—but not tax rates. International coordination exists—except that countries are not coordinating on the key component of tax policy. The OECD hopes that thanks to its effort there will soon be no profit shifting: companies will be taxed in the country where they actually operate, fair and square. But the question remains, taxed at what rate? Even if BEPS eventually succeeded in curbing profit shifting, absent any coordination on the tax rates themselves, there would always be some countries for which it would be profitable to cut their tax rates. Slashing the corporate tax rate may be more transparent than signing backroom deals, more forthright than offering tailor-made loopholes, more honest than keeping one's eyes shut on aberrant intragroup transactions. But it has the same implication: reducing the tax liabilities of big companies and of the shareholders who own them.

At its core, slashing rates is just another form of commercialization of state sovereignty. It's a profitable business for the small countries that practice it: it boosts their revenue—and, in contrast to facilitating the pure shifting of paper profits, can even boost employment and wages. But as with other forms of commercialization of state sovereignty, these gains come at the expense of the rest of the planet. The breaks that tax havens offer to big companies impose a cost on the rest of us, a "negative externality" in economics lingo. They feed a race to the bottom, leading to a world where, to prevent capital from moving abroad, most nations are compelled to adopt tax rates that are too low—lower than the rates they would otherwise democratically choose. The fundamental problem behind the current forms of international coordination is that they do not tackle, and in fact legitimize, the undemocratic forces of tax competition.

And indeed, tax competition has intensified since the start of the BEPS process, and the global race to the bottom in corporate tax rates has accelerated. Since 2013, Japan cut its rate from 40% to 31%; the United States from 35% to 21%; Italy from 31% to 24%; Hungary from 19% to 9%; a number of Eastern European states are following the same route. Between 1985 and 2018, in what is perhaps the most striking development in tax policy throughout the world, the global average statutory corporate tax rate has fallen by more than half, from 49% to 24%. If the current trend is sustained, the global average corporate tax rate will reach 0% before the middle of the twenty-first century.

Chapter 5

SPIRAL

While they may lament the most extreme forms of dumping, like Bermuda's zero tax rate, there is broad agreement among world leaders that the decline in corporate taxation is not necessarily a bad thing. Less tax means, after all, more profits that a firm can invest. And corporate investment is an engine of growth: business expansion supports employment and wages and ultimately benefits workers. Lowering taxes on capital can benefit the working class.

But does it? If the rich pay higher taxes, does it eventually hurt the rest of us? And conversely, does slashing the taxation of capital boost investment and wages?

Unfortunately, the public debate on these questions is mired in sterile, fact-free ideological posturing. There is no shortage of prophets who predict wonders from unfettered capital, offering grandiose growth forecasts if only "tax burdens" were to fall a bit more. These seers can divine a surge of investments and higher wages when after-tax profits are allowed to rise. Let's try to think this through.

LABOR AND CAPITAL: THE SOURCES OF ALL INCOME

To understand what happens when governments tax capital, we must first define precisely the notions of "labor" and "capital." Before any taxes are collected, all of the nation's income is received by either workers or the owners of capital, because everything that we produce is made using labor and capital (machines, land, buildings, patents, and other capital assets). In some sectors of the economy such as restaurants, production mostly uses labor; economists say that sector is labor-intensive. Other sectors such as energy are capital-intensive. Sometimes capital can produce output on its own (houses produce "housing services" with no help from us humans). Sometimes labor can produce output on its own (this would happen, for instance, if Beyoncé gave a concert a cappella in a public place). Sometimes capital is tangible (houses, machines, etc.) and sometimes it is intangible (patents, algorithms, etc.). But always and everywhere, everything that is produced—and hence any income that we earn—derives from labor, capital, or some combination thereof.

Labor income is paid to workers. It is equal to the wages, salaries, and employment fringe benefits such as health insurance and pension benefits. Capital income accrues to the owners of capital independently of any work effort. It includes the profits earned by the owners of corporations (whether they are paid in dividends or reinvested), the interest paid to bondholders, the rents paid to landlords, and so on. Following common practice, we include under capital income 30% of the "mixed income" earned by self-employed individuals—such as private lawyers and doctors—and under labor income 70% of this self-employment income (the reason being that 30/70 is the capital/labor split observed by economists in the corporate sector).[1]

By definition, every dollar of income that does not go to labor goes to capital, and vice versa. Saying this is not making a judgment about whether workers and capital owners deserve their share of the pie: economists and the public at large have different views on this question, which has been a central factor in political conflict ever since capitalism was born. To observe this fact of labor and capital is merely to describe how the economy works.

Let's take a concrete example. In 2018, according to its official accounts, Apple produced about $85 billion worth of goods and services (net of the cost of the raw materials and other inputs the company bought to produce its iPhones, iMacs, and other products). Out of that $85 billion, it paid about $15 billion to its employees: this is labor income.[2] The remaining $70 billion accrued to Apple's owners and creditors: this is capital income. Some of this capital income was distributed in dividends, some of it was paid in interest to bondholders and banks, some was reinvested. Similarly, some of the labor income was paid to Apple's executives, some to entry-level engineers, some to salespersons in Apple stores. There are many forms of labor and many forms of capital, which encompass many different social realities, legal arrangements, and power relationships.

Economists have long observed that the labor share does not fluctuate much, with capital earning 25% of national income and labor the remaining 75%. Keynes famously described this stability as "a bit of a miracle." This miracle, however, was not permanent.[3] From 1980 to 2018, the labor income share has fallen from 75% to 70% in the United States (while the capital income share has increased from 25% to 30%). The trend has been particularly marked over the last two decades. Since the turn of the twenty-first century, the average labor income per adult has almost stagnated in the United States (+0.4% a year on average), while capital income rose +1.6% a year per adult—driven by the surging profits of corporate behemoths in tech, pharma, and finance. Capital prospers while labor lags behind.

CAPITAL IS TAXED LESS AND LESS; LABOR MORE AND MORE

Just as all forms of income derive from labor and capital, all taxes fall either on labor or capital. When choosing how much tax to impose on each of the two factors of production, there is a trade-off. Because capital is useful, we do not want to tax it too much, lest we reduce the productive capacity of the economy. But taxing it less means that labor must bear a heavier burden, making it harder for people who have not inherited assets to accumulate wealth, especially in a world of quasi-stagnant wages.

Where does the United States split the tax burden today? The most comprehensive way to answer this question is to contrast the evolution of three tax rates. The first is the average macroeconomic tax rate: the total amount of taxes paid divided by national income. The second is the average tax rate on capital income, that is, the total amount of capital taxes—adding up the corporate income tax, property taxes, the estate tax, and the fraction of the income tax that corresponds to levies on dividends, interest, and other forms of capital income— divided by the economy's total flow of capital income. The third and last factor is the average tax rate on labor income, defined similarly as the ratio of total labor taxes to total labor income.[4] What do we see?

In contrast to other wealthy countries, where they have stabilized over the last decades, taxes in the United States have fallen. The macroeconomic tax rate is significantly lower today than at the end of the twentieth century. It is only recently, with the tax cuts of 2018, that this trend has become fully apparent: in the short run, tax revenues rise with economic expansions and fall in recessions, and these business cycle effects can obscure the trend line. But the medium-run trend is now clear. During the second half of the 1990s, the overall US tax rate peaked at about 31.5%. In 2019, following nine years of economic growth, and with unemployment at a historically low level, it is almost four points lower, at around 28%. Given that tax collections typically fall by several percentage points during recessions, it is safe to predict that when the next recession hits, the ratio of taxes to national income will reach its lowest level since . . . the 1960s!

A decline in the tax-to-GDP ratio of almost four percentage points over the course of two decades is an exceptional historical development. Until recently, nobody—neither Ronald Reagan, nor Margaret Thatcher, nor any other conservative leader—had managed to pull off such a feat. Under Reagan, tax revenues fluctuated as a share of GDP, with no discernible trend. In the United Kingdom, tax collections were higher when the Iron Lady left Downing Street in 1990 than when she arrived in 1979. In both cases taxes fell for the wealthy. But they rose for the rest of the population, leaving total tax collection mostly unchanged. The United States over the last twenty years is the first example of a large and sustained decline in the tax take in a developed country.

All of the decline in the macroeconomic tax rate in the United States comes from the collapse in capital taxation. In the second half of the 1990s, the average tax rate on capital was 36%. In the wake of Trump's tax reform, it barely reaches 26%.

Except for property taxes, which have remained broadly stable, all capital taxes have contributed to this downfall. The corporate tax, as we've seen, has collapsed. Dividend taxation has been halved, as the top tax rate fell from 39.6% under Clinton to 20% today. Revenues from the estate tax have been reduced by a factor of almost four, from 0.4% of national income in the late 1990s to about 0.1% today.

Taking a longer perspective, the changes in the balance of taxation across labor and capital are even more striking. From wealth taxation in Massachusetts as far back as the seventeenth century to the 50% effective corporate income tax rates under Eisenhower, capital taxes have contributed prominently to the public coffers in

5.1 THE COLLAPSE OF CAPITAL TAXATION

(Macroeconomic tax rates on labor and capital in the United States)

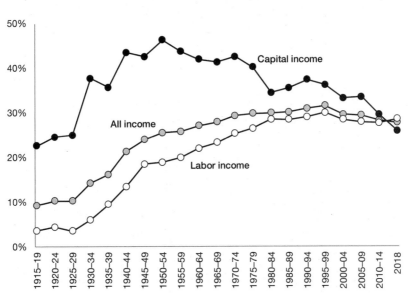

Notes: The figure depicts the evolution of the macroeconomic tax rates on capital income, labor income, and total income since 1915. Capital income and labor income add up to total national income. All federal, state, and local taxes are included and allocated to either capital or labor. Historically, the tax rate on capital was much higher than the tax rate on labor. This gap has shrunk a lot. In 2018, for the first time, the tax rate on labor is higher than on capital. Complete details at *taxjusticenow.org.*

America. From the 1940s to the 1980s, the average tax rate on capital exceeded 40%, while labor paid less than 25%. Since its peak of the 1950s, however, the average capital tax rate has been cut by twenty percentage points. At the same time, labor taxation has risen more than ten points, driven by the upsurge in payroll taxes. To capital owners who have prospered, the tax system has given more. From workers whose wages have stagnated, it has taken more. In 2018, for the first time in the modern history of the United States, capital has been taxed less than labor.

HEALTH INSURANCE:
A BIG BUT HIDDEN LABOR TAX

Even these numbers grossly underestimate the fiscal advantage that capital owners now have over workers. For these statistics only take into account public—but not private—mandatory levies. Taxes paid to governments are included, but those paid to private collectors are disregarded. Amid these taxes in everything but name, the most prominent one is health insurance paid by workers to insurance companies through their employers. Because the cost of health care is exorbitant in America (due to the much higher prices for standard medical procedures than in other wealthy nations),[5] this hidden labor tax is gigantic. The average contribution for workers covered through their employers exceeds $13,000 a year today. And it has skyrocketed over the last decades.[6]

To better understand this hidden tax, it's worth reviewing how health care is financed in the United States. Elderly Americans and low-income families are covered by public insurance programs (Medicare and Medicaid, respectively), funded by tax dollars (payroll taxes and general government revenue). The rest of the population must seek coverage by a private company; insurance, in that case, is funded by nontax payments. In practice, people most often obtain private insurance through their employers rather than pay separately. Since the passage of the Affordable Care Act in 2010, it has become compulsory to be insured: contributing to a private plan—for those not covered by Medicare or Medicaid—is mandatory. Conservatives dislike this obligation and are still trying to weaken it, but even if they succeed the situation would not fundamentally change. Whether insurance premiums are paid to a public monopoly (the government) or to a private monopoly (the notoriously uncompetitive US private health insurance system)[7] makes little difference. Both payments reduce the take-home pay of workers; and although it's always possible to evade taxes or to refuse to pay one thin dime to insurance companies, in practice almost everyone abides.

The main difference between these two forms of health coverage is their effect on the overall tax-to-GDP ratio. A greater reliance on private insurers lowers the official macroeconomic tax rate. This bias is particularly pronounced in the United States, but it also exists in countries like Switzerland and Japan that rely on compulsory or quasi-compulsory private health insurance (managed by unions, employers, or nonprofits) for the provision of health care. Like the United States, they can boast low tax-to-GDP ratios compared to the countries (such as the United Kingdom, Sweden, and France) where health insurance is fully or primarily funded by tax revenue.[8] But the boast isn't all that meaningful.

To provide a more accurate and internationally comparable picture, Figure 5.2 treats mandatory premiums paid to private insurers as taxes. These hidden taxes alone add up to 6% of national income in 2019[9]—the equivalent of one-third of all federal income tax payments! They increase the macroeconomic tax rate from 28% of national income to 34%, which is comparable to Canada and New Zealand, and barely lower than in the United Kingdom and Spain.[10] Since, by definition, these hidden taxes only fall on labor, the labor tax rate jumps even more sharply, from 29% to 37%. With this extended (and in our view more meaningful) view of taxation, we can see that during the 1980s and 1990s labor and capital tax rates converged. Since the turn of the twenty-first century—and particularly after the 2018 tax reform—capital has been taxed much less than labor.

In this broader view we can also see that the United States, con-

5.2 THE RISE OF LABOR TAXATION

(Macroeconomic tax rates on labor and capital in the United States)

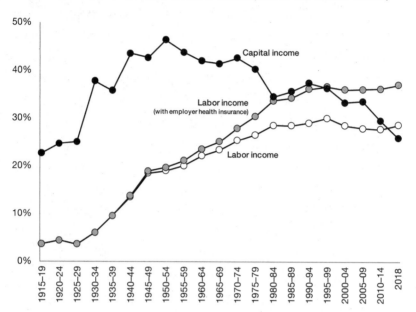

Notes: The figure depicts the evolution of the macroeconomic tax rates on capital income and labor income since 1915. Capital income and labor income add up to total national income. All federal, state, and local taxes are included and allocated to either capital or labor. The figure also includes a series where employer sponsored health insurance is added to labor taxes. Health insurance costs create an increasing and now very large extra burden on labor. In 2018, when including health insurance, the tax rate on labor is about 40%, much higher than on capital. Complete details at *taxjusticenow.org*.

trary to a widely held belief, is not a particularly low-tax country—at least once we make apples-to-apples international comparisons. After including mandatory private health insurance contributions, America's macroeconomic tax rate (34%) is still lower than France's (52%). But that's for the most part because in France, virtually all contributions to pensions (16.5% of national income) are counted as taxes too, while in the United States only contributions to Social

Security (4.5% of national income) are. In the end, the basic truth is that after they've paid their taxes, health insurance (privatized taxes), and pension contributions, Americans on average keep about the same fraction of their pre-tax income as their European brethren; the main difference is that Europeans then pay higher consumption taxes (13% of national income in France against 5% on the other side of the Atlantic). In both Europe and the United States, moreover, the burden of funding the government and health expenditures increasingly falls on labor.

THE OPTIMAL TAX RATE ON CAPITAL: 0%?

Should we worry about the decline in capital taxation and the concomitant rise of labor taxes? There is no doubt that this process is a powerful inequality engine. Always and everywhere, working- and middle-class families derive the bulk of their income from labor. Eighty-five percent of the pre-tax income earned by Americans in the bottom 90% of the income distribution comes from labor today—capital contributes only 15%. For the wealthy, it's the opposite. Top one-percenters derive more than half of their income from capital, the top 0.1% more than two-thirds.[11] It's a constant of capitalist societies: as one moves up the income ladder, the capital share of income rises—until it reaches 100% at the tip-top. When governments reduce the tax burden on capital, they almost always reduce taxes for the wealthy.

Less capital taxation means that the wealthy—who derive most of their income from capital—can mechanically accumulate more. This feeds a snowball effect: wealth generates income, income that is easily saved at a high rate when capital taxes are low; this saving adds to the existing stock of wealth, which in turn generates more income, and so on.[12] This snowballing effect contributes significantly to the surge in wealth concentration in America. The share of wealth

5.3 THE UPSURGE IN US WEALTH INEQUALITY

(Top 1% and bottom 90% shares of total private US wealth)

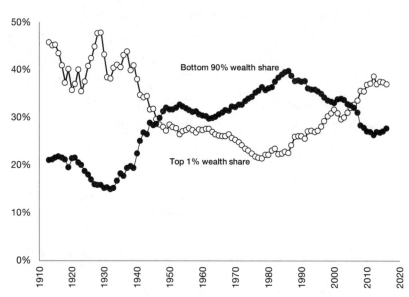

Notes: The figure depicts the evolution of shares of total household wealth owned by the top 1% wealthiest adults and the bottom 90% poorest adults. Wealth includes all private assets owned directly or indirectly by households (including housing, pension funds, and all financial assets) net of all debt. Wealth within married couples is split equally. The top 1% wealth share has almost doubled from 20% in the late 1970s to almost 40% today. Meanwhile, the bottom 90% wealth share has collapsed from 40% to about 25%. Complete details at *taxjusticenow.org.*

owned by the top 1% richest adults has exploded from 22% in the late 1970s to 37% in 2018. Conversely, the wealth share of the bottom 90% of adults has declined from 40% to 27%. Since 1980, the top 1% and the bottom 90% have exchanged their slices of the total wealth pie: what the bottom 90% has lost, the top 1% has gained.[13]

Yet if we subscribe to certain economic theories, we should rejoice at this development. For the collapse in capital taxation moves us closer to what's in the long-run interest . . . of ordinary workers. According to these theories, developed in the 1970s and 1980s, the optimal tax rate on capital is zero: all taxes on corporate profits, interest, dividends, capital gains, rents, residential properties, business properties, personal wealth, estates, and inheritances should be abolished and replaced by higher taxes on labor income or consumption.[14] Taken literally, this logic leads to striking recommendations: the Bill Gateses of the world should go completely tax-free, and governments should make up for the lost tax revenue by imposing on secretaries and retirees more. Even the poorest members of society—who own no wealth at all and earn no capital income—would benefit from such a move, at least in the long run, because they would see their pre-tax income rise.

This may sound like mere ivory-tower speculation, until you realize that it is the canonical theory taught to graduate economics students all over the world, and it's a standard benchmark in policy discussions in Washington, DC. There are, of course, numerous variations on the basic theory, according to which rates higher than zero are desirable. But these refinements often tend to be lost in policy discussions. Ask American tax law experts whether capital should be taxed. You will be surprised (it's been our experience) how many assert that "economists have proven" it should not. No large country, to be sure, has cut all its capital taxes, and in practice few people advocate for an immediate repeal of all capital taxes. But the notion that capital taxation is particularly harmful is mainstream.

Where does this belief come from? Essentially from the view that the supply of capital (the fraction of its income that the population saves each year plus the net flow of capital a country attracts from abroad) is very sensitive to changes in after-tax rates of return. So sensitive that even tiny taxes invariably end up destroying a huge swath of the capital stock in the long run. Since capital is useful—it makes workers more productive—taxing it ends up hurting wages. In economics lingo, capital taxes are entirely shifted to labor. The corporate tax, in this world view, is perceived as particularly likely to be shifted to workers. Tax companies and plants will move abroad; firms will stop purchasing capital assets, depleting the capital stock and reducing wages. In this analysis, the incidence of the corporate tax, in the jargon of economists, is on labor.

Incidence is a key part of any tax policy analysis, so let's pause on this concept to understand the merit of the arguments wielded by the opponents of capital taxation. What would happen if the corporate tax were slashed? Dividends and share buybacks might soar, boosting the income of shareholders. But firms could also increase their purchases of machines and equipment, making workers more productive and thus leading to higher wages. Or they could cut the price of the products they sell, in effect benefitting both labor and capital (to the extent that both forms of income are ultimately consumed). Tracing the myriad ways in which changes in taxation affect economic behavior, the level of economic output, and the distribution of income across the population is what tax incidence is all about.

The main result from economic research in this area is intuitive: the most inelastic factor of production bears the burden of taxes, while the most elastic factor dodges them. Concretely, if capital is very elastic—saving and investment collapse whenever capital is taxed—then labor bears the burden of capital taxation. But just as capital taxes can be shifted to labor, so too can labor taxes be shifted to capital. This happens if labor is very elastic—that is, if people work substantially less when the taxation of their earnings rises. In one of the oldest and most famous analyses of tax incidence, Adam Smith in *The Wealth of Nations* explained how taxes on wages could be shifted to capital. If farmers are at the subsistence level (they earn no more than what they need to barely survive), taxing their wage would make them starve. In that event a wage tax would be shifted away from poor peasants toward wealthier landowners, as those owners would be forced to increase pay to keep their workforce alive.

Tax incidence boils down to simple empirical questions: How

elastic are capital and labor? Does the capital stock, in particular, vanish when capital taxes rise? If it does, then taxing capital is indeed harmful and slashing corporate taxation can be in the long-run interest of workers.

A LONG-RUN PERSPECTIVE ON CAPITAL TAXATION AND ACCUMULATION

According to most commentators, capital's extreme elasticity is a law of nature, as certain as gravity. But this belief—like other stark predictions from basic economic theory (for instance, that the minimum wage must destroy employment)—needs a reality check. Although there are many ways to conduct such a check, a reasonable starting point involves comparing the long-run evolution of investment rates and capital taxes. Historically, has US investment significantly declined when capital was more highly taxed? If yes, this would mean that capital taxes reduce the capital stock and ultimately impoverish workers.

The short answer, however, is no. With data on saving and investment going back to the early twentieth century, we can contrast those figures with the average tax rates on capital incomes. It turns out that the period of high capital taxation—from the 1950s to the 1980s—was also a time when saving and investment were historically high, above 10% of national income on average. This is true whatever the measure of capital accumulation one looks at: private saving (the saving of individuals and corporations), national saving (private saving plus government saving), or domestic investment (national saving minus net foreign saving—in practice, because net foreign saving is most of the time quite small, domestic investment is close to national saving). There is no indication that capital accumulation has risen since capital tax rates started their descent in the 1980s. Quite the contrary: the national saving rate gradually fell

5.4 CAPITAL TAXATION AND CAPITAL ACCUMULATION

(Macroeconomic capital tax rate versus saving rates
in the United States)

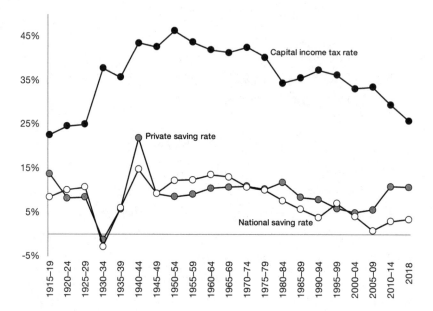

Notes: The figure depicts the evolution of the macroeconomic tax rate on capital income (total taxes on capital over total capital income), the private saving rate (household plus corporate saving, as a percent of national income), and the national saving rate (private plus government saving, as a percent of national income). From 1940 to 1980, the United States had both a high tax rate on capital and high saving rates. Since 1980, the tax rate on capital has come down and saving rates have also declined. In the macroeconomic data, taxing capital does not seem to reduce saving. Complete details at *taxjusticenow.org*.

after 1980, to reach close to 0% in the middle of the aughts. The saving rate of the rich remained stable but that of the bottom 99% of the population (and of the government) collapsed. This is the opposite of what the "zero-capital-tax" theory must assume to arrive at its strong policy recommendation.

Over the last hundred years, there is no observable correlation between capital taxation and capital accumulation. Before 1980 the saving and investment rates in the United States fluctuated around 10% of national income despite enormous variation in capital taxation. The main exceptions involve the Great Depression, when saving collapsed in a context of massive unemployment and unprecedented decline in real income, and World War II, when saving rose as consumption was rationed. Apart from these exceptional historical episodes, US saving was trendless. A similar regularity is observed in France, Germany, and the United Kingdom, three countries for which savings data go back to the nineteenth century. With the exception of the world wars, the private saving rate in these economies has fluctuated around 10% of national income, despite considerable changes in the average capital tax rate over time, from less than 5% in the nineteenth century, to more than 50% in the post–World War II decades.[15]

Let's be clear: this evidence does not prove that capital taxation has no economic cost. What it shows is that since saving and investment rates do not change much, capital taxes are borne by capital owners in the long run—not labor. Since the capital stock is no lower (and hence wages no lower) when capital taxes are high, the incidence of capital taxes falls squarely on capital. Because the rich derive most of their income from capital, while the working class and the middle class derive most of theirs from labor, capital taxes primarily hurt the rich—not the working class. Of course, saving decisions are not completely insensitive to taxes. If capital were taxed at 100%, there would probably be much less wealth in the economy. But for a broad range of after-tax returns to capital (say for returns between 2% and 5%, as has been the case over the course of the twentieth century), the available empirical evidence suggests these effects are small.

WHAT BOOSTS CAPITAL ACCUMULATION: REGULATION, NOT TAXES

Which brings us to a fundamental question: Why does capital accumulation seem to respond relatively little to capital taxation? In a nutshell, capital taxation is only one factor—and a relatively minor one—in the myriad of economic and social forces that affect wealth accumulation. The more important of these forces are the regulations that affect private saving behavior.

For most Americans, wealth primarily consists of housing and retirement savings on the asset side, and mortgage debt, consumer credit, and student loans on the liability side.[16] Public policies directly affect each of these forms of assets and liabilities. In the post–World War II decades, regulations encouraged firms to provide funded pensions to their employees. The federal government sponsored the creation of thirty-year mortgages, providing an effective tool to save over a lifetime—because paying down your mortgage debt and building home equity, now that's saving. After the 1980s, by contrast, student loans boomed as public funding for higher education retreated. Financial deregulation made it easier for people to get into debt, for example by facilitating the perpetual rollover of mortgage debt through refinancing, or by boosting the supply of consumer credit.

This is perhaps the main lesson of behavioral economics, the fast-growing field of research that strives to take a more realistic view of human behavior than the standard, hyper-rational economic model: when it comes to influencing the saving rate, nontax policies swamp tax incentives.[17] Take default options, for example. Newly hired workers are four times more likely to enroll in a 401(k) retirement savings account—the now dominant form of retirement saving in the United States—when that's the default option offered to them

(80%, in that case, do enroll) than when they have to voluntarily opt in (20%).[18] Default options not only boost retirement saving, they increase the *overall* saving rate of workers: the money put in retirement saving accounts does not crowd out other forms of wealth accumulation (such as the reimbursement of housing debt). By contrast, the traditional tax incentive that's supposed to boost retirement saving—namely, exempting investment returns from taxation—encourages people to shift money from nonretirement investments into tax-free retirement saving accounts without measurably increasing saving rates.[19] Simple "nudges" like default options have dramatically larger real effects on wealth accumulation than tax incentives.[20]

This is not to say that capital taxation has no effect. Capital is not very elastic, but it can be obscured. Rich people can hide wealth offshore. Multinational companies can shift profits to Bermuda. People can shift their investments into tax-free accounts. Because the supply of tax dodges is targeted at the rich, and capital income is primarily earned by the rich, the opportunities to dodge capital taxes are numerous when the tax-avoidance industry is not kept in check. But none of this tax dodging affects the *real* accumulation of wealth—how much stocks, bonds, and real estate people own. Therein lies a source of confusion in the debate about these questions. Yes, capital can respond strongly to taxes. But that response is to the countless ways to shift paper around—not because people start consuming much more today whenever the taxation of their saving increases. And that avoidance response is not a law of nature, but a choice that governments make. It's been large since the 1980s because governments have tolerated tax dodging, but it was weaker before.

The same conclusion holds true for the taxation of corporate profits, the form of capital income that's widely seen as most elastic. The way that corporations respond to international differences in tax rates is not primarily by moving their factories to low-tax places, but by shifting paper profits to tax havens. Profit shifting swamps true capital mobility. More generally, a host of evidence suggests that the corporate tax rate affects behavior in various domains.[21] When it rises, businesses are less likely to incorporate and more likely to opt for organizational forms that are not subject to corporate taxation, like partnerships. Companies also tend to borrow more money, as interest is tax deductible. If they get a temporary investment tax credit, firms will accelerate their investment plans. None of these choices, however, changes a firm's long-run capital stock—its stock of buildings, machines, and equipment. None of this implies that taxing corporate profits less will increase workers' wages.

Contrary to what many ideologues would like you to believe, economics has not "proven" that workers "bear the burden" of the corporate income tax. If this were true, then unions all over the world would be begging governments to slash it. In the real world, the most vocal proponents of the view that ordinary workers—not wealthy shareholders—suffer from high corporate taxes are . . . wealthy shareholders. During the 2018 US midterm elections, lobbies supported by the Koch brothers (worth about $50 billion each) spent $20 million to convince voters that President Trump's corporate tax cut was good for wages.[22] By the same token, economics has not proven that labor taxes are borne by capital. In the long run, capital taxes fall by and large on capital, and labor taxes fall by and large on labor. Poor people do not suffer from the taxes levied on the wealthy, no more than the wealthy suffer from the taxes levied on the poor.

TOWARD THE DEATH OF THE PROGRESSIVE INCOME TAX

Taxing capital less and labor more does not have proven benefits, but it has real costs. It not only undermines the sustainability of globalization—increasing the risk of a protectionist backlash, should globalization remain synonymous with lower taxes for its main winners. But it also opens the door to a potentially lethal form of tax avoidance: the shifting of income away from labor toward capital. Low capital tax rates encourage the wealthy to reclassify their highly taxed wages into lightly taxed capital income. The higher the gap in tax rates between the two forms of income, the greater the incentives to shift. As that shift takes hold, it creates a big problem: the death of the individual income tax, the main progressive component of modern tax systems.

There are, of course, many instances when it's not possible to shift income. Teachers, clerks, and most other employees will never be able to pretend their wages are in fact dividends. But for the wealthy, shifting income is child's play. The way this is done in practice is by incorporating.

Take John, a successful lawyer who earns a million dollars a year but only spends $400,000 for his ordinary personal expenditures. And picture yourself in 2050, in a world where tax competition has finally done away with the corporate tax. In such a world, what would John do? He would create his company, John LLC, which would pay him (as dividends) the $400,000 he needs to buy his meals, suits, vacations, etc., and would save the remaining $600,000. Despite earning a million, John would thus pay individual income taxes on $400,000 only. No tax would be charged on the rest: his savings would be tax-free. The income tax would be a simple consumption tax.

Any number of rich people can morph into companies and benefit when corporate tax rates are low. Lawyers, doctors, architects, and other self-employed individuals can choose to operate as corporations. Owners of financial assets can move their portfolios of stocks and bonds into holding companies. The owner-managers of private businesses can decide to slash their wages to keep more of their earnings within their firm. Even highly paid employees—software engineers, financial analysts, columnists—can become independent contractors, incorporate, and bill Google, Citigroup, or the *Washington Post* for their labor.

The threat of wealthy individuals incorporating is why all countries that have a progressive income tax also have a corporate tax. The corporate tax is a safeguard: it prevents wealthy individuals from shielding their income from the taxman by pretending it's been earned by a firm. This is not its only role; the corporate tax also ensures that companies contribute to funding the infrastructure from which they benefit, for example. But preventing tax dodging has always been its prime justification—and the reason why, historically, corporate income taxes were created at the same time as individual income taxes. Like the O-rings of the space shuttle *Challenger*, if the corporate tax malfunctions, the whole system of progressive income taxation collapses.

Once every rich person has become a company, not only is the progressive income tax dead (it is now a mere consumption tax), but the possibilities of evading this residual consumption tax become limitless. How so? By consuming within firms. Instead of paying John a (taxable) dividend, John LLC will pay for John's meals, suits, vacation, and other personal expenses. This is tax evasion, pure and simple: an allowable corporate expense is strictly regulated and does not include spending on personal consumption. But enforcing these rules and monitoring firms becomes impossible when everybody's a company—a fake company that's not accountable to anybody but its single owner. For a striking illustration, look no further than Chile today, where the vast majority of rich people have their own personal companies and routinely evade taxes by charging them for their personal expenses.[23]

The fundamental problem now comes into view: With the sharp cut in the American corporate tax rate to 21% in 2018—and the similar trend followed by corporate taxes globally—incorporating is becoming more valuable than ever for the rich. For anybody who can save a significant fraction of their income, morphing into a company is now worth the trouble, for all income that's not consumed is taxed at 21% only.

Is this idle fantasy? Examples of shifting abound throughout the world.[24] There is just one difference between the available historical record and today's situation: Until recently, governments were careful to limit the gap between labor and capital tax rates for the wealthy. Differences existed, but they were typically a few percentage points. With the collapse of capital taxation globally, we're entering unchartered territory.

If you've been appalled by the tax shelters of the 1980s, dismayed by the profit-shifting frenzy of America's corporate behemoths, hold your breath—we're now entering a third phase of tax injustice. Nothing is permanent, and positive change may well arrive in time. But under business as usual, a new wave of tax dodging is about to break. As tax competition rages and pushes corporate rates down globally, it is high noon on the clock of the next disaster.

Chapter 6

HOW TO STOP
THE SPIRAL

I n 2019, the International Monetary Fund asked a slate of experts for their views on the future of corporate taxation and tax competition. Most of the fund's interlocutors answered that tax competition was "likely to intensify" in the foreseeable future.[1] Since each nation has a sovereign right to choose its form of taxation, who could possibly force tax havens to stop their dumping? Some countries, the experts agreed, will always offer lower taxes than their neighbors if it's in their interest to do so. Mobile profits will seek the lowest tax burden. There may be ways to fix egregious forms of abuse. But taxing multinational companies at high rates? In a more and more tightly integrated global economy? Hopeless.

This view is wrong. There is nothing in globalization that requires that the corporate tax should disappear. The choice is ours. The race to the bottom that rages today is a decision we've collectively made—perhaps not fully consciously or explicitly, certainly not a choice that was debated transparently and democratically, but a choice nonetheless. We could have chosen to coordinate, and we've chosen not to. We could have chosen to prevent multinationals from booking profits in low-tax places, but we let them do it. We can make other choices, starting today.

WHY HAVE COUNTRIES FAILED SO FAR TO COORDINATE?

To see how we could escape our current predicament, we must start by understanding why we have failed, so far, to address the fiscal challenges presented by globalization.

There are, to start with, a number of relatively benign and circumstantial explanations. Financial globalization is a recent phenomenon. Close to 20% of the world's corporate profits are made by companies outside of the country where they are headquartered today.[2] Before the 2000s, that figure was less than 5%. Whether this modest amount of profits was appropriately taxed or not didn't matter much for public coffers, and so few people—in academia or in the policy world—cared. That's how the surge in multinational profits caught people off guard. In ministries of finance, the default assumption was that the 1920s-era system of transfer pricing would hold up. This assumption, as we saw in the previous chapter, was far too optimistic. But few people had thought about which system could replace it. This cluelessness allowed firms to exploit frailties in the law with quasi-impunity.

It also took time for the scale of corporate tax dodging to become clear, for the simple reason that the activities of multinational corporations are opaque. Companies are generally not required to publicly disclose in which countries they book their profits. In its annual report to the US Securities and Exchange Commission, Apple provides information on its worldwide consolidated profits. But the Cupertino-based giant doesn't publicly reveal *where* it books these profits—how much are booked in its Irish subsidiary (and thus taxed in Ireland), in Germany, or in Jersey. There is no way for the public to know how much money Apple shifts to tax havens. The same is true of most other giant multinationals.

6.1 THE RISE OF MULTINATIONAL PROFITS

(Percentage of global profits made by firms outside of the
country where they are headquartered)

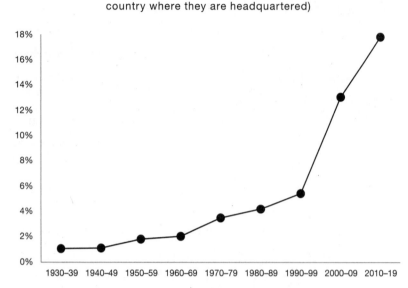

Notes: The figure depicts the evolution of the share of global corporate
profits that are made by corporations outside of the country where they
are headquartered. Decades ago, this share was small (less than 5%) but it
has grown over the last two decades to about 18% in the 2010s. Complete
details at *taxjusticenow.org*.

Ignorance is too convenient a culprit, however. No enhanced data
sources or special wisdom are needed to realize the dramatic decline
in corporate tax rates. Beyond simply not knowing, there are less
benign explanations for the choices that were made.

First among these is successful lobbying by the tax-dodging complex. The transfer pricing industry lives by the system of corporate
taxation created in the 1920s; it has a vital stake in preserving it.
For example, if companies, instead of being taxed subsidiary by
subsidiary, were taxed as consolidated entities, there would be no
point in computing the prices of transactions between subsidiaries.
The transfer pricing industry would become obsolete overnight.

The stakes are huge: today, 250,000 people work as transfer pricing professionals in private firms, either in the Big Four or as direct employees of multinationals.[3] It would be naïve to think that they are passive bystanders when it comes to the policies that condition the existence of their livelihoods.

The tax-dodging industry also has a vested interest in ensuring as little international coordination as possible. If all countries had the same tax rate, after all, firms would not care about shifting profits from one place to the other; there would be no point in moving patents across subsidiaries; no reason to borrow money from affiliates in Luxembourg. The corporate tax policy of Bermuda is a bane for the world, but it is a boon to PricewaterhouseCoopers. The Big Four would rather have you believe that tax competition is inevitable, or good, or both. Without tax competition their business wouldn't be much of a business.

Their lobbying has been legitimized by the view that tax competition in and of itself is a good thing—without it, governments would be too big. According to this world view, defended by political scientist Geoffrey Brennan and economist James Buchanan among others,[4] democratically elected majorities tend to overtax property owners, who then become victims of the tyranny of the majority. To prevent this risk, governments need to be subject to powerful constraints, such as the one imposed by international competition. The idea fits into a long intellectual tradition that seeks to curtail democracy—especially the democratic regulation of property—via nondemocratic institutions, such as constitutional rules and courts.

At its core, the notion that the power to collect taxes needs to be subject to checks and balances is not absurd. We can debate the proper way to design tax policy, and constitutional and legal constraints certainly have a role to play. The view that tax competition is a boon, however, pushes mistrust in democracy to a new level: Courts, constitutions, checks and balances—none of them are enough. We need Bermuda to protect us from the tyranny of the majority and tame the Leviathan; even rules frozen in constitutional marble might risk falling short of safeguarding property. According to this view, when it comes to taxation, people are unable to govern themselves rationally.

Although it can be tempting to dismiss this theory as a fringe libertarian fantasy and an American oddity, it would be a mistake to underestimate its influence. The ideology has made an impression beyond America, including in the European Union. By requiring the unanimity of all member states for any common tax policy, the Treaty on European Union—the closest thing the European Union has to a Constitution—casts tax competition in stone. Any country, no matter how small, can block efforts at harmonizing tax rates within the union. Luxembourg (population: 600,000) can dictate its will to 500 million Europeans. Given the divergent economic interests of small and large European nations (with the smaller ones having a lot to win from tax competition), this rule de facto prevents any form of tax coordination. Although it's rarely formulated explicitly, the underlying rationale appears to be that the European welfare states are too large and that tax competition is required to make them more frugal. Democracy, in this world view, is insufficient to the task. Even the elaborate post-democratic European institutions (the unelected, impartial policymakers of the European Commission) would be unable to rein in social spending. Italy needs Malta to become more sparing; France needs Luxembourg; Greece needs Cyprus.

In the real world, the costs of tax competition far outweigh its supposed benefits. As we've seen, there is no progressive income tax possible without a strong enough corporate tax, because with low corporate rates, rich people morph into companies and transform the income tax into a (hardly enforceable) consumption tax. And without progressive income taxation, our chances to address rising inequality are close to nil. There are certainly an array of policies that can help reduce inequality, from raising the minimum wage to reforming corporate governance, equalizing access to higher education, better regulating intellectual property, and curbing the excesses of the finance industry. But the progressive income tax has historically been the most potent tool to curb the concentration of riches.[5]

As peoples, and as interconnected nations, we're at a crossroads. Down the path of tax competition, tax injustice will prosper and inequality will keep rising. Fortunately, there are other, equally feasible paths. Halting the spiral of tax competition is possible: it is anything but utopian to expect that big multinational corporations will pay a decent amount of tax soon. An effective action plan has four pillars: exemplarity; coordination; defensive measures; and sanctions against free riders.

EACH COUNTRY MUST POLICE ITS MULTINATIONALS

Exemplarity, first, means that each country should police its own multinationals. The United States should make sure that US companies, if they don't pay enough abroad, at least pay their dime in America. Italy should do the same with Italian firms, and France with its own national champions.

To understand how this could work, let's consider a concrete example. Imagine that, by shifting intangibles and manipulating intragroup transactions, the Italian automaker Fiat had managed to make $1 billion in profits in Ireland—taxed at 5%—and $1 billion in Jersey, one of the Channel Islands—taxed at 0%. There's a problem here: Fiat pays much less tax than it should; much less, in particular, than domestic Italian businesses. We call this a *tax deficit*. The good news is that nothing prevents Italy from curbing this deficit itself, by collecting the taxes that tax havens choose not to levy. Concretely, Rome could tax Fiat's Irish income at 20%. It could tax its Jersey bounty at 25%. More generally, it could easily impose *remedial taxes* such that Fiat's effective tax rate, in each of the countries where it operates, equals 25%.

Such a reduction of Fiat's tax deficit would not violate any international treaty. It does not require the cooperation of tax havens. And what's perhaps more surprising, it doesn't even require new data: the necessary information exists. Under the pressure of civil society organizations, the veil of secrecy surrounding the activities of multinational companies has started to lift. As part of the OECD's base erosion and profit-shifting initiative, big companies are now required to report their profits and taxes on a country-by-country basis. Oh, we're still far from total financial transparency: these country-by-country reports are not public; they're only available to tax authorities. But they exist: Apple must now report to the IRS how much income it earns in each of the world's countries; L'Oréal must report similar information to France, and Fiat to Italy. About seventy-five countries have started collecting that information or promised to do so in the immediate future, including all large economies.[6]

This seems like a mundane tax administration issue until you realize that, thanks to this rich new information source, it has never been easier for big countries to police their own multinationals. The United States, France, Italy: any country could ensure its corporate champions pay a minimum tax rate of say 25% wherever they operate. Any country can in effect serve as the tax collector of last resort for its own multinationals. Apple pays 2% in Jersey? The United States could collect the missing 23%. The Paris-based luxury group Kering books profits in Switzerland, taxed at 5%? Paris could levy the missing 20%. Such a policy would immediately remove any incentive for multinationals to book profits in tax havens. They would still pay zero taxes on the profits booked in Bermuda, but it would be pointless since any tax saving would be fully offset by higher taxes at home.

Policing multinational companies this way would bring large sums home. Using tabulations of the 2016 country-by-country reports of US companies published for the first time by the IRS in 2019, we can compute how much America would collect if it levied remedial taxes on its multinationals. In 2016, large US companies made about $1.3 trillion in profits globally. On that sum they paid $262 billion in tax (to the United States and to foreign governments), corresponding to a global average effective tax rate of 20%. But in many countries they paid much less: 0% on the $22 billion they booked in the Bahamas, 0% too on the $24 billion booked in the Cayman Islands, 2% on the $39 billion shifted to Puerto Rico, etc. By imposing a 25% country-by-country minimum tax, the United States would have collected close to an extra $100 billion in revenue all else being equal in 2016—equivalent to increasing the global effective tax rate of US multinationals by seven points, from 20% to 27%.[7]

Of course, if such a remedial tax had been in place in 2016, US companies would have booked fewer earnings in Bermuda and more in high-tax countries (this is, after all, the whole point of this policy). Some of the Bermuda bounty would have been booked and taxed in the United States, increasing Uncle Sam's revenue. But some would also have been booked in Germany and France, which means that the United States would have collected less than $100 billion in extra revenue by applying the remedial tax we describe. The important point is that US firms—and ultimately their shareholders, the majority of whom are Americans—would have been compelled to pay $100 billion more globally. Moreover, the United States would benefit from remedial taxes imposed by other countries: if France tomorrow applied a minimum tax to its national champions, French firms would reduce their earnings in Luxembourg and report more income in the United States, boosting Uncle Sam's coffers.

Is it realistic to expect big countries to start policing their multinationals in the foreseeable future? Very much so, for it is in their interest. Unlike trade, tax competition makes some countries win and others lose, and all large economies are in the losers' camp. They have a clear incentive to stop this shell game. As we saw in Chapter 4, small countries that apply tiny tax rates collect a lot of corporate income tax revenue as a fraction of their national income. They benefit handsomely because they attract a huge amount of foreign profits relative to their domestic tax base. But large countries do not have anything to gain by emulating this strategy. Yes, they might attract foreign profits by slashing their rates. But unlike smaller countries, any gains from foreign profits would be swamped by the amount of tax revenue they lost after taxing their domestic business sector at the reduced rate. In the end, whenever they slash their rates, large countries are certain to collect less corporate tax revenue overall. For a striking illustration, look no further than the US tax cut of 2018, which reduced federal corporate income tax revenue by a whopping 45%.[8] Unlike Malta, the United States will never boost its government's coffers by becoming a tax haven.

And here's the catch: because almost all multinational companies are headquartered in large economies, lawmakers in Rome, Berlin, and Washington can whistle the end of the game by collecting remedial taxes on profits booked by their multinationals in low-tax countries.[9]

A first key lesson: the spiral of international tax competition can be stopped even if tax havens do not increase their tax rates. Small countries may have a gigantic interest in applying low rates, but that's not an obstacle to other individual countries raising the effective taxation of corporate profits here and now.

INTERNATIONAL COORDINATION, NOW!

At this point you probably want to know what would happen if big countries really did police their multinationals and started acting as tax collectors of last resort. Wouldn't Fiat, Apple, and L'Oréal move their headquarters to tax havens? Fortunately, there is more than one way to address this threat—most importantly through international cooperation.

As we have seen, most countries have already agreed to harmonize their laws to limit the most blatant forms of profit shifting. The obvious next step is for big countries to agree on a common minimum tax: G20 countries (which include all the world's largest economies) could all agree that they will apply a 25% minimum tax rate to their multinationals, wherever they operate. These countries already have the information necessary to apply this minimum tax. And it's in their interest to take up the job of tax collector of last resort. Strange as it may seem, and although tax competition has intensified in recent years, a solution appears within reach.

A mutually agreed minimum tax among G20 countries would not solve all the problems. Companies could still dodge taxes by moving their headquarters to tax havens. This issue looms in the public debate. In the United States, the specter of "tax inversions"—US firms merging with foreign companies in Ireland or other low-tax places, and in doing so adopting the nationality of their partner—haunts policymakers.

But the danger is exaggerated. For all the talk about tax inversions, very few firms have moved their headquarters to tropical islands. There have admittedly been some high-profile cases: the consulting company Accenture inverted from Chicago to Bermuda in 2001 (before moving to Ireland in 2009); the financial advisory firm Lazard moved its New York headquarters to Bermuda in 2005; and the dietary supplement company Herbalife has been a proud resident of the Cayman Islands since 2002. According to a tracker of tax runaways maintained by Bloomberg, in total, eighty-five US companies have expatriated between 1982 and 2017 (many of them in the pharmaceutical sector, and most of whom you have never heard of).[10] To that total we can add the handful of firms that have been headquartered in offshore financial centers from the start (or that moved long ago), the most notable of which is probably the oilfield service giant Schlumberger, headquartered in the southern Caribbean island of Curaçao.

All of this sounds pretty concerning, until you realize that it adds up to a drop in the ocean. Among the world's two thousand largest companies, only eighteen are headquartered in Ireland, thirteen in Singapore, seven in Luxembourg, and four in Bermuda today.[11] Close to a thousand are headquartered in the United States and the European Union, while most of the others are to be found in China, Japan, South Korea, and other G20 countries.

The reason few companies invert, despite the incentives to do so, is probably because a business's nationality is not easy to manipulate. The definition of a company's nationality is constrained by strict rules. For instance, once it has been incorporated in the United States, a company cannot simply move its headquarters abroad: any firm that does so continues to be treated as a US company for tax purposes. American firms can only change their nationality in the context of foreign acquisition; that is, by merging with a foreign company. And for these mergers to result in a legally valid inversion, certain conditions must be met—conditions that have been strengthened over time, in particular by President Barack Obama in 2016. Most importantly, there must be a meaningful change in ownership: a US firm cannot become Bermudian by merging with a shell company in the middle of the Atlantic. In practice, it has thus become impossible for American giants to relocate to unpopulated Caribbean Islands. Ever since the Obama regulations (so far preserved by Trump) inversions have come to a complete halt.

A second key lesson: Even with only a handful of big countries on board, international coordination can curb tax dodging. Should G20 countries tomorrow impose a 25% minimum tax to their multinationals, more than 90% of the world's profits would immediately become effectively taxed at 25% or more.

HOW TO COLLECT THE TAX DEFICIT OF TAX DODGERS

International coordination will take time and may remain limited in the foreseeable future. That's why the third aspect of our plan involves defensive measures against corporations headquartered in countries that refuse to take part in international coordination.

Let's take a concrete example: the Swiss company Nestlé. Assume that Switzerland refuses to police its multinationals, perhaps because it believes going rogue is in its national interest, or because its policymakers are captured by wealthy shareholders. Nestlé therefore is taxed at very low rates and Switzerland declines to apply the 25% country-by-country minimum tax. There you have it: a corporate behemoth that dodges taxes and can shift its profits to offshore havens with complete impunity. What should be done?

In a nutshell, high-tax countries should collect the taxes that Switzerland refuses to collect. The simplest mechanism involves apportioning Nestlé's global profits to where the Swiss giant makes its sales. If Nestlé makes 20% of its global sales in the United States, then—whatever the countries where Nestlé employs its workers or has its factories, wherever its headquarters are located, wherever it holds its patents—the United States can assert that 20% of the company's global profits have been made in America and are taxable there. If 10% of Nestlé's global sales are made in France, then Paris can similarly consider that 10% of Nestlé's global profits are taxable in France.

Is this idle fantasy? Not at all, for this is already how most US states collect their own corporate tax revenues. Forty-four states have their own state corporate tax (at a rate of up to 12%, in Iowa) which adds to the federal corporate tax. To determine how much of Coca-Cola's profits are taxable in California, the Golden State's tax authority apportions Coca-Cola's US-wide profits to where the company makes its sales. A few states, such as Kansas, Alaska, and Maryland, use more complicated apportionment formulas that take into account not only the geography of sales, but also the location of firms' properties and employees. But over time the majority of US states have converged on a formula based only on the location of sales. The apportionment of profits is a time-tested mechanism, which is also used by Canadian provinces and German municipalities.[12] Nothing prevents countries (and not only local governments) from applying this system.

In practice, an even more robust mechanism can be used to fight tax dodgers. Instead of apportioning Nestlé's global profits, high-tax countries could apportion Nestlé's tax deficit. Concretely, the United States (and any other nation that wished to do so) would compute Nestlé's global tax deficit—that is, the extra tax that Nestlé would pay if it were subject to an effective tax rate of 25% in each of the countries in which it operates. Then if the Swiss giant made 20% of its global sales in the United States, Uncle Sam would collect 20% of Nestlé's global tax deficit. In effect, the United States and the other countries where Nestlé sells its products would take up the role that Switzerland refuses to play—tax collector of last resort.

This solution, which to our knowledge has never been proposed before, has many advantages.

First, it's immediately doable. As we've seen, information about the country-by-country profits, taxes, and sales of multinational companies already exists. In the case of Nestlé, it's gathered by the Swiss tax authority, but since 2018 it has been automatically exchanged with foreign countries. As of February 2019, according to the OECD, there were over 2,000 pairs of countries exchanging country-by-country reports automatically.[13] France, the United States, and most other countries where Nestlé sells its products already have the information in hand to compute Nestlé's global tax deficit and collect their share of these unpaid taxes. Even if they didn't have the information, they could easily request it. In granting firms access to domestic markets, countries already set all sorts of conditions, such as safety regulations. Nothing prevents adding a bare minimum of accounting transparency to the list.

The second advantage of our solution is that it doesn't violate an existing international treaty. Over the years countries have signed myriad conventions to prevent the risk that firms would be taxed twice. In practice these treaties—and the inconsistencies therein—have opened the floodgates to all sorts of tax dodging. Despite that, many governments and the OECD are still attached to them, and other attempts at reforming corporate taxation have been blocked on the grounds that they would infringe these sacrosanct conventions. But since the defensive tax we propose is collected only to the extent that a firm pays less than the minimum standard of 25%, our solution by construction does not introduce any form of double taxation. As a result, it does not violate double-taxation treaties.

All countries would have an incentive to apply the defensive tax we describe, for the simple reason that each has an interest in being among the tax collectors of last resort. Not doing so would mean leaving money on the table for others to grab! If the countries where multinationals make the bulk of their sales all applied this defensive tax, the tax deficit of each company would be fully apportioned.

Even firms headquartered in Bermuda would face a minimum effective tax rate of 25%. There would be no place to hide.

SANCTIONS AGAINST TAX HAVENS

We should, of course, not underestimate the ingenuity of the tax-dodging complex. Lawyers may find new loopholes in the future. That's why any effective plan of action has a fourth component: sanctions for the tax havens that sell their sovereignty and enable tax dodgers.

Imposing sanctions on uncooperative tax havens is well-founded in economic reasoning. Each country is entitled to its laws, but when these laws have a major negative externality, victims are entitled to retaliate. Refusing to take part in a minimal global standard such as an effective tax rate of 25%, which is not particularly high in international or historical perspective, should be seen for what it is: an extreme form of dumping that fills the coffers of some small states (and more importantly of global shareholders) at the expense of everyone else. Practices of this type must be discouraged, for instance by imposing taxes on financial transactions with uncooperative havens. As we have seen in Chapter 3, the United States has successfully used the threat of taxes on financial transactions to force tax havens to share bank data automatically with the IRS, paving the way for a new form of global cooperation deemed impossible by many. The same approach could be used to convince holdouts to join the common corporate tax standard.

The main argument against this approach has been that taxation is a national prerogative and that pressuring a country to increase its corporate tax rate infringes upon its sovereignty. This is exactly how Switzerland used to defend its bank secrecy and lack of cooperation with other countries' tax agencies, before changing course under American pressure. The United States started pressuring Switzerland after a series of scandals made the scale of offshore abuse apparent. What is key for change to happen is to quantify the size of the negative externality imposed by tax havens on other nations. Now that data are finally becoming available on the amount of profits booked by multinationals in each of the countries where they operate, it becomes possible to estimate by how much, exactly, Ireland's tax policy reduces the tax collection of the United States and France. There is no excuse anymore for ignoring the fiscal externalities that some countries impose on others.

FROM THE RACE TO THE BOTTOM TO THE RACE TO THE TOP

What's a politically realistic path forward? It is probably too optimistic to expect that all G20 countries will agree to police their own multinationals, join the club of tax collectors of last resort, and apply sanctions against tax havens. But it is not unreasonable to hope that at least some will. About half of the world's multinationals are headquartered in the United States and the European Union; these two economies together also account for more than 50% of the world's consumption. If they jointly adopted the system we propose, up to 75% of the world's profits would be taxed at 25% or more: all the profits made by US and European multinationals (50% of global profits), plus up to half of the profits made by all other firms (25%). In our view, an agreement of this nature should be the primary goal for all proponents of transatlantic cooperation in the years to come.

More broadly, the way to make progress politically involves putting tax matters at the center of trade policies. Future trade deals should not be signed unless they contain an agreement on tax coordination. What sense does it make to sign treaties that go to great lengths to protect the property rights of foreign investors—which is what most of free-trade agreements are these days—while ignoring taxes entirely? Ownership cannot come with only rights and no tax duty.

With a high enough tax floor, the logic of international competition would be turned on its head. Once taxes are out of the picture, companies would go where the workforce is productive, infrastructure is high quality, and consumers have enough purchasing power to buy their products. Instead of competing by slashing rates, countries would compete by boosting infrastructure spending, investing in access to education, and funding research. Instead of primarily improving the bottom line of shareholders, international competition would contribute to more equality within countries.

Moreover, nothing would prevent countries from increasing their corporate tax rate above a minimum rate of 25%. To take one example, imagine the United States unilaterally adopts a 50% corporate tax rate tomorrow. Historically, very few US companies have inverted to avoid taxation, even when the US tax rate was significantly higher than the tax rate of other OECD countries, as was the case from the late 1990s until 2018. But let's imagine that, facing a 50% rate, many US firms would be tempted to move their headquarters abroad. Taking it one step further, what if all newly created firms were formed exclusively outside of the United States? In either case Uncle Sam could still collect significant revenues by deploying a defensive tax at a rate of 50%. There is nothing that firms can do to avoid this measure: to the extent that they have sales in America and pay less than 50% abroad, they would have to pay in the United States.

Contrary to what the experts polled by the IMF may believe, globalization does not prevent countries from taxing corporations at high rates. Those who profess that the race to the bottom in corporate income tax rates is natural, that imposing sanctions against tax havens is a crime against free-trade—they are not the defenders of globalization. What will make globalization sustainable is not the disappearance of capital taxation, but its reinvention. It is not competition; it is coordination. It is not free-trade agreements that ignore fiscal issues, but international deals that advance tax harmonization. When people embrace these ideas, it will become apparent that progressive taxation is not doomed to disappear—but that it can be reinvented and expanded in an integrated global economy.

Chapter 7

TAXING
THE RICH

After bragging that dodging taxes made him smart, then-candidate Donald Trump eventually offered more specifics about his accounting prowess. "I have a write-off. A lot of it is depreciation, which is a wonderful charge," Trump said in the second presidential debate. "I love depreciation." To bolster his case that the tax system was a rigged game, he went on to invoke Hillary Clinton's wealthy backers who, he claimed, did not pay much tax either. "Many of her friends took bigger deductions. Warren Buffett took a massive deduction."

What this "massive deduction" Trump had in mind is not clear, but since Buffett had famously pledged to give most of his wealth away during his lifetime, the deduction for charitable giving is a likely contender. Stung by the accusation, the chairman and CEO of Berkshire Hathaway issued a statement the next day detailing his tax affairs. "My 2015 return," Buffett said, "shows adjusted gross income of $11,563,931." Contrary to what Trump had claimed on television, there was no massive deduction. And Buffett did pay taxes: "My federal income tax for the year was $1,845,557. Returns for previous years are of a similar nature. I have paid federal income tax every year since 1944, when I was 13." The statement was offered as proof that the Oracle of Omaha was a responsible citizen who, unlike the reality-show celebrity, did not eschew his duties to society.

In fact, it showed just the opposite. According to *Forbes*, Buffett owned $65.3 billion in wealth in 2015. We don't know his exact rate of return on his wealth, but let's conservatively assume that it is 5%. If true, it means that Buffett's pre-tax income amounted to at least 5% of $65.3 billion in 2015, or $3.2 billion. Out of this sum, Buffett proudly disclosed he paid federal income taxes of about $1.8 million. You do the math: while Trump bragged he didn't pay tax, Buffett countered that he was of a different moral character, really, with an effective income tax rate of around . . . 0.055%.

Conscientious taxpayers are all alike; every tax dodger avoids taxes in its own way. Trump skirted estate tax duties on the huge fortune he inherited from his father, and then cut his income tax bill by exploiting all sorts of dodges customized to his needs by the tax-planning industry.[1] Buffett followed another route. His wealth primarily consists of shares in his company Berkshire Hathaway. The company does not pay dividends. When it invests in other corporations, it forces them to stop paying dividends too. The consequences of this maneuver? For decades, Buffett's wealth has been accumulating, free of individual income taxes, within his firm. The perpetually reinvested profits boost Berkshire Hathaway's share price, year after year. It now costs some $300,000 to buy one share in Berkshire Hathaway, thirty times more than in 1992. To finance any consumption needs, Buffett simply needs to sell a few shares. By selling forty shares at a price of $300,000, for example, he can move $12 million to his personal bank account. He then pays tax—a modest one—on the small amount of capital gains he just realized. And that's all.

Buffett has famously lamented that he pays too little in taxes, and lawmakers have made proposals to correct this injustice. The most famous of these efforts, advocated by Barack Obama in 2011 and

Hillary Clinton in 2016, involves applying a minimum tax rate of 30% on individuals making more than one million dollars in income a year. This "Buffett rule" has become a mainstay of Democratic tax platforms. It is supposed to address the problem that because the top tax rate on capital gains (20% in 2019) is lower than on wage income (37%), Buffett (who mostly earns capital gains) is subject to rates lower than his secretary's (who mostly earns wages). But a problem remains: the 20% tax rate Buffett faces when selling a handful of shares applies to a nanoscale fraction of his true income. Thirty percent of this nanoscale fraction would still be infinitesimal. If enacted, the "Buffett rule" would not make a meaningful difference to Buffett's own tax bill.

By their own admission, both Trump and Buffett pay trivial amounts of taxes. Even billionaires who celebrate paying their taxes do not contribute much to the public coffers. As we've seen, when taking into account all taxes, the ultra-rich as a whole have lower effective tax rates than the middle class. Most proposals on the table today would do very little to remedy the problem. How do we get out of this mess?

WHY TAX THE RICH? TO HELP THE POOR

The first question to ask concerns the objective—what is the ideal tax rate to apply to the wealthy? There are several ways to think about this problem, but a good starting point is the theory of social justice formalized by philosopher John Rawls, which has broad support among social scientists. It is acceptable, according to Rawls, to have social and economic inequalities if these inequalities increase the living standards of the most vulnerable members of society.[2] When applied to tax policy, this perspective suggests we should not concern ourselves with the monetary interests of the rich. We should care only about how taxing them affects the rest of the population. The goal should not be to "to make the rich pay their fair share" (a somewhat nebulous concept), but to ensure that the great wealth of some benefits the least well off.

Concretely, this means that if raising the top tax rate reduces taxes collected (for instance, because it makes the wealthy work less), the tax rate should be cut. In this case a reduction in taxes on the rich would increase the amount of revenues that governments can spend on health, child care, and other social services that improve the living conditions of the poor. Conversely, as long as increasing the tax rate generates additional revenue, the rate should continue to be raised, for higher revenues would be in the interest of the most disadvantaged members of society. The optimal tax rate on the rich is simply the rate that raises the maximum possible revenue. It's not a controversial objective among economists. And it makes intuitive sense: everybody can agree that an extra dollar is much more valuable in the hands of a poor person than in Bill Gates's. Taxing the wealthy a bit more is not going to prevent them from affording good child care, but if raising rates allows those who serve them coffee or clean their houses to do so, too, it's worth it.[3]

With this objective in mind, taxation becomes an applied engineering problem. In the 1920s, the prodigy mathematician and economist Frank Ramsey formally proved that if all taxpayers faced the same tax rate, the rate that maximizes government revenue is inversely proportional to the elasticity of taxable income.[4] What does this mean? We ran into the notion of elasticity in Chapter 5. If taxable income is inelastic, it means that when tax rates rise, reported income does not change much. In that case, the US Treasury mechanically collects more revenue by hiking tax rates. By contrast if taxable income is very elastic, then high tax rates reduce the tax base so significantly that they don't raise much revenue and are undesirable. That's the cardinal rule of optimal taxation, called the Ramsey rule: governments should not tax too much what's elastic.

Ramsey's approach was limited. It considered only a single tax rate, what is known as a flat tax, but the flat tax is a crude instrument. In principle, the income tax can be made progressive, with higher incomes subject to higher marginal tax rates. In practice, as we've seen, that's how the income tax works in almost all democracies. Researchers in the late 1990s extended the Ramsey result and investigated the optimal tax rate for the rich when the income tax is progressive. As in the standard Ramsey rule, the top marginal income tax rate that maximizes government revenue is inversely proportional to the elasticity of taxable income. But with a twist: the elasticity that matters is only that of the rich. Moreover, the optimal rate now also depends on the level of inequality: the higher the concentration of income, the larger the optimal rate to be imposed on the affluent.[5]

THE OPTIMAL AVERAGE TAX RATE ON THE RICH: 60%

With this theory in mind, we can see that when it comes to selecting a top tax rate, the way the rich change their behavior in response is a key parameter. In the public debate, the view that the reported income of the wealthy must be very elastic—hence that they can't be taxed too much—is often taken as self-evident. In reality things are more complicated, because elasticities are not immutable parameters. They are heavily influenced by public policies.

There are two ways, after all, that the wealthy can respond to higher taxes. The first is by changing their real economic behavior: working fewer hours, for example, or choosing less-lucrative careers.

There's not much that can be done to prevent them from doing so, it's their right. The second—and far more common—response is tax avoidance. And tax avoidance, in contrast to more fundamental responses to taxes, can be drastically reduced by policymakers.

When companies book profits in tropical islands, when lawyers incorporate, when doctors invest in tax shelters—they are not driven by laws of nature. Such actions arise when the tax code favors certain forms of income over others, and when governments let people exploit these differences. But what's at times tolerated, or even encouraged, can also be regulated and forbidden. When all income—whether it derives from capital or labor, whether consumed or saved, whether booked in Bermuda or in the United States, whether paid to a bank account in Zurich or in Paris—is taxed at the same rate, and when the supply of tax dodges is strictly constrained, tax avoidance can almost disappear. In that case, the wealthy cannot dodge taxes other than by reducing their true economic resources—that is, by choosing to become poorer.

People rarely volunteer to become much poorer, even for such a noble cause as eschewing taxes. The changes in real behavior provoked by the tax code are generally quite limited. It's unlikely that Steve Jobs would have invented another iMarvel if only his tax rate had been zero. Or that Mark Zuckerberg would have opted for a career in fine arts if the Internal Revenue Code had been penned differently. Yes, Apple does shift profits to Jersey, Facebook does create shell companies in the Cayman Islands, and a sprawling industry helps the wealthy slash their tax bills. But that's tax avoidance, which flourishes in a light regulatory environment.

For example, the 1986 Tax Reform Act—which reduced the top marginal income tax rate to 28%—led to a rise in the amount of income reported by the rich. But this increase was mostly due to changes in tax-avoidance strategies (as it became profitable to avoid the 35% corporate tax rate by organizing businesses as partnerships, subject to the individual income tax) and not an increase in labor supply.[6] When tax avoidance is kept in check, the lesson from modern research is that the elasticity of taxable income is generally quite low—and therefore the optimal tax rate quite high.

How high exactly? Not as high as 100%: at that point, most people would prefer spending time with their family or tending their vegetable garden rather than work solely for the benefit of society at large. But a body of work suggests that the top marginal tax rate that collects the most revenue possible from the rich hovers around 75%. By the rich we mean the members of the top 1%, people with more than $500,000 in income in 2019.[7] This estimate is the best that exists today on the basis of many empirical studies conducted over the last two decades. If there are limited tax-avoidance opportunities, the rich respond only modestly to tax changes: whenever their keep rate rises by 1% (instead of keeping 70 cents after taxes out of any extra dollar earned, they keep 70.7 cents), they work harder and increase their pre-tax earnings by about 0.25% in response.[8] This means that the tax base does not shrink much when the rich are taxed more heavily, implying optimal top marginal tax rates in the vicinity of 75%.

There are a few things to consider about this result. First, we're talking about a *marginal* tax rate, a rate applied only to income earned above a high threshold, $500,000 today. The associated *average* tax rate is lower than that, because any dollar earned below this high threshold is taxed less. It's only for the ultra-wealthy that marginal and average tax rates are the same. Concretely, if tomorrow the marginal tax rate on income above $500,000 were increased to 75%, the average tax rate of the top 1% richest Americans would reach 60%.[9] In other words, the optimal *average* tax rate on top bracket taxpayers is 60%—less than 60% for people at the bottom of the top 1%, up to 75% for the ultra-rich, and 60% on average among top one percenters. In many ways it is more transparent to reason in terms of average tax rates, which give a more concrete sense of the true contribution made by the various groups of the population to the community's funding needs. Given that the average macroeconomic tax rate is around 30%, an average rate of 60% means that the top 1% richest Americans would pay twice as much in tax, as a fraction of their income, as the average person.

Second, these optimal tax rates take into account all taxes, at all levels of government. The optimal average tax rate of 60% for the rich should be seen as including not only the federal income tax, but also state income taxes, the fraction of the corporate tax paid by the affluent, payroll taxes, sales taxes, and so on. Since payroll taxes are capped and sales taxes are insignificant at the top, the optimal top marginal rate of 75% should be thought of as combining the federal income tax, any state income taxes, and the corporate income tax.

Last, and it must be said clearly: Hiking top tax rates without any other change to the tax code or to enforcement would be a bad idea. The supply of tax dodges in circulation is too large. Before we can effectively tax the wealthy more, avoidance must be curtailed. We need to create the institutions that make a robust tax system sustainable in the long run, even in the era of extreme inequality.

HOW TO STOP THE RICH FROM DODGING TAXES: A PUBLIC PROTECTION BUREAU

The first step would be to create what we'll call a Public Protection Bureau, charged with regulating the tax-dodging industry. Just as the United States has federal agencies to regulate the financial sector (the Consumer Financial Protection Bureau), the aviation sector (the Federal Aviation Agency), and the pharmaceutical industry (the

Food and Drug Administration), it should also monitor businesses that offer tax-related services and ensure that their practices are not hurting the public interest.

For as we've seen throughout this book, tax avoidance and evasion are spurred by the suppliers of tax dodges, not by the taxpayers themselves. Behind every epidemic of tax avoidance there's an outburst of creativity in the market for dodges. There is, of course, a long list of loopholes in current law that ought to be closed (more on this later). But plugging these loopholes does not strike at the heart of the problem. When income tax avoidance surged in the 1980s, it was not in response to freshly introduced tax breaks, but as a direct consequence of innovation in the tax-dodging industry. When corporate tax avoidance exploded in the 1990s and 2000s, we saw the same thing: the system of transfer pricing that facilitated the new abuses had been in place since the 1920s. To curb tax injustice, we must weed out the supply of tax scams.

Unfortunately, when it comes to regulating the tax-dodging industry, the IRS brings a knife to a gunfight. That's due to several reasons. The first is the dramatic decline in the service's enforcement budget: Over the last decade, the IRS budget has decreased by over 20% adjusted for inflation.[10] Lower budgets mean fewer auditors: in 2017, the IRS had only 9,510 auditors—down from over 14,000 in 2010. The last time it had fewer than 10,000 auditors was in the mid-1950s, when the US population was half what it is today. The second problem is compensation: given the rewards one reaps by creating a successful tax dodge, it pays much more to work for the Big Four accounting firms than to work in public service to fight tax evasion.

The last—and critical—problem is that the IRS is vulnerable to political vagaries. The risk is not primarily direct interference by the executive branch in the day-do-day operations of the service. It is more subtle—and more fundamental—than that. Congress and the prevailing administration affect enforcement: they determine the resources available for audits, they influence how aggressively the IRS challenges the tax-lowering strategies of the wealthy, they have an impact on the application of the economic substance doctrine.[11] Even if these choice are not dictated by the president directly, they are shaped by the ideology that dominates in Washington. When the party in power vilifies the estate tax as an attack against sacrosanct property rights, for example, the IRS is unlikely to devote large resources to enforcing it (and indeed the frequency of estate tax audits has collapsed since 1980, as we saw in Chapter 3). This stealth erosion of tax enforcement is undemocratic. It is a threat to any progressive tax system. To avoid a new tax-sheltering frenzy à la Reagan in the twenty-first century, we need an agency that everybody—the public, the tax-accountancy industry, the IRS—can trust to apply the spirit of the law regardless of the party in power. The IRS itself will always be seen as one-sided actor, which is why an independent agency can play a useful role.

The Public Protection Bureau should have two broad missions. First, and most important, it should enforce the economic substance doctrine—the principle that makes illegal all transactions undertaken with the sole purpose of dodging taxes. That enforcement starts with collecting the necessary information. The bureau should automatically be made aware, by law, of any new product commercialized by the tax-planning industry: intragroup sales of intellectual property, investments in sham partnerships, generation-skipping trusts, and so on. In that way, it could spot the new products created to help the wealthy and corporations dodge taxes. Businesses that do not disclose their practices should face stiff penalties. And all the products that violate the economic substance doctrine should be immediately outlawed.

Second, the Public Protection Bureau would monitor foreign tax practices, and instruct Treasury to apply economic sanctions against tax havens that siphon off the US tax base. When the British Virgin

Islands enables money launderers to create anonymous companies for a penny or when Luxembourg offers sweet, secret deals to multinationals, they steal the revenue of foreign nations. Nothing in the logic of free exchange justifies this theft. The commerce of sovereignty needs to be more tightly regulated, for example through taxes on financial transactions with free-riding tax havens.[12]

PLUGGING LOOPHOLES: SAME INCOME, SAME RATE

Another key step to curbing tax avoidance is a simple application of common sense: people with the same amount of income should pay the same amount of tax. This seems obvious, until you realize that most of the reforms of the first two decades of the twenty-first century have done the opposite. From a preferential rate for dividends in 2003 to a lower business income tax in 2018, the main preoccupation of American lawmakers has been to tax capital less than labor. The same trend can be observed in France, where the government of Emmanuel Macron adopted a flat tax for interest and dividends in 2018, and indeed in the rest of Europe.

Taxing people with the same income at the same rate is the concrete application of calls to "plug loopholes." It has several implications.

First, it means that every income source should be subject to the progressive individual income tax: not only wages, dividends, interest, rents, and business profits, but also capital gains, which in many countries (including France and the United States) are currently taxed at lower, flat rates. There is no compelling reason to tax capital gains less than other income sources. The practice merely encourages the wealthy to reclassify their labor income and business profits into capital gains. The reason why many countries have historically resorted to this second-best policy is because tax authorities did not track the purchase price of assets (stocks, bonds, houses, etc.), making it hard to enforce a tax on capital gains. In the United States, the IRS only started to collect this information systematically in 2012. But with today's ample and inexpensive computing capacities, progressive capital gains taxes can be enforced, including when assets have appreciated over more than a generation.[13] The frequent objection that capital gains taxes impose unfairly hefty tax bills when businesses are sold (because capital gains are a one-time windfall) can be addressed by spreading payments out, as is routinely done in the context of estate taxation.

Further still, given that today's governments now know the purchase date of assets, they could improve the tax code by removing from capital gains the mechanical effect of price inflation. In our current tax system, an asset bought for $100 in 2012 and sold for $150 in 2020 generates a taxable capital gain of $50. This makes little sense: out of the $50 increase in value, $20 corresponds to general price inflation, which is not income; only $30 corresponds to a true capital gain. The tax imposed on the $20 is equivalent to a wealth tax—an opaque and random type of wealth tax, since it's determined by the inflation rate. This hidden wealth tax should be ditched, and only the $30 in pure capital gains should be subject to progressive income taxation. Here's a tax cut we can all agree on!

ENDING CORPORATE TAX SHELTERS: INTEGRATION

A second application of the "equal income means equal tax" principle: the corporate and individual income taxes should be integrated—like European countries used to do and countries such as Australia and Canada, among others, still do. Integrating the corporate and individual income taxes means that once corporate profits are distributed to shareholders, any corporate tax paid by the firm is credited against the amount of personal income tax owed. Take the case of John, a wealthy shareholder subject to a marginal individual income tax rate of 50%. Assume that John owns a firm that makes $100 in profits, pays $20 in corporate tax, and distributes the remaining $80 in dividends. Here's how an integration system works: John would include the full $100 profit (not only the $80 dividend) in his taxable individual income. He would pay $50 tax on that income, corresponding to his marginal income tax rate of 50% times $100. But in recognition of the fact that the company he owns has already paid $20 in corporate tax, his tax bill would be reduced by $20, bringing it down to $50 − $20 = $30.

Such a system recognizes the basic truth that the corporate income tax is only a prepayment for the individual income tax. It has many advantages. To start with, it dramatically reduces the incentives for firms to dodge corporate taxes. Imagine that Apple, carefully advised by the Big Four, had avoided taxation entirely: in an integrated system, its wealthy shareholders would get no tax credits and would have to pay (in the above example) the full rate of 50% on their portion of Apple's profits. Any tax paid by Apple would reduce the bill at the shareholder level dollar for dollar. You can bet that in such a world, Apple would be instructed to slash its tax-dodging budget.

Another advantage of an integrated system is that it removes distortions. For instance, it becomes neutral for a business to be incorporated (subject to the corporate tax) or not (with all its profits passed to its owners and subject to individual income taxes, like partnerships in the United States). It makes it neutral for corporations to issue debt or equity, because both interest and dividend payments have the same tax implications. More broadly, an integrated system ensures that capital is taxed like labor—no less, but no more. In John's case, above, we see that the total tax on $100 of profit is $50: $20 paid by the firm, plus $30 paid by John. That's a tax rate of 50%—the same tax rate John would face if, instead of earning profits, he earned wages. It's never a good idea to depart from the ideal of treating labor and capital the same for tax purposes, because doing so always creates opportunities for tax avoidance. And tax avoidance reduces the amount of revenue collected. If the goal is tax progressivity, it should be achieved not by taxing capital more than labor, but by taxing all income more progressively via higher top marginal income tax rates.

Although the United States has never had an integrated income tax, this system was the norm in Europe during most of the twentieth century: the United Kingdom, Germany, Italy, and France, among other countries, used to rely on it. Integration, however, gradually disappeared. Why? In a nutshell, because of a poor response to globalization. Up until the 1990s, people barely invested in foreign companies. When cross-border investments surged in the 1990s and 2000s, governments found it unacceptable to give tax credits to domestic shareholders to offset the corporate taxes levied by foreign countries. France, for example, did not give credits to the French shareholders of General Motors, which thus paid more taxes than the French owners of Renault. In 2004, the European Court of Justice ruled that the uneven treatment of foreign companies was discriminatory, leading France, among other nations, to abandon its integration system in 2005.[14]

The solution to this problem is simple: Foreign corporate taxes should be credited like domestic taxes. France should give tax credits to the French shareholders of US companies, and the United States should do the same with American owners of French firms. This reciprocity already exists in the case of wages earned by people working in one country but who are residents in another for tax purposes. It could easily be negotiated in bilateral tax treaties, or even better in the context of the kind of corporate tax coordination discussed in the previous chapter. Nothing in globalization prevents an integration system from working well.

There is a third implication of the "equal income means equal tax" principle. A major advantage of an integrated corporate tax is that a dollar of wage would always be taxed the same as a dollar of distributed profit. While it would be a step in the right direction, integrated taxation would still leave a thorny issue unaddressed: retained earnings—profits made by companies but not distributed as dividends—would still be taxed less than other income sources. John would be better off if his company did not pay dividends and instead reinvested its profits, for the $100 in profit would only be subject to the 20% corporate tax—and not to the individual income tax. Always and everywhere, wealthy shareholders have incentives to retain earnings within their firms; it allows them to avoid the dividend tax and save tax-free. In practice, the risk is particularly severe for closely held businesses, that is, corporations with few owners that can directly control dividend policy for their own benefit. The way to deal with this issue is by forcing closely held businesses to pass through all their profits to their owners for tax purposes. A business that is not publicly listed should always be treated as a partnership: free from corporate tax, but with all its profits subject to the progressive individual income tax of its owners. Since the Tax Reform Act of 1986, most closely held firms, including many large and complex ones, have been organized as pass-through businesses. The US experience shows that it is technically feasible to tax closely held companies at the shareholder level.[15]

This rule would make it impossible for the wealthy to reinvest their income tax-free, one of the most potent sources of tax injustice today. It would also destroy the shell company business that has ballooned since the 1980s, since shell companies would stop conferring any tax advantage to their creators. Shell corporations, it goes without saying, are not corporations. Recognizing them as corporations for tax purposes—with the associated tax benefits—is absurd and must stop.

HOW MUCH TAX COULD THE TOP 1% PAY?

With tax avoidance reduced to a minimum, there's a wide consensus that increasing the amount of revenue collected from the wealthy is possible. But by how much exactly? According to our computations, by about four percentage points of national income, or $750 billion a year in 2019.

To see how we arrived at that number, recall that the members of the top 1% earn, as a group, 20% of national income. And as we saw in the first chapter, taking into account all taxes, their average tax rate is 30% today. Their tax payments add up to 20% of America's national income times 30%—or 6% of national income. As the editorial board of the *Wall Street Journal* never fails to remind us, the rich do contribute to the public coffers. But contrary to what they'd like us to believe, that's not because the effective tax rate on the wealthy is high (it's almost the same as the average macroeconomic tax rate in the economy) but because in America the rich have a lot of income.

As we've seen, after cracking down on tax dodges, the average tax rate that would maximize tax collection at the top is much higher than the current rate of 30%—it is close to 60%. Admittedly, should their tax rate double, the wealthy would report less income, even with tax avoidance kept in check: thought leaders would perhaps give fewer paid speeches, company executives may retire somewhat earlier, and so on. As a result, the inequality of pre-tax income would fall; according to the best available estimates, the top 1% share of pre-tax national income would decline from 20% to about 16%.[16] Let's run the math again: should their average tax rate double, America's affluent families would pay 60% of 16% of national income in tax, which is about 9.5% of national income. According to standard economic theory, this is, then, the maximum amount of tax that can be collected from the top 1%: 9.5% of national income.

Raising the tax rate of people just below the top 1% slightly (for instance via an increase in the corporate tax rate) would generate an extra half percentage point in revenue, bringing the total amount of tax paid by the affluent to 10% of national income. That's four percentage points more than today.

Is doubling the average tax rate at the top, from 30% to 60%, realistic? As we have seen, it's not without precedent. The average tax rate of the top 0.1% income earners neared 60% in the 1950s and reached close to 70% for the top 0.01% in 1950, when higher corporate taxation generated massive revenue and equity ownership was still highly concentrated. The effective tax rates that prevailed among the rich at midcentury were much higher than the tax rates paid by the rest of the population. In 1950 the bottom 90% paid 18% of its income in taxes, forty points less than the top 0.1%. The notion that it would be a drastic departure to implement high, progressive tax rates at the top of the income pyramid doesn't hold up to scrutiny.

It is true, arguably, that even in the heyday of progressive taxation, the average tax rate among the merely rich (in the top 1% but not in the top 0.1%) was more like 40%. As a result, the average tax rate for the entire top 1% was close to 50%—less than the 60% that would be optimal today. The rich, however, captured a much smaller fraction of national income at midcentury than today. When income is more concentrated, economic theory suggests the rich should be taxed more.

Implementing a more progressive tax system today is not a matter of simply going back in time. The progressive post–World War II tax system, for all its virtue, was far from perfect. In violation of the "equal income means equal tax" principle, capital gains were taxed less than ordinary income. The individual income tax had loopholes. Each of these flaws meant that the rich had scope to dodge taxation. By leveraging modern technology and drawing the lessons from the past and from other countries, it is possible to do better today.

7.1 WHEN AMERICA TAXED THE RICH HEAVILY

(Average tax rate of the top 0.1% versus bottom 90%)

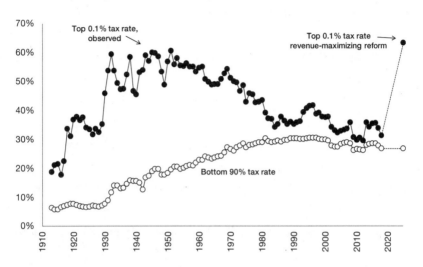

Notes: The figure depicts the average tax rates paid by the top 0.1% pre-tax income earners and the bottom 90% earners. All federal, state, and local taxes are included. Taxes are expressed as a fraction of pre-tax income. The revenue maximizing tax rate for the top 0.1% is around 65% today, similar to the effective tax rates reached at midcentury. Complete details at *taxjusticenow.org*.

A WEALTH TAX: THE PROPER WAY TO TAX BILLIONAIRES

The proper way to tax the wealthy in the twenty-first century—and in particular to arrive at the optimal rate of 60%—involves three essential and complementary ingredients: a progressive income tax, a corporate tax, and a progressive wealth tax. The corporate tax ensures that all profits are taxed, whether distributed or not: it acts as a de facto minimum tax on the affluent. The progressive income tax ensures high earners pay more. And a progressive wealth tax gets the ultra-wealthy to contribute an amount that reflects their true capacity to pay.

Why isn't the income tax enough? Quite simply because among the most advantaged members of society, many people possess substantial wealth while having low taxable income. Maybe they own a valuable business that does not make much profit, but which, everybody anticipates, will be immensely profitable in the future (see: Bezos, Jeff). Or, as is more frequently the case, they may structure their already profitable business so that it generates little taxable income (see: Buffett, Warren). In both cases, these billionaires can today live almost tax-free. As we saw in Chapter 5, even from the strict vantage point of economic efficiency, there is no cogent reason why the uber-wealthy should be permitted to grow their billions without contributing to their community's needs.

Without a wealth tax, it will be hard to reach average rates of 60% at the highest reaches of the wealth scale. Raising the top marginal income tax rate wouldn't affect the tax bill of Jeff Bezos or Warren Buffett notably, since neither of them has much taxable income in the first place. Raising other taxes, such as the estate tax, would not do either. We might take comfort in the idea that the richest man in the world, Jeff Bezos, will one day pay estate taxes on his immense wealth. But since the founder of Amazon turned fifty-five in 2019, that won't (hopefully) happen before 2050. And let's not mention Mark Zuckerberg, born in 1984—is it wise to wait until 2075 for him to contribute to the public coffers? The way to address this issue is by taxing wealth itself, today and not at some distant future date.[17]

A wealth tax will never replace the income tax; its goal is more limited: to ensure that the ultra-wealthy do not pay less than the rest of the population. Top executives, athletes, or movie stars—who earn a lot of income—can be appropriately taxed by a comprehensive income tax. It's the super-rich—most of whom own a lot of wealth but have little taxable income—for whom a wealth tax is essential.

There are many ways to combine a wealth tax with the progressive income tax and the corporate tax to arrive at an effective tax rate of 60%

7.2 ONE POSSIBLE OBJECTIVE: RETURNING TO THE TAX PROGRESSIVITY OF THE TRUMAN-EISENHOWER ERA

(Average tax rates by pre-tax income groups)

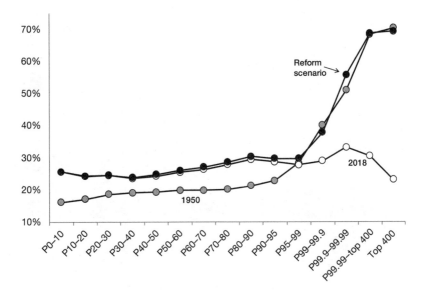

Notes: The figure depicts average tax rates by income groups in 1950 and 2018 and under a reform scenario that increases the corporate income tax, increases the progressivity of the individual income tax, and adds a progressive wealth tax. This reform scenario would restore the tax progressivity of the 1950 tax system. Complete details at *taxjusticenow.org*.

among the richest Americans.* In Figure 7.2, the effective corporate tax rate is multiplied by 2 (essentially returning tax revenues to their pre-2018 reform level, which is not impossible); the income tax is made more comprehensive (by treating capital like labor) and progressive (with a top marginal income tax rate of 60%); estate tax revenues are doubled (with better enforcement); and an annual wealth tax at a rate of 2% above $50 million in wealth and 3.5% above $1 billion is introduced.

---

* On *taxjusticenow.org*, any interested reader can simulate the effect of any imaginable tax combination.

7.3 THE WEALTH TAX:
A KEY INGREDIENT FOR A PROGRESSIVE TAX SYSTEM

(Average tax rates by pre-tax income groups)

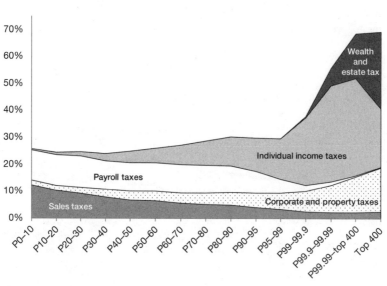

Notes: The figure depicts average tax rates by income groups under a tax reform scenario that increases the corporate income tax, increases the progressivity of the individual income tax, and introduces a progressive wealth tax. The progressive wealth tax is a crucial component to restoring tax progressivity at the very top. Complete details at *taxjusticenow.org*.

The result? A tax system that, at the top, would closely resemble that of the 1950s.

The primary departure from the 1950s tax system is the progressive wealth tax. The 1950s did not have one, and instead the system achieved its sharp progressivity mainly through a high corporate tax rate of 52%—which applied to profitable companies that, at the time, had relatively few owners, essentially individuals rather than institutional investors.[18] Since more than 20% of listed US equities are owned by foreigners and 30% by pension funds today,[19] even the measures described in the previous chapter (a systematic collection of the taxes not paid by multinationals), coupled with a massive hike in the corporate tax rate, would not create the same degree of tax progressivity as the 1950s. The corporate tax, which is not progressive, is too blunt an instrument to restore tax justice. And as we've seen, even with a much-improved income tax, it would not be possible to tax the ultra-rich properly. That's why the wealth tax is a critically important component to any reform.

HOW TO TAX WEALTH: LEVERAGE THE POWER OF MARKETS

A progressive wealth tax is possible because in contrast to taxable income, which can be artificially reduced, wealth is well defined at the very top. Wealth is the market value of one's assets net of all debts. Warren Buffett reports a tiny amount of taxable income to the IRS compared to his true economic income. But he cannot hide the fact that he's worth more than $50 billion. With a wealth tax at a rate of 2% on the fortunes above $50 million and 3% above $1 billion (such as the one proposed by Senator Elizabeth Warren in 2019), Buffett would pay around $1.8 billion a year, a thousand times his 2015 income tax bill of $1.8 million.

Not all forms of wealth are easy to value. As a publicly traded company, Berkshire Hathaway has a well-defined market value; because Buffett's wealth is fully invested in Berkshire Hathaway shares, it is easy to tax him. But the affluent can also own shares in unlisted (also called private or closely held) businesses. Other forms of wealth—like art or jewelry—are sometimes hard to value. But overall, these concerns about valuation are overblown.

Modern capitalist economies like the United States have well-defined property rights and put a value on most assets. According to our computations, 80% of the wealth owned by the top 0.1% richest Americans consists of listed equities, bonds, shares in collective investment funds, real estate, and other assets with easily accessible market values. As for the remaining 20%—mostly shares in private businesses—valuation raises fewer problems than you might think. Although not publicly listed, shares in large private businesses are regularly bought and sold. Even before Lyft and Uber went public in 2019, for instance, it was possible for rich people to invest in the ride-sharing service companies. Private companies regularly issue new stock to banks, venture capitalists, wealthy individuals, and other "accredited investors" with deep enough pockets. These transactions de facto put a value on private firms.

Admittedly, in some cases no transactions can take place for years. It's often true for mature private businesses that are controlled by a small number of owners. Let's look at the agribusiness giant Cargill, the largest private company in the United States, which is 90% owned by a hundred or so members of the Cargill and MacMillan families. The last time shares in Cargill were transacted was in 1992, when 17% of the company's shares were sold for $700 million—thus valuing the entire firm at a bit more than $4 billion.[20] Here is a striking case where taxing wealth might seem hopeless: What's the value of Cargill today, almost thirty years after this last share transaction? Isn't any estimate fraught with countless risks of abuse?

Taxing the Cargills and the MacMillans equitably is not impossible. To start with, the tax administration can take the 1992 Cargill valuation and update it based on any changes in the company's profits since then. If the company makes three times more profits today, it's not unreasonable to believe it's worth about three times as much as in 1992. Of course, much more data ought to inform a reliable valuation. For example, data about Cargill's direct competitors that are listed as public companies, such as Archer Daniels Midland and Bunge. To better assess Cargill, the IRS can consider how much a dollar of earnings made by these firms is valued by the stock market. It can study how the price-to-earnings ratios of Archer Daniels Midland and Bunge have changed since 1992. Valuing private firms in this and more sophisticated ways is what hundreds of financial analysts do every day. The United States has no shortage of expertise in this area. Drawing on standard private sector practices, it would not be terribly complicated for the IRS to come up with a reasonable estimate of Cargill's market value at the end of each year.

But here's the most interesting part. Let's assume that the Cargills and MacMillans feel cheated by the IRS—that is, they feel that the tax authority overestimates the value of their firm. Perhaps Cargill has fundamentally changed since 1992, in ways that state-of-the-art valuation techniques may fail to capture. Perhaps it has weaknesses that its competitors do not share. What is to be done?

At the heart of the problem there is a missing market: while there is an active, liquid market for Archer Daniels Midland and Bunge shares, no such market exists for Cargill's stock. The solution to this problem, in our view, is for the government to step in and create the market that's missing. The IRS would give the option to Cargill's shareholders to pay the wealth tax in kind—with Cargill shares—rather than in cash. If they used this option (which they would, by definition, only do if they believed the IRS valuation was exaggerated), the tax authority would then sell the shares to the highest bidders on a market open to any and all bidders—venture capitalists, private equity funds, foundations, or other families interested in acquiring a stake in the agribusiness giant.

This solution, which to our knowledge had not been proposed before, addresses a serious impediment to deploying a wealth tax. Just as a well-functioning income tax should treat all income equally, a good wealth tax should assess all forms of wealth in the same way, at their current market value. If some values are missing, the solution is to create them. And there's nothing better to create a market value than, well, to create a market. For a wealth tax imposed at an average rate of 2%, Cargill's shareholders would hand in 2% of their shares each year (or the cash equivalent, if they prefer to retain full control of the company). Like Buffett's Berkshire Hathaway, there would be no getting away.[21] Transforming Cargill's shares into cash would be the government's job.

This solution also addresses another frequent objection to wealth taxation—the problem of liquidity. Very rich people may have a lot of wealth and yet not enough income to pay their tax bills. Isn't it unfair to force them to pay a tax when they don't have cash in hand? To be frank, liquidity concerns are often put forward in bad faith. Most of the time, the notion that people worth a hundred million may not have enough cash to pay a million dollars in tax does not withstand scrutiny. When ultra-rich individuals pretend they have little cash, it's usually because they *choose* to realize little income to avoid the income tax. They organize their own illiquidity.

But there are instances where liquidity problems are real. The most relevant case is that of a highly valued start-up that makes no profit. Generating cash each year may turn out to be complicated or costly for anyone whose primary source of wealth is shares in the company, since young firms typically do not pay dividends. In that case, allowing taxpayers to pay in kind—with shares of the companies—addresses the problem. Because the wealth of the rich mostly consists of equity, and equity (in contrast to real estate) can always be divided, it can be used to pay for the tax. If the wealth tax can be paid with assets rather than cash, a progressive wealth tax isn't harder to implement than a progressive income tax.

The middle class already pays tax on its wealth, in the form of property taxes. The wealthy don't, since most of their wealth consists of financial assets, which are exempt from the property tax. In the nineteenth century, the property taxes of most states fell on all assets, both real and financial—in contrast to today. In the beginning of the twentieth century, the United States pioneered the progressive taxation of property with its federal estate tax—now moribund. Before turning its back to this distinguished tradition, America was at the forefront of the democratic regulation of property via the tax system. With a progressive tax on extreme wealth, the United States would be in a position to lead again.

Chapter 8

BEYOND LAFFER

Since 2015, visitors to the National Museum of American History in Washington, DC, have been able to admire a cloth napkin with a drawing by Arthur Laffer. Although perhaps not the original napkin on which Laffer drew his namesake curve at the restaurant Two Continents in 1974—more likely a keepsake created years later—all the ingredients are there. There's the economy's tax rate on one axis and the amount of tax revenue collected on the other. When the tax rate is zero, no revenue is collected, which makes sense. As the tax rate rises, revenues first increase, but as the rate is further hiked, at some point they begin to fall. When the tax rate reaches 100%, revenues are back to zero. The lesson is simple: Too much tax kills tax. The napkin is dedicated to Donald Rumsfeld, who served as secretary of defense from 1975 to 1977 under Gerald Ford, and again from 2001 to 2006 under George W. Bush.

As a diagram, the napkin displayed in the museum is incomprehensible. It has everything upside down: the axes are inverted, and the equations all have the wrong signs. But while Laffer may not have been the mathematical wizard Frank Ramsey was, he had a point. If starting tomorrow all incomes were to be taxed at 100%, people either would expend a lot of effort hiding their earnings or they would stop working. Since a rate of 0% and a rate of 100% would both collect nothing, there must be some rate in between these two extremes, often called the Laffer rate, where tax revenues peak.

It is hard, of course, to know what this rate is: 50%? 60%? 80%? On purely logical grounds anything is possible, depending on how sensitive people are to taxation. But whatever rate corresponds to peak revenue, it seems we should never want to go beyond it. If we did it would mean collecting *less* revenue than with a lesser tax rate. No society should ever want to be on the "wrong" side of the Laffer curve, where revenues fall as tax rates rise. Right?

In this chapter, we want to explain why democratic governments may reasonably decide to pick tax rates that are above the revenue-maximizing rate for the rich, why destroying part of the tax base can be in the interest of the community. If this notion seems crazy to you, it's because too much of the discussion about taxes has been based on napkin diagrams that ignore history, politics, and power relationships in a market economy. It's time to move beyond Laffer.

TOP INCOME TAXATION BEFORE LAFFER

In one sense, the idea that very high tax rates can be good policy even if they raise little revenue should not be surprising, at least to an American reader. This was, after all, the official stance of the US government for many decades. As we saw in Chapter 2, from 1930 to 1980, the top marginal income tax rate averaged 78%; it exceeded 90% from 1951 to 1963. Policymakers understood, well before Laffer's napkin, that faced with marginal tax rates of 90% even the most profit-driven individuals would be discouraged from raking in more income. From the presidency of Franklin Roosevelt to that of Dwight Eisenhower, it was clear that the top marginal income tax rates did not add revenue. They were of the "wrong" side on the Laffer curve. They destroyed income.

This was not a bug: it was the goal of the policy. The quasi-confiscatory top rates championed by Roosevelt and his successors in office were meant to reduce the income of the super-rich and thereby compress the income distribution. Recall that they applied to extraordinarily high incomes only, the equivalent of more than several million dollars today. Only the ultra-rich were subjected to them. In 1960, for example, the top marginal tax rate of 91% started biting above an income threshold that was nearly a hundred times the average national income per adult, the equivalent of $6.7 million in income today.[1] The merely rich—high-earning professionals, medium-size company executives, people with incomes in the hundreds of thousands in today's dollars—were taxed at marginal rates in a range of 25% to 50%, in line with what's typical nowadays (for instance, in states like California and New York, when you count state income taxes).

The policy of quasi-confiscatory tax rates for sky-high incomes, according to the available evidence, achieved its objective. From the late 1930s to the early 1970s, income inequality fell. The share of pre-tax national income earned by the top 1% was reduced by a factor of two, from close to 20% on the eve of World War II to barely more than 10% in the early 1970s. In 1960, for example, only 306 families earned more than $6.7 million in taxable income a year, the threshold above which income was taxed at 91%.[2] Meanwhile, the economy grew strongly. And as we saw in Chapter 2, the decline in inequality is not a fiscal illusion; it was a real phenomenon. There was, of course, tax avoidance. But it's not the case that the wealthy sheltered enormous sums off the IRS radar. The fall in the top 1% income share we measure includes all forms of income earned, whether reported to the IRS or not—among them profits retained within companies, investments in tax-exempt bonds, and other tax shelters available at the time. The quasi-confiscatory top rates truly reduced the concentration of pre-tax income.

America was not alone in pursuing this policy. The United Kingdom went further, with top marginal income tax rates as high as 98% from 1941 to 1952 and in the mid-1970s (and always above 89% in between). Just like in the United States, these high rates applied to very few people and did not raise a significant amount of revenue. And just like in the United States, the concentration of income and wealth in the UK fell dramatically in the 1940s and remained at historically low levels until the late 1970s.

THE CASE FOR CONFISCATORY TOP INCOME TAX RATES

On both sides of the Atlantic during these eras, tax policy reflected the view that extreme inequality hurts the community; that the economy works better when rent extraction is discouraged; and that unfettered markets lead to a concentration of wealth that threatens our democratic and meritocratic ideals.

This view is at least as old as the United States itself, and not the appanage of Anglo-Saxon liberals. The idea that excessive wealth concentration corrodes the social contract is shared by illustrious conservatives. James Madison wrote in the late eighteenth century: "The great object [of political parties] should be to combat the evil: 1. By establishing a political equality among all. 2. By withholding unnecessary opportunities from a few, to increase the inequality of property, by an immoderate, and especially an unmerited, accumulation of riches."[3] Conservatives are more likely to argue that extreme wealth is "merited" (with arguments often involving sharp distinctions between good, "job-creating" American billionaires and bad Russian or African "kleptocrats"—arguments that ignore the frequent commonalities between these actors, such as their monopoly power and influence on lawmaking). This important difference notwithstanding, even conservatives often agree that extreme wealth can in and of itself be a bad thing, which is probably one of the reasons why the FDR policy of quasi-confiscatory top income taxation was continued by Republican administrations until Reagan. Excessive wealth concentration, in Madison's view, was as poisonous for democracy as war. "In war, too, the discretionary power of the Executive is extended; its influence in dealing out offices, honors, and emoluments is multiplied . . . The same malignant aspect in republicanism may be traced in the inequality of fortunes."[4]

Wealth is power. An extreme concentration of wealth means an extreme concentration of power. The power to influence government policy. The power to stifle competition. The power to shape ideology. Together, they are the power to tilt the distribution of income to one's advantage—in the marketplace, in governments, in the media. This is, and has always been, the core reason why extreme wealth owned by some can reduce what remains for the rest of us. Why the income of today's super-rich can be gained at the expense of the rest of society. That's what earned John Astor, Andrew Carnegie, John Rockefeller, and other Gilded Age industrialists their epithet of "robber barons."

What do Apple, Jeff Bezos, and the Walton heirs do today? They protect their wealth. They defend their established positions. They buy new entrants before they become a threat to their business. They fight competitors, regulators, and the IRS. They buy newspapers. That's what those who've accumulated billions, always and everywhere, do. The founders of Apple, Amazon, and Walmart all innovated a great deal and created new products and services. Some have not stopped. But tomorrow's greatest innovations aren't likely to come from the heirs of successful founders, nor from companies that for years have topped the Fortune 500 ranking.

This is the theoretical case for going beyond Laffer. Extreme wealth, like carbon emissions, imposes a negative externality on the rest of us. The point of taxing carbon is not to raise revenue but to reduce carbon emissions. The same goes for high tax rates on the very highest incomes: They are not aimed at funding government programs in the long run. They are aimed at reducing the income of the ultra-wealthy. They prevent or impede the various forms of rent extraction associated with extreme and entrenched wealth and with the reality of the market economy in unequal societies.[5] What's the point of negotiating a $20-million salary, of earning millions by creating zero-sum financial products, of spiking the price of patented drugs, when out of any extra dollar earned, 90 cents will go the IRS? When in place, quasi-confiscatory tax rates redistribute economic power, equalize the distribution of pre-tax income, and make the marketplace more competitive.

From a purely logical perspective, this argument—the standard justification for tamping down the inequalities generated by free-market economies—can also work in the other direction. Maybe the externality of extreme wealth and huge incomes is positive. Maybe the ultra-rich bring more to society than what they privately earn. Maybe we all benefit from Bill Gates earning billions today and would all be worse off if these billions were taxed away—for instance because it would mean less funding for the Bill & Melinda Gates Foundation, which according to some observers spends its funds better than the government. This is a variation on the famous trickle-down theory, according to which the fortunes of the rich ultimately trickle down to the rest of society.

To think more deeply about whether the theoretical case for going beyond Laffer has empirical merit today, we need one thing that's too often missing from this debate: data.

THE BENEFITS OF EXTREME WEALTH: A DEBATE WITHOUT DATA

A scientific perspective on these questions requires a great deal of data. How does the prosperity of the ultra-wealthy—and the public policies that influence it—affect not only the overall growth rate of the economy, but also the dynamics of income for each social group? Do working-class incomes blossom when the rich are taxed less? To start with, we need to study the growth of income across the various groups of the population.

The national accounts, unfortunately, only provide information about the growth of total national income. They offer no data on how income grows in each social group. It's a major lacuna of government statistics. A few years ago, we embarked on a journey to remedy this gap. Our goal? Track who has really benefited from economic growth over the last decades—for instance how growth has been distributed to the working class, the middle class, the affluent, and the super-rich. Headline growth numbers matter for this assessment, but they are too coarse: what matters is how income is growing for teachers and bankers; for retirees and working-age adults—for every profession and every condition.

We created "distributional national accounts," a database that systematically allocates national income among all adults who live in the United States each year. It is impossible to know how much each person earns exactly—there is no administrative file anywhere that records this information in a comprehensive way—so the observations in our database do not correspond to any real person. They are synthetic observations, constructed by statistically combining tax returns data, surveys of household income and wealth, Social Security statistics, and many other sources of official data.

Altogether, the synthetic, fictitious Americans in our database are fully representative of the US population. Their income adds up to total national income in the economy, and their income has grown on average 1.4% a year since 1980, matching the macroeconomic statistics.

Our computations are in no way definitive. Our hope is that this work will be taken over and improved by government statisticians, and eventually that public agencies will publish their own official distributional national accounts. The national accounts we use today were created in much the same way in the middle of the twentieth century. In the meantime, we believe the merit of our work is its consistency (growth across the income ladder adds up to macroeconomic growth), transparency (our code and sources are publicly available), and universality (similar statistical methods are applied in other countries).[6]

1946–1980: HIGH AND EQUITABLE GROWTH

What really happened in the era of quasi-confiscatory top marginal income tax rates?

To visualize who benefited from growth at that time, we divide the population into a hundred equal-sized groups (100 percentiles) and compute the growth rate of average income in each of these groups over time. Given that the top percentile earns a large fraction of national income, we switch to finer subgroups at the top: dividing the top 1% into ten groups, and in turn dividing the top 0.1% into ten subgroups. With these groups in place we can compute growth rates from minimum-wage workers up to billionaires.

What do we see? In the decades after World War II, growth was strong and widely shared. From 1946 to 1980, average per adult national income rose 2.0% a year, one of the highest growth rates recorded over a generation in a country at the world's technological frontier. Nearly every group saw its income grow at the macro-economic rate of 2.0% a year (see Figure 8.1). The only exception involves the 1% highest income earners, who grew more slowly than the wider economy. But apart from that one dot, the similarity in the growth experience of the various social groups is stunning. One easily understands why economists chose, during this period, to model the economy on a single "representative agent." Almost every social group was behaving like the economy as a whole.

1980–2018: THE WORKING CLASS SHUT OFF FROM ECONOMIC GROWTH

The picture for the period from 1980 to 2018 looks completely different.

First, average growth slowed down. The first characteristic of the Reagan and post-Reagan US economy is poor growth performance. Since the financial crisis of 2008–2009 growth has picked up slightly (especially compared to what has happened in Europe), but if we look at a longer period—one that averages booms and busts, reces-

Notes to Figure 8.1: The figure depicts the annual real pre-tax income growth per adult for each percentile of the income distribution in the 1946–1980 period (upper panel) and 1980–2018 period (lower panel). From 1946 to 1980, growth was evenly distributed with all income groups growing at the macroeconomic average 2% annual rate (except the top 1%, which grew slower). From 1980 to 2018, growth has been unevenly distributed with very low growth for bottom income groups, mediocre growth for the middle class, and very high growth at the very top. Complete details at *taxjusticenow.org.*

8.1 FROM A RISING TIDE THAT LIFTS ALL BOATS
TO ONE THAT LIFTS ALL YACHTS

Annual growth of pre-tax income by income group, 1946–1980

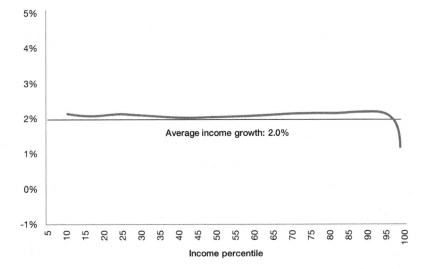

Annual growth of pre-tax income by income group, 1980–2018

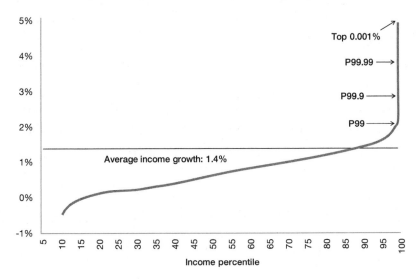

sions and the recoveries that follow—things do not look good. Since 1980, national income per adult has grown only 1.4% on average per year. And since the turn of the twenty-first century, it's grown by even less than that: 0.8% a year.

Second, most social groups did not experience anything close to the headline rate of growth of 1.4%. For almost 90% of the population, growth has been below—often much below—that figure. Only the top 10% highest income earners have experienced growth at or above 1.4%. If you pick a group at random, its income growth will most likely have no relation to how well the economy performed. There has been a massive disconnect between the economy's growth (1.4%) and people's growth (the average growth of each person's income is 0.65%). The fiction of a "representative agent" is dead.

Meanwhile, America's affluent have prospered. Look at the spike on Figure 8.1. It shows that the rich—adults within the top 1%, with more than $500,000 in income today—have received big raises. And for a tiny minority, growth has skyrocketed. For the highest 0.1% of earners, incomes have grown 320% since 1980; for the top 0.01%, incomes have grown by as much as 430%. And for the tip-top 0.001%—the 2,300 richest Americans—incomes have grown by more than 600%.

Over those same forty years, the working class—the half of the population with the lowest incomes—has received almost no raise. The average pre-tax income of the bottom 50%, which amounts to $18,500 in 2018, has barely increased: adjusted for inflation, it was around $17,500 in the late 1970s. This corresponds to an annual growth rate of 0.1% over four decades. It's not only that the share of income going to the top has risen since 1980. It's that their absolute income has skyrocketed, while that of half of the population *flatlined*. There is no evidence that the income of the rich has "trickled down" to the working class. The working class has been shut off from economic growth.

This evidence, we are aware, does not prove that trickle-down policies have hurt the working class. It doesn't prove that the fortunes earned by the ultra-rich have been gained at the expense of the rest of the population. From a purely logical perspective, it is possible that the working class would have fared even worse if tax policy had not favored the wealthy. That instead of growing 0.1% a year on average over the last four decades, the group's real income would have fallen. It doesn't seem very plausible, but it cannot a priori be ruled out. Statistics of income growth by percentile are extremely useful, but considered alone they cannot provide definitive answers on the merits and demerits of various public policies. We can't, alas, time-travel back to 1980 and run an experiment where tax rates would remain at their 1980 level to see what would have happened.

But a comparison with income growth in the post–World War II decades does not vindicate the trickle-down theory, to say the least.

WORKING-CLASS INCOME GROWTH: A TALE OF TWO COUNTRIES

Comparing US results with countries that have implemented other policies since 1980 does not vindicate trickle-down theory either.

Let's look at France, a country that is broadly representative of continental Europe. Average national income per adult is higher in the United States than in France: today, about 30% higher. This is not because Americans are more productive on average, but because they work more: they start working earlier in life (in part to pay for higher college costs), they retire later (in part to make up for smaller Social Security benefits), and in between they get fewer holidays and shorter parental leaves. In terms of productivity, the United States and France look the same. Gross domestic product divided by the number of hours worked—the most meaningful way to gauge productivity—is comparable, at around $75 today, and it has been following the same trend for some time.[7]

Despite Americans working longer hours, if we restrict our analysis to the bottom 50% of the population the average income per adult is 11% higher in France. On strictly monetary terms (disregarding its better health outcomes and more extensive leisure time) the working class—half of the population—is better off in France. The French welfare state is not responsible for this feat: we're talking here about income *before* government taxes and transfers. Once you account for public funding devoted to childcare, health, and education, the working class fares even better in France—not a huge surprise. What's interesting is that for most of the population, the *market* delivers higher incomes in France than it does in the United States.

This was not always the case. While the income of the working class has stagnated in America over the last four decades, in France it has grown. At 0.8% a year on average that growth has not been stellar, and since the Great Recession of 2008–2009 it has stopped altogether. But 0.8% a year over a generation, even if it's not much, is better than 0.1%. It's been enough for the French working class to surpass its American counterpart: While average income for the bottom half of the population is $2,000 lower in the United States than in France today, it was $2,000 higher in 1980.

Some argue that the stagnation of the American working class was inevitable. They cite a confluence of economic forces—technological progress, increased international trade—that have made workers durably less productive and what they produce less in demand. Comparing the United States and France makes the problem with this world view clear. Both the French and the American economies have been subject to the same waves of technological progress—the use of computers is no more prevalent on one shore of the Atlantic than on the other. Both trade with emerging economies. Many workers, in both countries, have been displaced by machines in the automobile

8.2 THE PLIGHT OF THE AMERICAN WORKING CLASS

(Average pre-tax income of the bottom 50%,
United States versus France, 2018 US dollars)

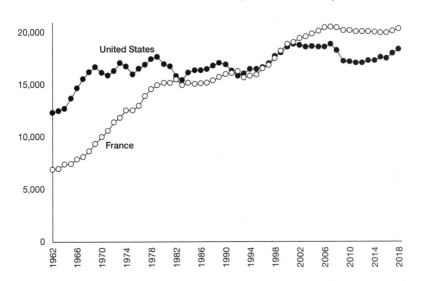

Notes: The figure shows the average income per adult for the bottom 50% of income earners in the United States and in France since 1962, before government taxes and transfers. The series are expressed in 2018 US dollars, using purchasing power parity exchange rates to convert euros into US dollars. In France, bottom 50% incomes have grown faster and are now higher than in the United States. Complete details at *taxjusticenow.org.*

sector and other industries. Yet in France, working-class income has grown—not a lot to be sure, but it has increased 30% since 1980—while it has flatlined in America. There lies a key lesson: technological change and pressures from globalization cannot be the main culprits for the woes of America's working class.

The notion that the working class has suddenly become less productive in America does not bear scrutiny. The international evidence suggests that government policies have redistributed income away from the working class and toward the top. Successive administrations since the 1980s have made deliberate choices in this regard, including letting the federal minimum wage erode, cutting taxes on the wealthy, restricting the power of unions, and increasing the costs of access to public universities.[8] France and most other rich countries have experienced some of the same policy changes themselves, but the turn to market fundamentalism has been more drastic in America.

IS GROWTH UNDERESTIMATED?

The stagnation of working-class income over more than a generation is perhaps the most fundamental development in the US economy, one with profound political and economic implications. It is so striking that to some observers, it must be wrong. We must be underestimating the true progress in living conditions. This is an objection that we must discuss before we can draw policy lessons. It comes in three flavors.

The first is that official statistics underestimate growth rates because they overestimate the true inflation rate. When measuring growth, statisticians try hard to tease out what fraction of the increase in national income comes from a real increase in production and what merely owes to the general rise in prices. This is not a perfect science. If we produced the exact same goods and services every year, it would be a straightforward task. But the nature of economic growth means that over time product quality tends to increase. When the price of a good rises, is it because its quality has improved or because of a general increase in prices? Sometimes quality changes are directly observable and statisticians can easily account for improvements—for instance, TV screens are larger than they were twenty years ago. But sometimes quality improvements are less easy to quantify—as in the case of less invasive surgery or more user-friendly computer software. Another difficulty is that businesses, among them Google and Facebook, sometimes provide services for which they don't charge their customers. We don't pay for the geolocation service provided by Google maps and as a result that service doesn't get counted into national income.

These knottier questions have led some observers to suggest that national account statistics (and therefore our distributional national accounts) underestimate growth. More or less everyone who's been involved at a high level in economic policymaking over the last decades, or an influential figure in the new economy, says it. Martin Feldstein, chair of President Reagan's Council of Economic Advisers: "the official data understate the changes of real output and productivity."[9] Bill Gates: "GDP understates growth even in rich countries."[10] The line of argument is a favorite of Silicon Valley–linked economists: "There is a lack of appreciation for what's happening in Silicon Valley, because we don't have a good way to measure it," according to Google's chief economist Hal Varian.[11] All of these comments suggest there's a hidden growth miracle acting on the economy, if only we can find a way to measure it.

As a matter of principle, these objections are legitimate. However, recent academic work suggests that once we account for these hurdles, the picture painted by the official numbers does not improve much. If anything, the growth slowdown between the 1946–1980 period and the post-1980 period may be even stronger than we think.[12] The reason is simple: the concerns outlined by Bill Gates and others aren't new; they are inherent to the process of economic growth itself. The same issues arose before the 1980s—and mattered perhaps even more back then. Yes, there have been improvements in the quality of our smartphones—just like the quality of cars and household appliances increased in the decades after World War II. Yes, some of the new services produced by Silicon Valley are free—but so was radio and television programming. Overall, US national income per adult might have grown 1.5% a year on average since 1980 instead of 1.4% as in the official data. But by that same token, growth from 1946 to 1980 was also probably stronger than what we believe—2.2% instead of 2.0%, perhaps. Correcting the full time series of official data would make the growth slowdown even starker. And it would barely affect the income growth of the working class (0.2% a year, perhaps, instead of 0.1%).

The official statistics, instead of being too dark, may in fact be too rosy. Why? Because if quality improvements are sometimes hard to quantify, so too are quality deteriorations. Air travel is a classic example of a service whose quality has declined since the 1980s. More seriously the growth statistics omit the dramatic deterioration of the climate and the decline in biodiversity. On balance these mismeasured degradations are likely to matter more than the mismeasured increases in output. Google Maps is wonderful, but perhaps not as important as the future of the planet.

The second argument that growth statistics misrepresent the true economic progress of the working class centers on mobility. The individuals who make up the bottom 50% change from one year to the next. Some ascend the income ladder and leave the group as others enter. Immigrants also come into the United States. If, instead of comparing average income in each group over time, you follow a single person over the years, some commentators believe the working class can be shown to have flourished. This argument expresses the popular belief in America as "the land of opportunity."

Alas, it's a fallacy. There is income mobility: People's incomes typically rise over their lifetime. Wages increase with job experience, workers get promoted, and so on. But what the statistics show is simple: working-class Americans do not earn more, on average, than their parents did at the same age.[13] At every stage of their life cycle, they're no better off than the previous generation. To understand why it's fallacious to claim that the working class has flourished when you follow people over time, consider the following thought experiment. Imagine we lived in a world with zero national income growth, a world where old cohorts are replaced year after year by younger generations who start with relatively little income. In such a world, everybody's income would grow over their lifetime, despite the stability of national income. Looking at this zero-growth economy, would it make sense to extol the virtues of progress? No. That working-class peoples' incomes rise over their life cycle does not indicate that the working class is prospering in any meaningful sense.

And what about immigration? Is it the case that many working-class people in America have arrived from foreign countries where their wage was even lower? Some new Americans do meet these criteria, but overall their statistical effect is too small to matter much. From 2010 to 2016, the annual inflow of permanent immigrants in the United States averaged 0.33% of the population—two to three times less than in nations like Canada, Germany, the Scandinavian countries, and the United Kingdom.[14] The United States had been a low-immigration country since well before the arrival of the Trump administration.

THE LIMITS OF REDISTRIBUTION

The last argument that growth statistics misrepresent the true growth of the working class involves government redistribution. Our estimate that average working-class income has grown only 0.1% a year since 1980 captures income before taxes and government transfers. As we've seen, taxes have increased. But government transfers have increased even more. As a result, on a post-tax and transfer basis, average working-class income has grown a bit more.

The effect is not large. After taxes and transfers, growth for the bottom 50% remains scant, about 0.6% a year since 1980. And before praising the equalizing effects of government transfers too quickly, let's pause. What are these transfers that have increased? The answer is simple: Medicare and Medicaid, chiefly. It's not that the government has been protecting the most vulnerable among us through cash transfers. Or alleviating the growing costs of raising kids by subsidizing parents. Instead, it's been paying for a large share of the soaring health bill of the country. The "beneficiaries" of this largess cannot choose to spend it as they see fit. The money is not flowing to their bank account. It's flowing to the bank accounts of health care providers, some of whom are comfortably in the top 1%. Are we sure the services provided in exchange are worth every penny?

In the end, the most striking indictment of market fundamentalism emerges from what has happened to life expectancy in the United States. Life expectancy is easier to measure than income; in many ways it is also more informative than the more materialistic notions of well-being discussed so far. Most people care about living a long, healthy life more than anything else. On average, for every five dollars they earn every year, Americans pay one dollar to doctors, hospitals, pharmaceuticals, and insurance companies. They have never spent as much on health care as they do today, and they spend much more on health care than residents of any other country. And yet, Americans' life expectancy is falling. It fell for the third straight year in 2017. In 1980, life expectancy in America exceeded that of other OECD nations by 1.5 years. Today it is almost two years less than in other wealthy countries.[15]

This deterioration took place gradually; its timing precisely mirrors the gradual worsening of relative living conditions for the working class. The affluent live longer, the poor die younger. In recent history, there is only one comparable example of life expectancy falling during peacetime—Russia during the chaotic transition away from communism in the first half of the 1990s.

This stunning inversion of life expectancy outcomes suggests there are good reasons to believe our income growth statistics do not exaggerate the woes of the American working class, but in fact underestimate them.

CURBING WEALTH CONCENTRATION: A RADICAL WEALTH TAX

This is, then, the empirical case for going beyond Laffer. Whether we compare the last four decades to the postwar period, or today's America to other wealthy nations, it seems that the upsurge of the super-rich has not benefited the rest of the population—but has been chiefly at the expense of the working class.

In retrospect, this should not be a terrible surprise. Supply-side policies boost, well, the supply. But the supply of what, exactly? Do these policies encourage teachers, inventors, and scientists to work more? Perhaps. It doesn't sound very plausible, but as a matter of logic it's not impossible that at least some of them are motivated by the lure of immense profits and work harder when taxes are low. Whatever their sensitivity to after-tax returns, however, it's clear they are not the people most responsive to monetary gains. The sellers of zero-sum financial products, the creators of deadly pills, the promoters of tax dodges and the lawyers who certify them, the price gougers, the patent trolls, the makers of fake university diplomas: *they* will rise to the occasion and supply more of their labor when taxes fall. These solely profit-driven individuals will innovate more boldly—faster and faster, making it harder and harder for regulators to catch up, or for people to learn about their fraud before falling for a new one. If low top tax rates encourage innovation, they must galvanize rent extraction.

Among the many policies that can curb the power of established wealth and contain rent-seeking, the quasi-confiscatory taxation of very high incomes historically has proved effective. But it faces a major limitation: as we've seen, it's become too easy for the very rich to own a lot of wealth while reporting little taxable income. Reinstating a 90% top marginal income tax rate would not make a meaningful difference to the tax bills of many of America's billionaires.

Overcoming this limitation requires taxing top wealth itself at high rates. A moderate wealth tax at a marginal tax rates of 2% above $50 million and 3% above $1 billion, such as the one discussed in the previous chapter, would generate a lot of revenue—about 1% of GDP each year, according to our estimates. It would be on the "good" side of the Laffer curve.

Consider now a radical wealth tax with a marginal tax rate of 10% above $1 billion. A person with $1 billion in wealth would pay the same $19 million as under a moderate wealth tax.* A radical wealth tax would not make it harder to become a billionaire; it would make it harder to remain a multibillionaire. A person with $2 billion would pay almost 5% a year, a decabillionaire like George Soros 9%, and a centibillionaire like Jeff Bezos 10%. Just as Roosevelt's 90% top marginal income tax sharply reduced the number of families earning more than $10 million of today's dollars, a radical wealth tax would lead to a reduction in the number of multibillionaires. More than collecting revenue, it would deconcentrate wealth.

There would still be multibillionaires, no doubt. If a wealth tax of this higher sort had been in place over the last decades, Mark Zuckerberg would still be worth $21 billion in 2018—instead of the $61 billion recorded by *Forbes*. Why? Because Zuckerberg's wealth has grown at a rate of 40% a year since 2008 when he first became a billionaire. A 10% annual wealth tax would not have stopped his stratospheric ascent. But a more mature billionaire such as Bill Gates would be worth $4 billion "only"—instead of $97 billion in 2018—because he has been a billionaire for over three decades now, giving the radical tax more time to grind his wealth down. If a radical wealth tax had been in place since 1982, most of the

---

* Since the tax is 2% above $50 million, a person with $1 billion in wealth pays 2% of $950 million, which is $19 million.

8.3 A WEALTH TAX TO LIMIT THE RISE OF INEQUALITY . . . OR DE-CONCENTRATE WEALTH?

(Share of wealth owned by the Forbes 400:
actual versus with wealth taxation since 1982)

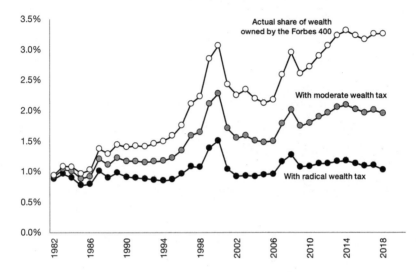

Notes: The figure depicts the share of total wealth owned by the top 400 richest Americans since 1982 from *Forbes* magazine. It also depicts what their wealth share would have been if a moderate or radical wealth tax had been in place since 1982. The moderate wealth tax has a 3% marginal tax rate above $1 billion while the radical wealth tax has a 10% marginal tax rate above $1 billion. The wealth share of the top 400 has increased from less than 1% in 1982 to almost 3.5% in 2018. With a moderate wealth tax in place since 1982, their wealth share would have been around 2% in 2018. With a radical wealth tax, it would have been about 1% in 2018, as in the early 1980s. Complete details at *taxjusticenow.org*.

400 richest Americans would still be billionaires in 2018, but they would be only one third as wealthy as they currently are. Their share of America's wealth would be similar to what it was back in 1982, before the huge increase in wealth inequality took place.

A radical wealth tax would have raised $250 billion in revenue from the 400 richest Americans alone in 2018, more than 1% of GDP. But if such a tax had been in place since 1982, it would have only raised $66 billion from these 400 wealthiest families in 2018, while a moderate wealth tax, despite its much lower rate, would have yielded almost as much—about $50 billion. In the long run, a radical wealth tax erodes top fortunes so much that it reduces the taxes paid by the ultra-rich: it goes beyond Laffer.[16]

Is a radical wealth tax worth it? Would society benefit from curbing huge fortunes with a 10% annual wealth tax above $1 billion, even if it means lower tax collection at the top end? Over the years, our own thinking about this question has evolved as the stagnation of working-class income and the boom in extreme wealth became clearer in the data. Perhaps yours will too.

Chapter 9

A WORLD
OF POSSIBILITY

There is a recurring fixture of most debates about public policy that might surprise you at this stage of the book: it's the argument that the progressivity of the tax system doesn't matter. The government, according to this view, can always achieve the redistribution it desires through public spending. As long as spending helps the more vulnerable among us, how taxes are levied is irrelevant; collecting revenues is what matters. This view is prevalent in the United States and in Europe and has informed most of the tax advice provided by the International Monetary Fund and the World Bank over the last decades. Governments in Asia or Africa have been encouraged to raise their value-added taxes—levies that burden the poor more than the rich—to fund social programs. Progressive income taxes? Inheritance taxes? Wealth taxes? These are unnecessary, and perhaps even politically dangerous.

This strategy is not entirely without merit: value-added taxes can generate a large flow of revenue that can help fund education, health care, and other public goods that raise standards of living. The problem lies with the underlying view of the development process that informs these well-meaning experts. Development is not primarily a matter of mechanically collecting taxes to fund spending, no matter how useful this spending may be. Development is about building trust in institutions, including, most importantly, governments. When governments take more from the poor than from the wealthy, sustained trust becomes impossible.

This insight is essential for understanding the history of taxation, from the tax revolts of the Middle Ages to the 2018 "yellow vests" movement in France. It will likely remain relevant in the future.[1] Take environmental taxes. Putting a price on carbon is critical to combat climate change, but since spending on fuel and other carbon-intensive goods absorbs a greater share of income for the poor than for the rich, carbon taxes are typically regressive. To offset this pain, fighting climate change will require additional progressive taxes. Governments that forget this basic truth will learn it the hard way.

Or take health care. In the United States, two of the most comprehensive efforts to introduce universal health insurance—the Clinton proposal of 1993, and the Vermont single-payer health care project of 2014—failed not for lack of general support, but largely because there was no palatable, fair funding solution. That's what happens when only spending matters, and not how the money is raised. Often, no spending occurs. Since the failure of Clinton's 1993 universal health care plan, thousands of Americans have died for lack of insurance;[2] millions have lived with the fear of losing theirs.

As we saw in Chapter 7, the United States could collect up to four points of national income in additional taxes by taxing the rich more. This would be enough to provide health care to the millions of currently uninsured Americans. But it could also be the starting point of a more ambitious expansion of the US social state, centered on the public funding of health care for all and education for all from early childhood to university. This expansion of the US social state would require funding above and beyond the extra taxes collected from the rich. In this chapter, we show one potential way to generate this funding.

THE RISE OF THE SOCIAL STATE

Why do most people think that the government should fund health care and education? For the same reasons they believe that retirement ought to be funded largely by the government. An adequate standard of living is recognized as a fundamental human right. In practice, without education, old-age income support, and health care, the right to an adequate standard of living cannot be fulfilled.

Before the twentieth century, families—rather than the government—did provide support for the elderly and the sick. Parents paid for the education of their children; children took care of their aging parents. Religious organizations aided those without family support. But that all occurred in a context where educations were short for most, medical care rudimentary, and the elderly could not expect to live long. As technology improved, life expectancy rose, and medical science progressed, the cost of education, retirement, and health increased—making collective funding necessary.

In the United States, the income of the working class (half of the population) is $18,500 a year per adult in 2019. That's at a time when America spends 20% of its national income on health care, or $15,000 per adult. All advanced economies spend at least 10% of their national income on health, even when they work hard to control costs.[3] If the United States emulated them and curbed health spending to 10% of national income, this would still amount to $7,500 per adult, a sum which is out of reach on a $18,500 income.

Can't the poor purchase discounted health care and education? No, because cheap health care, like cheap education, means in practice no education and no health care when you need it. The view that health care services are like haircuts or restaurant meals—services for which there is a product tailored to any budget—is a myth. The poor need as much health care as the rich, and as much education. Almost all American kids, no matter their background, graduate from high school after at least twelve years of education; and we all wish that more kids from disadvantaged backgrounds would attend college. Everybody needs their broken legs mended. No advanced economy succeeds in delivering decent health care and education on the cheap.

That's why all developed countries have, over the course of the twentieth century, gradually entrusted their governments with the task of funding education (including pre-kindergarten child care), old-age support, and health care. Of course, there is a legitimate debate about how much governments should spend, how much individuals should contribute, and how to regulate providers of education, retirement, and health services. But there is no example of a successful model for retirement, education, and health care that is not heavily funded through taxes or mandatory contributions equivalent to taxes. In all advanced economies, total taxes have increased from less than 10% of national income around 1900 to between 30% and 50% of national income today, primarily to fund the three pillars of the social state: education for the young, retirement benefits for the old, and health care for all.[4]

PRIVATE HEALTH INSURANCE: A HUGE POLL TAX

The United States is no different. Social Security, created in 1935 and funded by payroll taxes, now spends about 6% of national income each year on retirement and disability benefits. Mass secondary and higher education has always been organized primarily through government and funded by general tax revenue.[5] Even though tuition for higher education is high and student loans burden many, government still funds about two-thirds of all education spending in America. It also provides health insurance for the poor (Medicaid), the elderly (Medicare, starting at age sixty-five), and veterans.

The US social state, however, has major holes. The government spends very little on child care and early education, placing it near the bottom in international rankings on that metric. The world's richest countries guarantee mothers more than a year of paid maternity leave; the United States guarantees them nothing. Except for some US cities at the vanguard, there's no public school before age five; no public nursery in America. Other wealthy countries have long understood that education—including early education—is better and more efficiently provided by the community than by the market; the United States, not yet.

Because the cost of child care is prohibitively high—the annual cost of day care can easily reach $20,000 per infant—many families resort to parental care. In practice, this task falls primarily on mothers. The absence of government spending, in effect, imposes a huge tax on women's time—the most archaic possible form of tax. This tax has profound impacts on women's careers and deepens gender inequality. Earnings for American mothers fall 31% on average after the birth of a first child relative to fathers. That's how, despite the fact that women are more educated and more likely to graduate from college than men, massive gender disparities in earnings remain.[6] Isn't it absurd, even from a pure efficiency point of view, to devote resources to higher education, but then fail young mothers at a critical time in their careers by not providing early education to their children?

The other specificity of the United States compared to other advanced economies is that public health insurance is far from universal in America. About half of all health care spending (10% out of 20% of national income) is publicly funded. A large fraction of the population must purchase private insurance. The system of private insurance excludes millions of Americans and imposes a mammoth burden on workers.

As we saw in Chapter 5, private insurance premiums are akin to a huge private tax. Although most workers get insurance through their employers—and thus employers nominally foot the bill—the premiums are a labor cost as much as payroll taxes are. Just like payroll taxes, premiums are ultimately borne by employees. The only difference is they are even more regressive than payroll taxes, because the premiums are unrelated to earnings. They are equal to a fixed amount per employee (and only depend on age and family coverage), just like a poll tax.* The secretary literally pays the same dollar amount as an executive.

Poll taxes, unsurprisingly, are not popular. When Margaret Thatcher imposed a poll tax in 1988 to replace real estate property taxes, she faced an unprecedented revolt and was ousted from office in 1990. No government would out of the blue impose a poll tax to fund health care; it would be a crushing burden on moderate-income families. And yet in essence that's what the United States does today: employers are administering a huge poll tax on behalf of the government. Since the passage of the Affordable Care Act in 2010, employers with fifty or more employees are legally required to provide health insurance to their workers or pay a penalty of $2,500 per employee in 2019. Given how big the average annual health insurance premium has become ($13,000 per covered worker), this system is unsustainable.

To illustrate the magnitude of this poll tax, let's look at the distribution of US tax payments once we include mandatory private health insurance premiums. As we saw in the first chapter, considering regular taxes only the US tax system looks like a giant flat tax that becomes regressive at the top. But with the health care poll tax

---

* Historically, in American colonies and in some US states before 1964, voting registration was conditioned on the payment of "poll" taxes. In this book, we use the classic definition of a poll tax, namely a tax levied on every adult without reference to income or resources.

9.1 THE US TAX SYSTEM: FLAT . . .
OR MASSIVELY REGRESSIVE?

(Tax rates including compulsory health insurance, 2018)

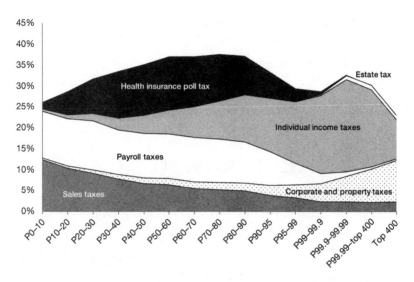

Notes: The figure depicts the average tax rate by income group and its composition by type of tax in 2018. All federal, state, and local taxes are included. The figure adds quasi-mandatory employer-sponsored health insurance premiums as an additional tax paid by enrolled workers. Including these quasi-taxes, the US tax system is sharply regressive, with the working class and especially the middle class paying more than the very rich. Complete details at *taxjusticenow.org.*

added, it is in fact frankly regressive: once private health insurance is factored in, the average tax rate rises from a bit less than 30% at the bottom of the income distribution to reach close to 40% for the middle class, before collapsing to 23% for billionaires.

The poll tax hammers the working and the middle class. At the bottom of the distribution, it's not as onerous as sales and payroll taxes. But that's because many working-class Americans do not get health insurance from their employers. They either face the burden of obtaining coverage themselves, rely on a family member to cover them, enroll into Medicaid, or go uninsured. The Affordable Care Act increased the pool of Americans eligible for Medicaid and subsidized the purchase of private insurance for low-income people who weren't otherwise covered, but the law still left about 14% of the adult population uninsured in 2019.[7] And it provided no relief for workers who fund their health care through a poll tax whose cost for the middle-class class far outweighed that of the income tax.

FUNDING THE SOCIAL STATE: BEYOND PAYROLL TAXES AND THE VAT

How do other rich countries—where health insurance is universal or near-universal and the provision of public child care much more prevalent—fund these essential social needs? Generally speaking, health insurance is funded by payroll taxes or general government revenue such as the value-added tax. While better than nothing, this style of funding is not ideal.

Payroll taxes are fairer than a poll tax, since they are proportional to wages, at least up to some limit. But they have a big limitation: They are typically imposed on labor income only. Capital income is exempt. Certain countries have tried to expand their payroll taxes to include some capital income into the base, but despite that effort labor carries the bulk of the burden of funding health care.[8]

If people have access to health care whether they earn labor or capital income, there's no reason why only labor should contribute. And, as we've seen, capital income is taxed less and less (despite rising faster than national income in most countries), while labor is taxed more and more (despite rising more slowly than national income, and sometimes stagnating). In that context, exempting capital from funding rising health expenditures seems neither sensible nor sustainable.

On top of payroll taxes, all advanced economies except the

United States have large value-added taxes. The principle of the VAT emerged in the early twentieth century, invented independently by a German industrialist, Wilhelm von Siemens, and the American economist Thomas Adams. France was the first country to experiment with VAT implementation in 1948, adopting it more broadly in 1954. The concept caught fire in the 1960s and was adopted by most countries in the decades that followed.[9] The VAT replaced earlier consumption taxes such as excise taxes on specific goods, sales taxes, and turnover taxes (which are similar to VAT with the difference that they tax intermediate goods).[10]

The VAT has clear advantages over the consumption taxes it replaced and that still exist in the United States today. It taxes services as well as goods. It does not create cascading taxes over the chain of production—as turnover taxes do—because the cost of intermediate products purchased by firms can be deducted from the value of the goods and services they sell. It is harder to evade than sales taxes because the tax is collected at each stage of production, not only at the time of the final sale. That's why, following France's lead, the VAT has been broadly adopted across the world.

To some observers, the solution is obvious: The United States should adopt a VAT to fund the expansion of its incomplete social state. In our view that would be a mistake. The VAT has two big flaws: it's regressive and its tax base, although larger than that of payroll taxes, is too small.

The VAT is regressive because it taxes consumption, not income. The working class and many in the middle class cannot afford to save: they consume all their income and, during some rainy days, more than their income. The VAT hits these groups hard. As one moves up to the top of the income pyramid, by contrast, consumption becomes smaller and smaller relative to income. There's only so much you can consume, even if you spend lavishly, and the ultra-wealthy barely pay any VAT relative to their incomes. At some point even the rich consume their savings, but that can be decades after income has been earned (if savings are used to fund retirement) or centuries after (if savings are passed to successive generations of heirs). The fundamental injustice of consumption taxes, relative to income taxes, is that the well-off can postpone them by saving, while the poor pay cash on the nail. "Justice too long delayed is justice denied":[11] this is true also when it comes to taxation.

Contrary to what is widely believed, the VAT exempts a significant fraction of the economy. Finance, education, and health care, three of the largest sectors in our modern economies, are typically exempt. Finance has contributed more than any other sector to the upsurge in income inequality in the United States; health care is high on the list too.[12] Introducing a new tax that exempts these sectors would not exactly advance the fight against inequality. VAT excludes finance because there's no easy way to compute "value-added" in the financial industry. For regular businesses, value-added is equal to sales to customers minus cost of intermediate inputs. The financial sector manages your funds (bank accounts, mutual and pension funds) by taking a cut on the returns, and it lends you money (credit cards, student loans, mortgages) at a high rate. But it does not explicitly and separately charge for its services.

Finance, health care, and education together were small sectors when value-added taxes were first introduced in the 1950s. Since then, however, they have grown fast. Moreover, because the VAT is (correctly) perceived as regressive, necessities such as food receive preferential rates. For all these reasons, France and Germany for example, which have standard VAT rates of 20% and 19% respectively, only raise about 8% of their national income via VAT.[13] In other words, the VAT only draws on 40% of their national income. In the United States—where the health care and finance sectors are larger than in Europe, but where people save less of their income overall—the base of the VAT would be a similarly low fraction of total national income. To raise 6% of national income in revenue, America would need to apply a 15% VAT rate.

The limitations of VAT and payroll taxes mean they aren't up to the job of funding the social state at a time of high inequality. These two options were popular in Europe in the postwar decades when inequality reached a historical nadir, but they are now outdated. We need to innovate.

FUNDING THE SOCIAL STATE IN THE TWENTY-FIRST CENTURY: THE NATIONAL INCOME TAX

The United States can leapfrog the VAT. It can pave the way in the creation of the fiscal institutions of the twenty-first century— as it did during the twentieth century. How? By creating a national income tax.

The basic idea is simple: the national income tax is a tax on all income, whether it derives from labor or from capital, and whether it originates from the manufacturing sector, finance, nonprofits, or any other sector of the economy. The tax does not exempt saving, which is highly concentrated among the well-off and is more effectively encouraged by government regulations (such as automatic enrollment in pension plans and financial regulation) than tax breaks. To keep administration simple, the national income tax has a single rate and offers no deductions.

Let's be clear: the national income tax is certainly not meant to replace the income tax, or any other progressive tax for that matter. It is meant to supplement progressive taxation and to replace *regressive* taxes that impose an unfairly high burden on the American working class and middle class, chief among which are private insurance premiums—the most regressive levy.

The national income tax is a true flat income tax. The "flat tax" proposed by the economists Robert Hall and Alvin Rabushka in 1985 and embraced by many conservatives is in reality a consumption tax at a flat rate, like a VAT, but it's often disguised as an income tax to make it more appealing.[14] The national income tax is more comprehensive and fairer, since it does not discriminate across different uses of your income (consumption versus saving).

To see how the tax would work, it is important to bear in mind that national income is the sum of labor income, business profits, and interest income. Concretely, taxing national income means taxing each of these income flows.

For labor income, the national income tax would be administered and remitted by employers. All employers—whether for-profit businesses, not-for-profit organizations, or governments—would pay a tax proportional to the full labor cost of all their employees. This would look like an employer payroll tax but levied on a larger base, including all fringe benefits and with no cap. All employee compensation, already reported on corporate and business tax returns and amounting to 62% of national income, would be covered by the national income tax.

Next, all businesses—from mom-and-pop restaurants to giant corporations—would have to pay the national income tax on their profits. The base would be the full amount of profits with no deductions or exemptions. Businesses would depreciate their capital assets to reflect normal wear and tear, but would not be allowed to deduct any tax paid. Business profits are already measured for income tax purposes on corporate or business tax returns.

The national income tax would also be levied on interest income. The interest businesses pay on their loans and bonds is deducted from business profits; the corresponding interest received by lenders must be taxed. For businesses, interest received is already included in profits. This leaves only interest received by individuals and nonprofits to be added to the tax base, which does not present any administrative difficulty. Foreign dividends received by individuals and nonprofits, as well as other income forms received from abroad, also would be liable for the tax.

Because a tax defined this way taxes all income sources only once, there is no need to tax US dividends (corporations have already paid the tax on their profits), retirement income (for labor income, including retirement contributions, has already been taxed), or any government transfer such as social security payments or unemployment benefits. That's a key difference with the VAT: the national income tax does not burden people who live off transfer income, who tend to be at the bottom of the income distribution. This makes the national income tax much more progressive than a VAT.

Our computations show that the national income tax has a base nearing 100% of national income. The rents that homeowners pay to themselves (which are part of national income, but not easy to tax) are excluded from the base; but the national income tax base does not deduct mortgage interest payments. In practice, tax evasion would make the base of the national income tax slightly lower than 100% of national income. The informal economy, including employees receiving wages off the books or self-employed workers paid in cash, would not be reached, and some businesses would underreport profits. According to the available estimates, these activities would reduce the base by about 7% of national income.[15]

Because it's so broad, the national income tax could raise substantial revenues with low rates. It would be a stable source of tax revenue—since national income does not vary much from one year to the other—which is important to fund the core, long-run missions of the social state. Occasionally it's argued that a carbon tax could provide some of the funding for health or childcare, but that's a mistake. Carbon taxation is, of course, necessary to fight climate change. But its goal should be only this: fight climate change. It should not aim at collecting revenue in the medium run, but instead aim at eradicating future carbon emissions. A successful carbon tax should eventually yield zero revenue.

If the national income tax is such a great idea, why hasn't it been proposed and implemented before? Probably because of international tax competition, since the national income tax does increase the taxation of corporate profits. However, with proper taxation of multinationals, as discussed in Chapter 6, concerns about tax competition would fall away.

UNIVERSAL HEALTH INSURANCE, NOW

The national income tax opens a world of possibility. In the United States, it might be used to fund universal health insurance, child care, and a more equal access to higher education, for instance through more funding for public universities. Higher education is particularly unequal in America, where only 30% of young adults from poor families attend college by age twenty-two (versus close to 100% for the rich),[16] and where students are burdened with skyrocketing loans that impede wealth building for the middle class. The national income tax could also be used to replace the states' archaic sales taxes, which are very regressive, and to provide states with a tool to fund their own social state, should the federal government fail to act. Other countries could implement a national income tax to reduce their VAT or payroll taxes on labor earnings, thereby making their tax systems less regressive.

For example, in America a national income tax at a rate of 6%, combined with a greater taxation of the rich, would generate about ten points of national income in government revenue. With six points going to health care, one point to universal child care, and half a point to higher education, America would acquire a social state worthy of the twenty-first century. The remaining revenue could be used

9.2 FUNDING THE SOCIAL STATE OF THE TWENTY-FIRST CENTURY

Tax revenue

	Type of tax	Revenue (% of national income)
Wealth tax	2% rate above $50 million	1.2%
	3.5% rate above $1 billion	
Income tax	Full taxation of dividends and capital gains	1.7%
	60% top marginal income tax rate	
Corporate tax	30% effective US corporate tax rate	1.2%
	25% country-by-country minimum tax	
National income tax	Flat 6% rate	5.6%
Total		**9.8%**

Spending

	Type of spending	Cost (% of national income)
Health care for all	$8,000 for currently covered workers	6.0%
	$8,000 for the currently uninsured	
Education for all	Public child care and early education	1.0%
	Free tuition for public universities	0.5%
Sales tax cut	Eliminate sales taxes and Trump tariffs	2.3%
Total		**9.8%**

Notes: Our proposed reform funds health care for all and education for all (from early child care to university), and eliminates regressive and archaic sales taxes (but keeps excise taxes, which primarily fall on gasoline, alcohol, and tobacco). This reform is funded by extra taxes on the rich (progressive wealth taxation, more progressive income taxation, and enhanced taxation of corporations) and a national income tax, fairer and broader than a VAT. Complete details at *taxjusticenow.org*.

to eliminate the archaic sales taxes (and the Trump tariffs) that currently hammer the working class.

Although it is difficult to quantify the economic effects of a healthier and more educated workforce, the evidence suggests that the effect on growth would be positive. Freed of the risk of losing their employer-provided health insurance, more people might start businesses. More college graduates would boost productivity. Universal child care would increase women's labor force participation. In turn, higher incomes would increase tax collection, eventually reducing the government deficit.

If a 6% national income tax was used to fund health care, here is how it would work. A rate of 4.5% would be enough to fund standard health insurance covering all medical needs for all workers who currently pay contributions through their employers. It would also allow the extension of Affordable Care Act exchange subsidies to all participants regardless of their family income. Increasing the rate to 6% would be enough to cover the 30 million Americans who are uninsured today—and achieve true universal health insurance.

With a national income tax of 6% funding health care, most Americans would come out ahead. Of course, such a tax would reduce labor earnings by 6%. But a large swath of workers pay more than 6% of their income today in health insurance. Suppose you earn $40,000 and your employer currently pays $12,000 for your health care. In reality your labor income is $52,000, but 23% of it is eaten by the health insurance poll tax. Covered workers would come out ahead if their insurance premiums are less than 6% of their total labor income, which is the case for over 90% of workers with employer-sponsored health insurance. On the flip side, high wage earners and individuals with capital income would pay more.

The main practical objection to embracing what amounts to a "Medicare for All" program is that currently covered employees do not want to give up the private insurance they know for a new public insurance program. One way to address this issue involves giving workers the option to keep their current plan. Suppose that you earn $40,000 and that your employer contributes $12,000 to a private plan today. Imagine again that the public health insurance is worth $8,000. In this case, the government would pay your employer

9.3 A PROGRESSIVE TAX SYSTEM
FOR THE TWENTY-FIRST CENTURY

(Tax rates, percentage of pre-tax income)

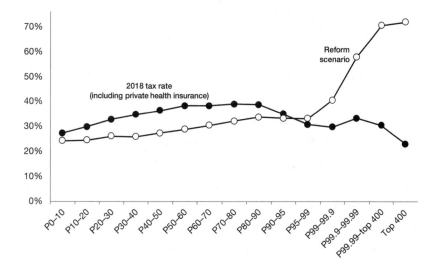

Notes: The figure depicts average tax rates by income groups in 2018, treating employer-sponsored health insurance premiums as taxes. The reform scenario abolishes all sales taxes and employer-sponsored health insurance premiums, introduces a national income tax at a rate of 6%, creates a progressive wealth tax, and increases the corporate income tax and the progressivity of the individual income tax. Complete details at *taxjusticenow.org.*

$8,000. The cost, for your employer, of subscribing to your preferred private plan would fall from $12,000 to $4,000. The law would mandate that employers pass on to workers the $8,000 received from the government; your take-home pay would thus increase by $8,000—a 20% jump. The alleviation of health insurance costs would be neutral for employers and directly show up on workers' paychecks.

Figure 9.3 illustrates what the US tax system would look like under our proposed reform: taxation of the rich up to the top of the

Laffer curve, a national income tax (fairer and broader than a VAT), the abolition of sales taxes, and the disappearance of the mammoth health insurance poll tax.

All social groups from the bottom up to roughly the ninety-fifth percentile would pay less than today when including health insurance premiums. The working class (which pays a lot in sales taxes) and the middle class (for which health care costs are currently prohibitive) would see their disposable income boosted. Around the median, the tax rate would fall from 38% to 28%: about thirteen points of health insurance premiums would disappear, as would three points of sales taxes, all of which would be replaced by six points of national income tax.

Would this tax system harm growth? Would it be the end of America as we know it? History does not suggest so. As we've seen, similar levels of tax progressivity were reached in the 1950s, before the collapse in taxes at the top, the explosion of health care costs, and the rise of payroll taxes transformed the US tax system into an engine of injustice. It's through collective spending on education, health, and other public goods that rich countries have become wealthy, not through the deification of a tiny minority of ultra-rich. If history is any guide, the prosperous nations of the future will continue to be those that invest in the success of all.

Conclusion

TAX JUSTICE NOW

We draw one principal conclusion from our investigation: Societies can choose whatever level of tax progressivity they want. Globalization has raised thorny issues about how to tax multinational companies and the wealthy—but international openness does not doom us to a world of ever-growing tax injustice. Tax evasion has been tolerated since the 1980s—but there is technically nothing that prevents us from curbing it. With the race to the bottom that's currently raging, progressivity is under threat—but just as it pioneered progressive taxation a century ago, the United States can create new fiscal institutions adapted to the challenges of the twenty-first century.

In these pages, we have made propositions to meet those challenges: a sharply progressive wealth tax to curb the forms of rent extraction associated with extreme and entrenched wealth, an effective taxation of globe-straddling companies to reconcile globalization with tax justice, a national income tax to fund the modern social state and alleviate the crushing cost of health care. Our solutions are imperfect. They are not, of course, the only possible ones. There is not one single path for the future of taxation, but a world of possibility. The ingenuity of human societies, history teaches us, is boundless. Where economists can be helpful is not in elevating some supposedly invincible constraints or universal law—which often are invincible and universal in their eyes only—but in making more concrete the multiplicity of possible futures.

This is why we have developed *taxjusticenow.org*. This book shows one set of solutions; the website shows the infinity of future paths that exist. The website starts from the current distribution of tax payments—the giant flat tax, regressive at the top end, that the US tax system has become and that we studied in Chapter 1. But it then does what no book—no matter how long—could do: it shows how adjusting any of the taxes that exist, removing some of them, adding brand-new levies, or strengthening enforcement would change the effective tax rate of each group of the population, from minimum-wage workers to billionaires. Anybody can quickly assess how a wealth tax, higher top income tax rates, or a stricter taxation of big companies would affect government revenue and the progressivity of the tax system.

A key novelty of our simulator is to show how taxes affect the dynamics of inequality over the longer run. Concretely, if your favorite wealth tax had been in place since 1980, how wealthy would Jeff Bezos, Bill Gates, Warren Buffett, and other billionaires be today? If the top marginal income tax rate was increased tomorrow to 70%, how would this affect the top 1% income share?

Let's say it at the outset: It is impossible to provide perfectly accurate answers to these questions. Although economists have made progress in understanding what economic forces shape the evolution of inequality and how taxation affects economic behavior, we're still far from being able to perfectly predict the effect of taxes on inequality. But this is no reason not to try our best. The main effect of the tax system is not to influence the overall growth rate of the economy, but to change the distribution of economic resources—because it changes the disposable income of each social group, but also and more importantly because it affects the incentives to earn income and accumulate wealth. Any serious thinking about taxation must put inequality front and center, even more so in today's world of rising wealth concentration.

That is what we've attempted to do with *taxjusticenow.org*. Our goal is not to provide a definitive model of the complex interplay between government policies and inequality, but to harness existing knowledge to foster a democratic fiscal debate. Our simulator is transparent and open-source: our code, data, and programs are available online; each of our results can be reproduced; each of our assumptions can be modified; each of our choices can be traced back to a body of recent research. But you do not need to be an expert to use it; it's a tool for the people, for all individuals who care about the future of collective action.[1] We plan to improve this tool in the years to come, as new knowledge emerges about taxes and their effect on inequality, and we thank our readers in advance for their reactions and suggestions.

Join us on *taxjusticenow.org*!

ACKNOWLEDGMENTS

This book would not have been possible without the numerous co-authors and colleagues who have worked with us and commented on our research on taxes and inequality over the years, and without the support of our home institution, UC Berkeley. We want to thank in particular Heather Boushey, Lucas Chancel, Kimberly Clausing, Camille Landais, Claire Montialoux, and Thomas Piketty for their detailed comments on the manuscript. We thank our research assistants Akcan Balkir, Katie Donnelly Moran, and Clancy Green, and our agent Raphael Sagalyn. Special thanks to our editor Brendan Curry and his W. W. Norton colleagues for their invaluable work.

NOTES

Chapter 1: INCOME AND TAXES IN AMERICA

1. See online appendix available at *taxjusticenow.org* for complete details on the statistics discussed in this chapter.
2. Barbier (2014).
3. Reeves (2017).
4. Alveredo et al. (2018). All the data are available online on the *World Inequality Database* at wid.world.
5. Custom duties are on pace to reach $75 billion in 2019, double the $38 billion collected in 2017 (US Department of Commerce Bureau of Economic Analysis, National Income and Product Accounts of the United States, Table 3.2, 2019-Q1). Yet, total consumption taxes including all levels of government are over $800 billion (ibid., Table 3.5, 2017, total taxes on production and imports excluding property taxes).
6. US Treasury (2018).
7. Okner and Pechman (1974). Federal agencies (the Congressional Budget Office, the US Treasury, or the Joint Committee on Taxation) and think tanks (such as the Tax Policy Center) produce statistics on the distribution of federal taxes by income groups but they ignore state and local taxes. See, e.g., US Congressional Budget Office (2018). The Institute on Taxation and Economic Policy (ITEP) has produced estimates of the distribution of state and local taxes for recent years (Institute on Taxation and Economic Policy, 2018). Piketty, Saez, and Zucman (2018) distribute all taxes and the results presented in this chapter update and improve this study.
8. We discuss this point in detail in Saez and Zucman (2019).

9. At the very bottom of the distribution, people do not earn labor, capital, or pension income but only transfer income; they pay consumption taxes out of this transfer income, which leads to high tax rates when expressed as a fraction of pre-tax income. We avoid this problem by restricting our population to adults with pre-tax income more than half the annual federal minimum wage ($7,250 per year). The average tax rate in that population is almost identical to the macroeconomic rate of taxation.

10. In 1950, the minimum wage was $0.75 per hour or $1,500 for a full-year, full-time job (50 weeks × 40 hours × $0.75). National income per adult in 1950 was $2,660.

11. See Organisation for Economic Co-operation and Development (2019) for a description of payroll taxes in France.

12. Institute on Taxation and Economic Policy (2018) provides the most comprehensive estimates of state and local tax progressivity.

13. In the national accounts, federal corporate tax receipts were $285 billion in 2017 and $158 billion in 2018 (US Bureau of Census, 2019, Table 3.2).

14. Business owners can deduct (up to the limit of 20% of income) 2.5% of their capital stock (excluding land, intangibles, and inventories) valued at its purchase price without depreciation. As long as the rate of return on their capital—the ratio of business income earned to the value of their capital stock—is below 12.5% (2.5% / 20%), the deduction is unlimited.

15. Landais, Piketty, and Saez (2011) and Bozio et al. (2018).

Chapter 2: FROM BOSTON TO RICHMOND

1. The top marginal income tax rate even reached 92% in 1952 and 1953.

2. The property tax records from colonies have been used by scholars to construct inequality statistics for antebellum America. Northern colonies had levels of inequality substantially lower than in England (Lindert, 2000).

3. Einhorn (2006).

4. Einhorn (2006).

5. This saying is attributed to John Steinbeck by Canadian author Ronald Wright (Wright, 2004) but is likely a paraphrase.

6. The Revenue Act of 1861 established the first federal income tax with a rate of 3% for incomes over $800 but it lacked an enforcement mechanism and was never applied. It was repealed and superseded by the Revenue Act of 1862.

7. In 1860 there were about 31 million inhabitants in the continental United States (US Bureau of the Census, 1949, series B2). The national income of the United States was about 5 billion current US dollars (the Historical Statistics of the United States report a total "private production income" of $4.1 billion in 1859 in series A154, which is likely to be slightly on the low end and must be adjusted upward for the small amount of government production), and hence average income per capita was around $150 in 1860, i.e., a fourth of the exemption threshold of $600. From 1860 to 1864 the price index increases by about 75% (Atack and Passell, 1994, p. 367, Table 13.5), so the average income per capita reached about $250 in 1864.

8. Huret (2014), p. 25.

9. The price index was multiplied by a factor of about forty between 1860 and 1864 in the Confederacy but increased only by about 75% in the Union. Confederacy: Lerner (1955); Union: Atack and Passell (1994), p. 367, Table 13.5.

10. Huret (2014, p. 40–41).

11. US Bureau of the Census (1975), series Y353–354.

12. Holmes (1893).

13. Sparh (1896), Pomeroy (1896), and Gallman (1969).

14. Lindert (2000).

15. Seligman (1894).

16. Huret (2014), p. 85.

17. See Mehrotra (2013) and Scheve and Stasavage (2017).

18. According to available estimates, the top 10% owned 90% of total wealth in Europe on the eve of World War I, against about 75% in the United States (Piketty, 2014; Piketty and Zucman 2015).

19. Fisher (1919).

20. Einhorn (2006), Chapter 6.

21. Plagge, Scheve, and Stasavage (2011), p. 14.

22. See Piketty, Saez, and Stancheva (2014) for presenting such a theoretical model and estimating it using modern data.

23. Kuznets (1953) pioneered the creation of top income shares using individual income tax statistics. See Piketty and Saez (2003) for modern estimates of top fiscal income shares. The statistics cited here refer to the top 0.01% income share excluding capital gains.

24. For a detailed description of how we account for untaxed income, and complete results, see Piketty, Saez, and Zucman (2018).

25. Norton-Taylor (1955).

Chapter 3: **HOW INJUSTICE TRIUMPHS**

1. Four polls carried out by ABC and Gallup in late 1986 showed that public support for the Tax Reform Act of 1986 was at best tepid with approval rates between 22% and 40% and a large fraction of the public not having a view. Approval/disapproval/don't know percentages stand at 22/15/63, 22/15/63, 38/36/26, 40/34/26 for each of the four polls (Kertcher, 2017).

2. Crystal (1992) shows that executive compensation soared after the Tax Reform Act of 1986. Hubmer, Krusell, and Smith (2016) find that the Tax Reform Act of 1986 has played a key role in the rise of US wealth concentration. See also Piketty, Saez, and Zucman (2018).

3. See, e.g., the symposium on the Tax Reform Act of 1986 in the *Journal of Economic Perspectives* in 1987 (online at https://www.aeaweb.org/issues/256). Even scholars in favor of progressive taxation such as Joseph Pechman or Richard Musgrave end up broadly supportive of the tax reform—or at least recognize its inevitability (Pechman, 1987; Musgrave, 1987).

4. On the Mont Pelerin society, Burgin (2012). On tax revolt of the rich, Martin (2015). On Goldwater, see Perlstein (2001). On the role of conservative foundations, see Mayer (2017) and Teles (2012).

5. Margaret Thatcher, interview for *Woman's Own*, September 1987.

6. See Slemrod (2007) and Slemrod and Bakija (2017), Chapter 5, for a discussion of tax evasion and tax enforcement.

7. Since 1922, when preferential tax rates on capital gains were first introduced, the maximum tax rate on long-term capital gains has always been below 40%. The maximum tax rate was 25% from 1942 to 1964, the era of quasi-confiscatory top marginal income tax rates.

8. Oblivious to this social norm, economists could not understand why firms were paying dividends and dubbed this the "dividend puzzle" (see e.g., Black, 1976).

9. Hall (1951), p. 54. Lewellen (1968), the classic study on executive compensation from the 1960s, entirely ignores company perks, perceived as negligible.

10. A long article in *Fortune* in 1955 described how top executives live (Ducan-Norton, 1955). The only mention of company perks is the following statement: "A common practice is for a company president, on his way to New York in the company plane, to fill the empty seats with family and friends. The return trip may include a detour into Canada

for some fishing." This can be compared to anecdotal evidence of company perks today, such as the gala in the palace of Versailles paid for by the automaker Renault (for over 600,000 euros) in 2014, on the sixtieth birthday of Renault's then-CEO Carlos Ghosn (officially to celebrate the fifteenth anniversary of the Renault-Nissan alliance).

11. US Joint Committee on Tax Evasion and Avoidance (1937).

12. Fack and Landais (2016), Figures 4.5 and 4.7.

13. Wang (2002), p. 1252.

14. These calculations are made by the authors using publicly available income tax data published by the Statistics of Income division of the IRS.

15. Even more, businesses losses from passive activities (where the taxpayer was just owning part of the business and did not perform any significant activity managing the business) would only be deductible against business gains from similar passive activities. See Auerbach and Slemrod (1997) for a more detailed discussion.

16. Thorndike (2003).

17. David Cay Johnston's 2003 book, *Perfectly Legal*, describes the surge in tax avoidance by the rich since the mid-1970s.

18. Ventry (2006).

19. These auditing statistics are published by the IRS annually and available online (US Treasury, Internal Revenue Service, 2018, Table 9a for year 2018 and US Treasury, Internal Revenue Service, 1975, Table 2, p. 89 for year 1975). The reporting series *Gutting the IRS* (ProPublica, 2018–2019) use these statistics to document the sharp reductions in IRS enforcement activities in recent decades.

20. It is possible to infer the wealth distribution among the full population from estate tax statistics using the estate multiplier method in which wealth at death is weighted by the inverse of the mortality rate conditional on age, gender, and wealth. See Saez and Zucman (2016) for a detailed discussion and evaluation.

21. Raub, Johnson, and Newcomb (2011).

22. See Cooper (1979) for a description of estate tax avoidance in the 1960s and 1970s.

23. Kopczuk and Saez (2004), Table 1, column 2.

24. Donald Trump provides a vivid illustration of estate tax dodging as documented by the *New York Times* (Barstow, Craig, and Buettner, 2018).

25. The academic literature on tax evasion finds small effects of marginal tax rates on tax evasion but very large effects of enforcement on evasion. See, e.g., Kleven et al. (2011).

26. This is known as the IRS National Research Program, previously called the Taxpayer Compliance Measurement Program. See, e.g., US Treasury, Internal Revenue Service (1996).

27. Guyton et al. (2019).

28. This is documented for the United States in the IRS National Research Program (see, e.g., US Treasury, Internal Revenue Service, 1996). This issue is analyzed in more detail in the context of Denmark by Kleven et al. (2011).

29. Alstadsæter, Johannesen, and Zucman (2019) and Zucman (2019).

30. International Consortium of Investigative Journalists (2016).

31. Zucman (2013, 2015) and Alstadsæter, Johannesen, and Zucman (2018).

32. Johannesen and Zucman (2014) study the weak information exchange regime prevailing before the automatic exchange of bank information. The incomplete network of cross-border information exchange treaties in place could be circumvented by tax evaders using offshore accounts in noncomplying tax havens.

Chapter 4: **WELCOME TO BERMULAND**

1. Zucman (2014).

2. Organisation for Economic Co-operation and Development (2017).

3. In the United States, employee representation plans and company unions—employee-elected bodies that consult with management on workplace issues—played an important role in corporations from World War I to the mid-1930s (see, e.g., Wartzman 2017).

4. Wright and Zucman (2018).

5. Zucman (2014).

6. https://www.sec.gov/Archives/edgar/data/1288776/000119312504143377/d424b4.htm.

7. Drucker (2010), Kleinbard (2011), pp. 707–714. Ireland has committed to phase out the scheme that enables a firm to be incorporated in Ireland but tax resident in Bermuda by 2020.

8. Bowers (2014).

9. Wright and Zucman (2018).

10. See US Treasury, Internal Revenue Service, Country-by-Country Report (Form 8975) (2018, Tax Year 2016, Table 1A).

11. Tørsløv, Wier, and Zucman (2018) and Clausing (2016, 2019).

12. See for instance Phillips et al. (2017) for estimates of how much profits

Fortune 500 companies held offshore on the eve of the Tax Cut and Jobs Act.

13. See for instance Hodge (2018).

14. Cook (2016).

15. Wearden and Elliott (2018).

16. On the notion of commercialization of state sovereignty, see Palan (2002).

17. Tørsløv, Wier, and Zucman (2018).

Chapter 5: **SPIRAL**

1. The income earned by self-employed workers is mixed in the sense that it conceptually corresponds to both a payment for their work (time spent curing patients or performing legal services) and their capital (medical devices, intangible assets such as the brand value of a law firm). Attributing 70% of self-employment income to labor is somewhat arbitrary, but because most workers are salaried individuals (not self-employed), varying this assumption is largely immaterial.

2. In public financial statements, total labor costs are not reported separately (they are lumped with other costs under "costs of goods sold"). However, we know that Apple had approximately 132,000 full-time equivalent employees in 2018, and thanks to a new rule implemented by the Securities and Exchange Commission in 2018 compelling companies to disclose the ratio of the CEO's to median employee pay, we know that the median Apple employee was paid $55,000 (excluding fringe benefits such as health insurance). We assume that the average employee was paid $95,000, to which we add $20,000 in health and retirement benefits, bringing total labor compensation to about $15 billion. We add this amount to the $70.9 in "operating income" reported in Apple's 2018 10-K report, p. 38, to form our estimate of Apple's value-added ($85 billion).

3. See Piketty and Zucman (2014) for a systematic analysis of capital versus labor shares at the macroeconomic level across countries and over time.

4. To be complete, we also assign sales taxes to labor and capital, in proportion to the share of labor and capital in national income. This ensures that the average macroeconomic tax rate is equal to the sum of the capital and labor rates, weighted by the respective shares of labor and capital in national income.

5. According to the Kaiser Family Foundation, an MRI scan cost five times more in the United States ($1,119 on average) than in a country like Australia ($215) in 2014. An appendectomy costs $15,930, the equivalent of an entire year of pre-tax income for the average American in the lower half of the income distribution (Kamal and Cox, 2018).

6. Kaiser Family Foundation Employer Health Benefits Survey, 2018; see also Kaiser/HRT Survey of employer-sponsored health benefits for statistics covering the period from 1999 to 2017. The Bureau of Labor Statistics Employee Benefits survey shows that in 2017, 58% of workers received health care benefits (US Bureau of Labor Statistics. National Compensation Survey, 2018, Table 9). There were 150.5 million full-time and part-time employees in the United States in 2017 (see US Department of Commerce, Bureau of Economic Analysis, 2019, Table 6.4D) and hence 87.3 million with health insurance at an average cost per insured worker of $12,000. The total cost of insurance premiums for employer sponsored benefits is $1.044 trillion in 2017 (see US Centers for Medicare and Medicaid Services, 2019, Table 05–06 of the National Health Expenditure Accounts). Assuming a 4% nominal growth rate in health care cost from 2017 to 2019, this is $13,000 per worker in 2019.

7. Dafny (2010).

8. Organisation for Economic Co-operation and Development (2018c, 2019c).

9. The total cost of insurance premiums for employer-sponsored benefits represented the equivalent of 6.2% of national income in 2017 ($1.044 trillion out of $16.756 trillion in national income, see US Centers for Medicare and Medicaid Services, 2019, Table 05–06 of the National Health Expenditure Accounts, US Department of Commerce, 2019, Table 1.12). As health care costs grow faster than national income, the corresponding figure for 2019 is slightly higher than 6.2%.

10. See Organisation for Economic Co-operation and Development (2018c) for macroeconomic tax rates across OECD countries.

11. Piketty, Saez, and Zucman (2018).

12. See Piketty (2014) for an analysis of the interplay between capital taxation, the rate of return to capital, and long-run wealth inequality.

13. Top wealth shares are estimated by capitalizing the capital income reported on income tax returns. See Saez and Zucman (2016) and updated data series in Piketty, Saez, and Zucman (2018).

14. These zero capital tax results are known as the Atkinson-Stiglitz theorem (Atkinson and Stiglitz, 1976) and the Chamley-Judd result (Cham-

ley, 1986, and Judd, 1985). These results, however, rely on very strong and unrealistic assumptions. In more realistic settings, capital taxes are actually desirable (see, e.g., Piketty, and Saez, 2013, and Saez and Stantcheva, 2018).

15. Piketty and Zucman (2014).

16. See Saez and Zucman (2016) for a detailed description of the evolution of bottom 90% savings and wealth over the last century.

17. Two broad-audience books provide overviews of the behavioral economics literature and summarize its implications for public policies: Thaler and Sunstein (2008) and Thaler (2015).

18. This result was first established by Madrian and Shea (2001). It has been replicated in many subsequent studies (see, e.g., Beshears et al., 2009).

19. Chetty et al. (2014).

20. This is apparent, for instance, in Denmark, which abolished its progressive wealth tax in 1997 and yet where wealth inequality did not rise, as the extra saving rate of the wealthy was more than offset by the boost in middle-class saving coming from changes in pension regulations. See Jakobsen et al. (2018).

21. See De Mooij and Ederveen (2003) for a survey of the empirical literature.

22. McCormick (2018).

23. Agostini et al. (2018).

24. In Israel, see Romanov (2006). In Sweden, see Edmark and Gordon (2013). In Norway, see Alstadsæter (2010). In Finland, see Pirttilä and Selin (2011).

Chapter 6: **HOW TO STOP THE SPIRAL**

1. International Monetary Fund (2019), Appendix 1, p. 47.

2. Tørsløv, Wier, and Zucman (2018).

3. Available estimates suggest that the compensation of transfer pricing professionals globally has been about $20 billion a year in recent years; see Tørsløv, Wier, and Zucman (2018).

4. Brennan and Buchanan (2000).

5. See, e.g., Atkinson, Piketty, and Saez (2011) and Piketty (2014).

6. Organisation for Economic Co-operation and Development (2018).

7. See online appendix available at *taxjusticenow.org.*

8. Federal corporate tax revenue fell from $285 billion in 2017 to $158 billion in 2018 (US Department of Commerce, 2019, Table 3.2). With state

corporate income taxes, the fall is 35% (from $338 billion in 2017 to $218 billion in 2017, ibid. Table 3.1).

9. The 2018 US tax reform introduced an embryo of remedial taxation with its GILTI ("global intangible low-tax income") provision. According to this rule, the foreign profits of US multinationals deemed abnormally high (that is, exceeding a 10% return on tangible capital) are taxed at a minimum tax rate of 10.5% in the United States. However this provision is insufficient for two key reasons: the 10.5% tax rate is too low, and the remedial tax does not apply on a country-by-country basis but on a consolidated basis (which means that a company that books profits in Bermuda but pays high enough taxes in Japan can avoid it). See Toder (2018) for more details.

10. Bloomberg (2017).

11. *Forbes* (2019), accessed July 4, 2019.

12. For an analysis of the US experience with the apportionment of corporate profits, see Clausing (2016b).

13. Organisation for Economic Co-operation and Development (2019b).

Chapter 7: **TAXING THE RICH**

1. Barstow, Craig, and Buettner (2018) and Buettner and Craig (2019).

2. Rawls (1971).

3. Economists rely primarily on the utilitarian principle of maximizing the sum of utilities across individuals in society. Individual utility increases with income but at a decreasing rate so that the kick in utility provided by an extra dollar of income becomes vanishingly small as income becomes very large. See Piketty and Saez (2013b).

4. Ramsey (1927).

5. Diamond (1998) and Saez (2001).

6. See Slemrod (1990) and Saez (2004) for a discussion of tax avoidance responses around the Tax Reform Act of 1986. Moffitt and Wilhelm (2000) show that the increase in the taxable income of high-income individuals around the tax reform was not accompanied by an increase in hours of work.

7. See Diamond and Saez (2011) for a summary of the theoretical analysis.

8. Saez, Slemrod, and Giertz (2012) review the empirical literature and show that large documented behavioral responses to tax changes always arise from tax avoidance. In the case of tax systems with few avoidance

opportunities such as Denmark, behavioral responses to tax changes are quantitatively small with elasticities in the range of 0.2–0.3 for top earners (Kleven and Schultz, 2014).

9. The average income above $500,000 is approximately $1,500,000 (Piketty, Saez, Zucman 2018). Hence top bracket taxpayers would pay 75% on $1,000,000 and a lower rate on their first $500,000. If we assume that the tax rate on their first $500,000 is the average macroeconomic tax rate of 30%, this gives a total tax rate on top bracket taxpayers of $(2/3) \times 75 + (1/3) \times 30 = 60\%$.

10. Kiel and Eisinger (2018) document the gutting of the IRS budget and enforcement activities since 2010.

11. See for instance Kiel and Eisinger (2019).

12. Zucman (2015).

13. In current US law, when assets are transferred to heirs, their purchase price is re-set to the price prevailing at the time of the transfer. This infamous loophole, known as stepped-up basis, means that people can avoid capital gains taxes by holding on to their assets until death. Most economists agree that this is a critical loophole to close.

14. Zucman (2014).

15. Profits accruing to nonindividual shareholders (such as pension plans and foundations) would remain subject to the corporate tax. Realized capital gains would be subject to the progressive income tax, but this does not imply that these capital gains would be taxed twice, for the following reason. In the integrated system that we describe, retained earnings would be considered as new investment from shareholders and hence factored in the shareholder stock basis (as for S corporations in the United States today). As a result, capital gains would not reflect retained earnings but would only reflect pure asset price appreciation.

16. We assume that the elasticity of income with respect to one minus the marginal tax rate is 0.25 for the top 1%. Under the current system, individuals in the top 1% pay an average tax rate of 30% and face a marginal tax rate of 35% on average. Shifting to a marginal tax rate of 75% would reduce top 1% pre-tax incomes by a factor of $((1 - 0.75) / (1 - 0.35))^{0.25}$ = 79%. The top 1% income share would fall to $20\% \times 79\% = 15.8\%$.

17. We discuss in more detail prospects for progressive wealth taxation in the United States in Saez and Zucman (2019b).

18. In the 1950s–1970s, wealth concentration was at a historically low level in America. Progressive wealth tax proposals usually follow from the empirical analysis of growing wealth concentration. Following his

research on the rise of wealth inequality in America in the 1980s (Wolff, 1995), Wolff (1996) proposed a progressive wealth tax (albeit with modest rates). More recently, Piketty (2014) proposes a global progressive wealth tax with top rates of up to 5%–10% in response to the rise of global wealth concentration. Piketty (2019) suggests top wealth tax rates up to 90% on multibillionaires to fund a capital endowment for each young adult.

19. Rosenthal and Austin (2016).

20. Meyer and Hume (2015).

21. For smaller businesses (like mom-and-pop companies with a single owner), the simplest way to proceed is to follow the best international practices. Switzerland has successfully taxed equity in small, single-owner private businesses by using formulas based on the book value of business assets and multiples of profits. In the United States, the IRS already collects data about the assets and profits of private businesses for business and corporate income tax purposes, so it would be straightforward to apply similar formulas.

Chapter 8: BEYOND LAFFER

1. Commentators often convert brackets using price inflation adjustment only, without factoring in economic growth. This exaggerates the tax burdens of the distant past as real incomes were much lower then.

2. See US Treasury Department, Internal Revenue Service (1962), p. 32.

3. Madison (1792).

4. Madison (1795).

5. Piketty, Saez, and Stantcheva (2014) develop a model of taxation along these lines. They find that if high top tax rates reduce rent extraction by top earners, then confiscatory top tax rates that go beyond the Laffer rate are desirable. Using international evidence on CEO pay, they show that indeed, high top tax rates play an important role in moderating top executive compensation.

6. Piketty, Saez, and Zucman (2018) present US distributional national accounts and Alvaredo et al. (2016) present the general methodology. The US census bureau and the Organisation for Economic Co-operation and Development have also developed initiatives in this direction for the United States and European countries (Fixler and Johnson 2014; Zwijnenburg et al. 2017).

7. Garbinti, Goupille-Lebret, and Piketty (2018).

8. College Board (2019).

9. Feldstein (2017).

10. Gates (2013).

11. Aeppel (2015).

12. Mouton (2018).

13. Chetty et al. (2017).

14. Organisation for Economic Co-operation and Development (2018b).

15. See OECD Health Statistics (Organisation for Economic Co-operation and Development 2019c). Case and Deaton (2015) document these mortality trends and show that the increase in mortality in the US is concentrated among whites in mid-life without college degrees. They show that this increase in mortality can be partly explained by "deaths of despair": poor economic prospects leading to drug or alcohol abuse and suicides.

16. Saez and Zucman (2019b) provide all the details on the computations of the wealth tax statistics discussed here.

Chapter 9: **A WORLD OF POSSIBILITY**

1. Kuziemko et al. (2015) show that in the United States, public support for redistribution in a high inequality context is much weaker when trust in government is low.

2. A large body of empirical work shows that public health insurance saves lives (although a precise quantification is difficult); see, e.g., Card, Dobkin, and Maestas (2009).

3. See OECD Health Statistics (Organisation for Economic Co-operation and Development 2019c).

4. Singapore is often cited as an example of an advanced economy with low taxes. The tax to GDP ratio in Singapore was only 13.5% in 2016. But this is misleading as Singapore imposes very large mandatory payroll contributions on workers' earnings for health and retirement benefits and education expenses, called the Central Provident Fund (www .cpf.gov.sg), which are essentially equivalent to payroll taxes. The rates are very high, with a combined employee and employer contribution of 37% of earnings for nonelderly workers (see Organisation for Economic Co-operation and Development, 2019d, Global Tax Statistics Database).

5. See OECD statistics for the level of public and private education funding

relative to GDP in OECD countries (Organisation for Economic Co-operation and Development, Revenue Statistics, 2019e).

6. See Goldin, Katz, and Kuziemko (2006) on the college graduation rate by gender and cohort. See Blau, Ferber, and Winkler (2014) for an analysis of the gender gap, and Kleven et al. (2019) for estimates of "child penalties" across countries.

7. See Gallup surveys (Witters, 2019).

8. This is the case of France for example with its Contribution Sociale Généralisée (see Landais, Piketty, and Saez, 2011).

9. See Ebrill, Keen, and Perry (2001) for a detailed history of the VAT.

10. Turnover taxes are taxes on gross sales that businesses make regardless of whether the sale is made to final consumers or another business. Some US states still use such turnover taxes (see Watson, 2019).

11. Martin Luther King, Jr. used the phrase "justice too long delayed is justice denied" in his "Letter from Birmingham Jail," smuggled out of jail in 1963.

12. Bakija, Cole, and Heim (2012).

13. Organisation for Economic Co-operation and Development, Revenue Statistics (2018c), Table 3.14.

14. Hall and Rabushka (1985) proposed the "flat tax." Viard and Carroll (2012) present a description of various consumption tax proposals. They lucidly point out that flat tax proposals disguised as income taxes are challenging to sell to the public because they would be "income taxes" exempting interest income, dividend income, and realized capital gains—that is, exempting the forms of income which are highly concentrated among the rich.

15. See US Department of Commerce, Bureau of Economic Analysis, National Income and Product Accounts of the United States (2019), Tables 7–14, 7–16, and 7–18. Misreported income in 2015 was $86.2 billion for wage earnings, $672 billion for unincorporated business income, and $367 billion for corporate profits. The total is $1,125 billion or 7.2% of national income in 2015. Complete details are provided in Saez and Zucman (2019c).

16. Chetty, Friedman et al. (2017) provide an analysis of college attendance by family income. They show that the likelihood of college attendance by age twenty-two grows linearly by percentile of parental income from 32% at the bottom to 95% at the top (Appendix, Figure I). Richer kids also attend better schools than poor kids.

Conclusion: **TAX JUSTICE NOW**

1. Tax simulators exist within government agencies, including the Congressional Budget Office, the US Treasury, and the Joint Committee on Taxation, as well as within think tanks such as the Tax Policy Center. These tools capture minute details of the tax code, making it possible to precisely simulate federal legislative changes, but they are not accessible to the public. Our tool is accessible to all and focused on the interplay between taxes and inequality. Combining these two approaches would be valuable and we hope to contribute to this task in the future.

BIBLIOGRAPHY

Aeppel, Timothy. "Silicon Valley Doesn't Believe U.S. Productivity Is Down." *Wall Street Journal*, July 16, 2015.

Agostini, Claudio A., Eduardo Engel, Andrea Repetto, and Damián Vergara. "Using Small Businesses for Individual Tax Planning: Evidence from Special Tax Regimes in Chile." *International Tax and Public Finance* 25, no. 6 (2018): 1449–1489.

Alstadsæter, Annette. "Small Corporations Income Shifting Through Choice of Ownership Structure—A Norwegian Case." *Finnish Economic Papers* 23, no. 2 (2010): 73–87.

Alstadsæter, Annette, Niels Johannesen, and Gabriel Zucman. "Who Owns the Wealth in Tax Havens? Macro Evidence and Implications for Global Inequality." *Journal of Public Economics* 162 (2018): 89–100.

———. "Tax Evasion and Inequality." *American Economic Review* 109, no. 6 (2019): 2073–2103.

Alvaredo, Facundo, Anthony Atkinson, Lucas Chancel, Thomas Piketty, Emmanuel Saez, and Gabriel Zucman. "Distributional National Accounts (DINA) Guidelines: Concepts and Methods Used in the World Wealth and Income Database." WID Working Paper 2016/1, 2016.

Alvaredo, Facundo, Lucas Chancel, Thomas Piketty, Emmanuel Saez, and Gabriel Zucman. *World Inequality Report 2018*. Cambridge, MA: Harvard University Press, 2018.

Atack, Jeremy, and Peter Passell. *A New Economic View of American History from Colonial Times to 1940*. 2nd ed. New York: W. W. Norton, 1994.

Atkinson, Anthony, Thomas Piketty, and Emmanuel Saez. "Top Incomes in the Long Run of History." *Journal of Economic Literature* 49, no. 1 (2011): 3–71.

Atkinson, Anthony, and Joseph E. Stiglitz. "The Design of Tax Structure: Direct Versus Indirect Taxation." *Journal of Public Economics* 6, no. 1–2 (1976): 55–75.

Auerbach, Alan J., and Joel Slemrod. "The Economic Effects of the Tax Reform Act of 1986." *Journal of Economic Literature* 35, no. 2 (1997): 589–632.

Bakija, Jon, Adam Cole, and Bradley T. Heim. "Jobs and Income Growth of Top Earners and the Causes of Changing Income Inequality: Evidence from US Tax Return Data." Williams College Department of Economics Working Paper 2010–22, revised January 2012.

Barbier, Edward B. "Account for Depreciation of Natural capital." *Nature* 515 (2014): 32–33.

Barstow, David, Susanne Craig, and Russ Buettner. "Trump Engaged in Suspect Tax Schemes as He Reaped Riches From His Father." *New York Times*, October 2, 2018.

Beshears, John, James J. Choi, David Laibson, and Brigitte C. Madrian. "The Importance of Default Options for Retirement Saving Outcomes: Evidence from the United States." In Jeffrey Brown, Jeffrey Liebman, and David Wise, eds., *Social Security Policy in a Changing Environment*, 167–195. Chicago: University of Chicago Press, 2009.

Black, Fischer. "The Dividend Puzzle." *Journal of Portfolio Management* 2, no. 2 (1976): 5–8.

Blau, Francine, Marianne A. Ferber, and Anne E. Winkler. *The Economics of Women, Men, and Work*. 7th ed., Upper Saddle River, NJ: Prentice Hall, 2014.

Bloomberg. "Tracking Tax Runaways," Bloomberg LP, March 1, 2017. Available at www.bloomberg.com/graphics/tax-inversion-tracker/.

Bowers, Simon. "Luxembourg Tax Files: How Juncker's Duchy Accommodated Skype and the Koch Empire." *The Guardian*, December 9, 2014.

Bozio, Antoine, Bertrand Garbinti, Jonathan Goupille-Lebret, Malka Guillot, and Thomas Piketty. "Inequality and Redistribution in France 1990–2018: Evidence from Post-tax Distributional National Accounts." WID. world Working Paper no. 2018/10, 2018.

Brennan, Geoffrey, and James M. Buchanan. *Collected Works: Analytical Foundations of a Fiscal Constitution. The Power to Tax*. Indianapolis: Liberty Fund, 2000.

Buettner, Russ, and Susanne Craig. "Decade in the Red: Trump Tax Figures Show Over $1 Billion in Business Losses." *New York Times*, May 8, 2019.

Burgin, Angus. *The Great Persuasion: Reinventing Free Markets since the Depression*. Cambridge, MA: Harvard University Press, 2012.

Card, David, Carlos Dobkin, and Nicole Maestas. "Does Medicare Save Lives?" *Quarterly Journal of Economics* 124, no. 2 (2009): 597–636.

Case, Anne, and Angus Deaton. "Rising Morbidity and Mortality in Midlife among White Non-Hispanic Americans in the 21st Century." *Proceedings of the National Academy of Sciences* 112, no. 49 (2015): 15078–15083.

Chamley, Christopher. "Optimal Taxation of Capital Income in General Equilibrium with Infinite Lives." *Econometrica* 54, no. 3 (1986): 607–622.

Chetty, Raj, John N. Friedman, Søren Leth-Petersen, Torben Heien Nielsen, and Tore Olsen. "Active vs. Passive Decisions and Crowd-out in Retirement Savings Accounts: Evidence from Denmark." *Quarterly Journal of Economics* 129, no. 3: (2014): 1141–1219.

Chetty, Raj, John Friedman, Emmanuel Saez, Nicholas Turner, and Danny Yagan. "Mobility Report Cards: The Role of Colleges in Intergenerational Mobility," National Bureau of Economic Research Working Paper no. 23618, July 2017.

Chetty, Raj, David Grusky, Maximilian Hell, Nathaniel Hendren, Robert Manduca, and Jimmy Narang. "The Fading American Dream: Trends in Absolute Income Mobility since 1940." *Science* 356, no. 6336 (2017): 398–406.

Clausing, Kimberly A. "The Effect of Profit Shifting on the Corporate Tax Base in the United States and Beyond." *National Tax Journal* 69, no. 4 (2016): 905–934.

———. "The U.S. State Experience under Formulary Apportionment: Are There Lessons for International Tax Reform?" *National Tax Journal*, 62, no. 2 (2016b): 353–386.

———. *Open: The Progressive Case for Free-Trade, Immigration, and Global Capital*. Cambridge, MA: Harvard University Press, 2019.

College Board. *Trends in Higher Education, Tuition and Fees and Room and Board over Time*, 2019.

Cook, Tim. "A Message to the Apple Community in Europe." Apple Inc., August 30, 2016.

Cooper, George. *A Voluntary Tax? New Perspectives on Sophisticated Tax Avoidance*. Studies of Government Finance. Washington, DC: Brookings Institution, 1979.

Crystal, Graef S. *In Search of Excess: The Overcompensation of American Executives*. New York: W. W. Norton, 1992.

Dafny, Leemore. "Are Health Insurance Markets Competitive?" *American Economic Review* 100, no. 4 (2010): 1399–1431.

De Mooij, Ruud A., and Sjef Ederveen. "Taxation and Foreign Direct Investment: A Synthesis of Empirical Research." *International Tax and Public Finance* 10, no. 6 (2003): 673–693.

Diamond, Peter A. "Optimal Income Taxation: An Example with a U-shaped Pattern of Optimal Marginal Tax Rates." *American Economic Review* 88, no. 1 (1998): 83–95.

———, and Emmanuel Saez. "The Case for a Progressive Tax: From Basic Research to Policy Recommendations." *Journal of Economic Perspectives* 25, no. 4 (2011): 165–190.

Drucker, Jesse. "Google 2.4% Rate Shows How $60 Billion Is Lost to Tax Loopholes." *Bloomberg*, October 21, 2010.

Ebrill, Liam, Michael Keen, and Victoria Perry. *The Modern VAT*. Washington, DC: International Monetary Fund, 2001.

Edmark, Karin, and Roger H. Gordon. "The Choice of Organizational Form by Closely-Held Firms in Sweden: Tax Versus Non-Tax Determinants." *Industrial and Corporate Change* 22, no. 1 (2013): 219–243.

Einhorn, Robin. *American Taxation, American Slavery*. Chicago: University of Chicago Press, 2006.

Fack, Gabrielle, and Camille Landais, eds. *Charitable Giving and Tax Policy: A Historical and Comparative Perspective*. Oxford: Oxford University Press, 2016.

Feldstein, Martin. "Underestimating the Real Growth of GDP, Personal Income, and Productivity." *Journal of Economic Perspectives* 31, no. 2 (2017): 145–164.

Fisher, Irving. "Economists in Public Service: Annual Address of the President." *American Economic Review* 9, no. 1 (1919): 5–21.

Fixler, Dennis, and David S. Johnson. "Accounting for the Distribution of Income in the U.S. National Accounts." In D. Jorgenson, J. S. Landefeld, and P. Schreyer, eds., *Measuring Economic Stability and Progress*. Chicago: University of Chicago Press, 2014. 213–244.

Forbes. "GLOBAL 2000: The World's Largest Public Companies." May 15, 2019. Available at www.forbes.com/global2000.

Gallman, Robert E. "Trends in the Size Distribution of Wealth in the Nineteenth Century: Some Speculation." *Six Papers on the Size Distribution of Wealth and Income*. 1–30. New York: National Bureau of Economic Research, 1969.

Garbinti, Bertrand, Jonathan Goupille-Lebret, and Thomas Piketty. "Income inequality in France, 1900–2014: Evidence from Distributional National Accounts (DINA)." *Journal of Public Economics* 162 (2018): 63–77.

Gates, Bill. "GDP Is a Terrible Way to Measure a Country's Economy." *Slate*, May 9, 2013.

Goldin, Claudia, Lawrence F. Katz, and Ilyana Kuziemko. "The Homecoming of American College Women: The Reversal of the College Gender Gap." *Journal of Economic Perspectives* 20, no. 4 (2006): 133–156.

Guyton, John, Patrick Langetieg, Daniel Reck, Max Risch, and Gabriel Zucman. "Tax Evasion by the Wealthy: Measurement and Implications," UC Berkeley Working Paper 2019.

Hall, Challis A. *Effects of Taxation on Executive Compensation and Retirement Plans*. Vol. 3. Division of Research, Graduate School of Business Administration, Cambridge MA: Harvard University Press, 1951.

Hall, Robert, and Alvin Rabushka. *The Flat Tax*. Stanford, CA: Hoover Institution Press, 1985.

Hodge, Scott A. "'The Missing Profits of Nations' Mistakes Tax Competition for Tax Evasion." Tax Foundation, Fiscal Fact no. 607, 2018.

Holmes, George K. "The Concentration of Wealth." *Political Science Quarterly* 8, no. 4 (1893).

Hubmer, Joachim, Per Krusell, and Anthony A. Smith, Jr. "The Historical Evolution of the Wealth Distribution: A Quantitative-Theoretic Investigation." National Bureau of Economic Research Working Paper No. 23011, 2016.

Huret, Romain D. *American Tax Resisters*. Cambridge, MA: Harvard University Press, 2014.

Institute on Taxation and Economic Policy. *Who Pays: A Distributional Analysis of the Tax Systems in All 50 States*. 6th ed., Washington DC: ITEP, 2018. Available at https://itep.org/whopays/.

International Consortium of Investigative Journalists. The Panama Papers: Exposing the Rogue Offshore Finance Industry. Available at www.icij.org/investigations/panama-papers/.

International Monetary Fund. "Corporate Taxation in the Global Economy," IMF Policy Paper no. 19/007, March 2019.

Jakobsen, Katrine, Kristian Jakobsen, Henrik Kleven, and Gabriel Zucman. "Wealth Taxation and Wealth Accumulation: Theory and Evidence from Denmark." National Bureau of Economic Research Working Paper no. 24371, 2018, forthcoming in *Quarterly Journal of Economics*.

Johannesen, Niels, and Gabriel Zucman. "The End of Bank Secrecy? An

Evaluation of the G20 Tax Haven Crackdown." *American Economic Journal: Economic Policy* 6, no. 1 (2014): 65–91.

Johnston, David Cay. *Perfectly Legal: The Covert Campaign to Rig Our Tax System to Benefit the Super Rich—and Cheat Everybody Else.* New York: Portfolio Books, 2003.

Judd, Kenneth L. "Redistributive Taxation in a Simple Perfect Foresight Model." *Journal of Public Economics* 28, no. 1 (1985): 59–83.

Kaiser Family Foundation. *2018 Employer Health Benefits Survey.* 2018. Available at www.kff.org/health-costs/report/2018-employer-health-benefits -survey/.

Kamal, Rabah, and Cynthia Cox. "How Do Healthcare Prices and Use in the U.S. Compare to Other Countries?" Peterson-Kaiser Health System Tracker, May 8, 2018.

Kertscher, Thomas. "Paul Ryan Claims 1986 Tax Reform, Like the Current One, Had Low Public Support Just Before Passage." *Politifact*, December 18, 2017.

Kiel, Paul, and Jesse Eisinger. "How the IRS Was Gutted." *ProPublica*, December 11, 2018.

———. "The IRS Tried to Take on the Ultrawealthy. It Didn't Go Well." *ProPublica*, April 5, 2019.

Kleinbard, Edward D. "Stateless Income." *Florida Tax Review* 11, no. 9 (2011): 699–774.

Kleven, Henrik, Camille Landais, Johanna Posch, Andreas Steinhauer, and Josef Zweimüller. "Child Penalties Across Countries: Evidence and Explanations." *AEA Papers and Proceedings* 109 (2019): 122–126.

———, Martin Knudsen, Claus Kreiner, Soren Pedersen, and Emmanuel Saez. "Unwilling or Unable to Cheat? Evidence from a Tax Audit Experiment in Denmark." *Econometrica* 79 no. 3 (2011): 651–692.

———, and Esben Anton Schultz. "Estimating Taxable Income Responses using Danish Tax Reforms." *American Economic Journal: Economic Policy* 6, no. 4 (2014): 271–301.

Kopczuk, Wojciech, and Emmanuel Saez. "Top Wealth Shares in the United States, 1916–2000: Evidence from Estate Tax Returns." *National Tax Journal* 57, no. 2, part 2 (2004): 445–487.

Kuziemko, Ilyana, Michael I. Norton, Emmanuel Saez, and Stefanie Stantcheva. "How Elastic are Preferences for Redistribution? Evidence from Randomized Survey Experiments." *American Economic Review* 105, no. 4 (2015): 1478–1508.

Kuznets, Simon. *Shares of Upper Income Groups in Income and Savings.* New York: National Bureau of Economic Research, 1953.

Landais, Camille, Thomas Piketty, and Emmanuel Saez. *Pour une Révolution Fiscale—Un Impôt sur le Revenu pour le 21e Siècle.* Le Seuil: République des Idées, 2011.

Lerner, Eugene. "Money, Prices and Wages in the Confederacy, 1861–65." *Journal of Political Economy* 63, no. 1, (1955): 20–40.

Lewellen, Wilbur G. *Executive Compensation in Large Industrial Corporations.* New York: National Bureau of Economic Research, 1968.

Lindert, Peter H. "Three Centuries of Inequality in Britain and America." In Anthony B. Atkinson and Francois Bourguignon, eds., *Handbook of Income Distribution*, Volume 1, 167–216. Amsterdam: Elsevier Science, North-Holland, 2000.

Madison, James. "Parties." *National Gazette*, January 23, 1792.

———, "Political Observations." April 20, 1795, in *Letters and Other Writings of James Madison*, Volume 4, Philadelphia: J.B. Lippincott & Co., 1865.

Madrian, Brigitte C., and Dennis F. Shea. "The Power of Suggestion: Inertia in 401 (k) Participation and Savings Behavior." *Quarterly Journal of Economics* 116 no. 4 (2001): 1149–1187.

Martin, Isaac William. *Rich People's Movements: Grassroots Campaigns to Untax the One Percent.* Oxford: Oxford University Press, 2015.

Mayer, Jane. *Dark Money: The Hidden History of the Billionaires Behind the Rise of the Radical Right.* New York: Anchor Books, 2017.

McCormick, John. "Koch-Backed Groups Are Selling Trump's Tax Cuts Door-to-Door Ahead of the Midterms." *Bloomberg Businessweek*, May 2, 2018.

Mehrotra, Ajay K. *Making the Modern American Fiscal State: Law, Politics, and the Rise of Progressive Taxation, 1877–1929.* Cambridge: Cambridge University Press, 2013.

Meyer, Gregory, and Neil Hume. "Cargill Guards Private Life in 150th Year." *Financial Times*, April 19, 2015.

Moffitt, Robert, and Mark Wilhelm. "Taxation and the Labor Supply Decisions of the Affluent." In Joel Slemrod, ed., *Does Atlas Shrug? The Economic Consequences of Taxing the Rich.* New York: Russell Sage Foundation, 2000. 193–234.

Mouton, Brent R. "The Measurement of Output, Prices, and Productivity—What's Changed Since the Boskin Commission?" *Brookings Institution*, July 25, 2018.

Musgrave, Richard A. "Short of Euphoria." *Journal of Economic Perspectives* 1, no. 1 (1987): 59–71.

Norton-Taylor, Duncan. "How Top Executives Live." *Fortune*, July 1955. Available at online at http://fortune.com/2012/05/06/how-top-executives -live-fortune-1955/.

Okner, Benjamin A., and Joseph A. Pechman. "Who Paid the Taxes in 1966?" *American Economic Review* 64, no. 2 (1974): 168–174.

Organisation for Economic Co-operation and Development (OECD). "Board-Level Employee Representation." *Collective Bargaining.* Paris: OECD Press, 2017.

———. Automatic Exchange Portal. Country-Specific Information on Country-by-Country Reporting Implementation. Paris: OECD Press, 2018. Available at www.oecd.org/tax/automatic-exchange/country-specific -information-on-country-by-country-reporting-implementation.htm.

———. *International Migration Outlook 2018*. Paris: OECD Press, 2018b.

———. *Revenue Statistics 2018*. Paris: OECD Press, 2018c.

———. *Taxing Wages 2019*. Paris: OECD Press, 2019.

———. Base erosion and profit shifting. Country-by-Country exchange relationships. Paris: OECD Press, 2019b. Available at www.oecd.org/tax/ beps/country-by-country-exchange-relationships.htm.

———. Health Statistics. Paris: OECD Press, 2019c. Available at www.oecd .org/els/health-systems/health-data.htm.

———. Global Tax Statistics Database. Paris: OECD Press, 2019d. Available at www.oecd.org/tax/tax-policy/global-revenue-statistics-database .htm.

———. Education Spending. Paris: OECD Press, 2019e. Available at https:// data.oecd.org/eduresource/education-spending.htm.

Palan, Ronen. "Tax Havens and the Commercialization of State Sovereignty." *International Organization* 56, no. 1 (2002): 151–176.

Pechman, Joseph A. "Tax Reform: Theory and Practice." *Journal of Economic Perspectives* 1, no. 1 (1987): 11–28.

Perlstein, Rick. *Before the Storm: Barry Goldwater and the Unmaking of the American Consensus*. New York: Hill and Wang, 2001.

Phillips, Richard, Matt Gardner, Alexandria Robins, and Michelle Surka. *Offshore Shell Games 2017: The Use of Offshore Tax Havens by Fortune 500 Companies*. Institute on Taxation and Economic Policy and U.S. PIRG Education Fund, 2017.

Piketty, Thomas. *Capital in the 21st Century*. Cambridge, MA: Harvard University Press, 2014.

———. *Capital et Idéologie*. Paris: Le Seuil, 2019.

———, and Emmanuel Saez. "Income Inequality in the United States, 1913–1998." *Quarterly Journal of Economics* 118, no. 1, (2003): 1–39.

———, and Emmanuel Saez. "A Theory of Optimal Inheritance Taxation." *Econometrica* 81, no. 5 (2013): 1851–1886.

———, and Emmanuel Saez. "Optimal Labor Income Taxation." In Alan Auerbach, Raj Chetty, Martin Feldstein, and Emmanuel Saez, eds., *Handbook of Public Economics*, Volume 5, 391–474. Amsterdam: Elsevier–North Holland, 2013.

———, Emmanuel Saez, and Stefanie Stantcheva. "Optimal Taxation of Top Labor Incomes: A Tale of Three Elasticities." *American Economic Journal: Economic Policy* 6, no. 1 (2014): 230–271.

———, Emmanuel Saez, and Gabriel Zucman. "Distributional National Accounts: Methods and Estimates for the United States." *Quarterly Journal of Economics* 133, no. 1 (2018): 553–609.

———, and Gabriel Zucman. "Capital Is Back: Wealth-Income Ratios in Rich Countries 1700–2010." *Quarterly Journal of Economics* 129, no. 3 (2014): 1255–1310.

———, and Gabriel Zucman. "Wealth and Inheritance in the Long Run," In Anthony B. Atkinson and Francois Bourguignon, eds., *Handbook of Income Distribution*, Volume 2, 1303–1368. Amsterdam: Elsevier Science, North Holland, 2015.

Pirttilä, Jukka, and Håkan Selin. "Income Shifting within a Dual Income Tax System: Evidence from the Finnish Tax Reform of 1993." *Scandinavian Journal of Economics* 113, no. 1 (2011): 120–144.

Plagge, Arnd, Kenneth Scheve, and David Stasavage. "Comparative Inheritance Taxation Database." Yale University, ISPS Data Archive, 2011.

Pomeroy, Eltweed. "The Concentration of Wealth." *Arena* 16 (1896): 82.

ProPublica, *Gutting the IRS: Who Wins When a Crucial Agency Is Defunded*. ProPublica series, 2018–2019.

Ramsey, Frank P. "A Contribution to the Theory of Taxation." *Economic Journal* 37, no. 145 (1927): 47–61.

Raub, Brian, Barry Johnson, and Joseph Newcomb. "A Comparison of Wealth Estimates for America's Wealthiest Decedents Using Tax Data and Data from the Forbes 400." *National Tax Association Proceedings*, 103rd Annual Conference on Taxation (2010): 128–135.

Rawls, John. *A Theory of Justice*. Cambridge, MA: Harvard University Press, 1971.

Reeves, Richard. *Dream Hoarders—How the American Upper Middle*

Class Is Leaving Everyone Else in the Dust, Why That Is a Problem, and What to Do About It. Washington, DC: Brookings Institution Press, 2017.

Romanov, Dmitri. "The Corporation as a Tax Shelter: Evidence from Recent Israeli Tax Changes." *Journal of Public Economics* 90, no. 10–11 (2006): 1939–1954.

Rosenthal, Steven M. and Lydia S. Austin. "The Dwindling Taxable Share of U.S. Corporate Stock." *Tax Notes*, May 16, 2016.

Saez, Emmanuel. "Using Elasticities to Derive Optimal Income Tax Rates." *Review of Economic Studies* 68, no. 1 (2001): 205–229.

———. "Reported Incomes and Marginal Income Tax Rates, 1960–2000: Evidence and Policy Implications." In James Poterba, ed., *Tax Policy and the Economy*, Volume 18. Cambridge, MA: MIT Press, 2004.

———, Joel Slemrod, and Seth Giertz. "The Elasticity of Taxable Income with Respect to Marginal Tax Rates: A Critical Review." *Journal of Economic Literature* 50, no. 1 (2012): 3–50.

———, and Stefanie Stantcheva. "A Simpler Theory of Optimal Capital Taxation." *Journal of Public Economics* 162 (2018): 120–142.

———, and Gabriel Zucman. "Wealth Inequality in the United States since 1913: Evidence from Capitalized Income Tax Data." *Quarterly Journal of Economics* 131, no. 2 (2016): 519–578.

———, and Gabriel Zucman. "Clarifying Distributional Tax Incidence: Who Pays Current Taxes vs. Tax Reform Analysis." UC Berkeley Working Paper 2019.

———, and Gabriel Zucman. "Progressive Wealth Taxation." *Brookings Papers on Economic Activity*, 2019b.

———, and Gabriel Zucman. "A National Income Tax." UC Berkeley Working Paper 2019c.

Scheve, Kenneth, and David Stasavage. *Taxing the Rich: A History of Fiscal Fairness in the United States and Europe.* Princeton, NJ: Princeton University Press, 2017.

Seligman, Edwin. "The Income Tax." *Political Science Quarterly* 9, no. 4 (1894): 610–648.

Slemrod, Joel. *Do Taxes Matter? The Impact of the Tax Reform Act of 1986.* Cambridge, MA: MIT Press 1990.

———. "Cheating Ourselves: The Economics of Tax Evasion." *Journal of Economic Perspectives* 21, no. 1 (2007): 25–48.

———, and Jon Bakija. *Taxing Ourselves: A Citizen's Guide to the Debate Over Taxes.* 5th ed. Cambridge, MA: MIT Press, 2017.

Spahr, Charles. *An Essay on the Present Distribution of Wealth in the United States.* New York: TY Crowell, 1896.

Teles, Steven. *The Rise of the Conservative Legal Movement: The Battle for Control of the Law.* Princeton, NJ: Princeton University Press, 2012.

Thaler, Richard H. *Misbehaving: The Making of Behavioral Economics.* New York: W. W. Norton, 2015.

———, and Cass R. Sunstein. *Nudge: Improving Decisions about Health, Wealth, and Happiness.* New Haven, CT: Yale University Press, 2008.

Thorndike, Joseph J. "Historical Perspective: Pecora Hearings Spark Tax Morality, Tax Reform Debate." *Tax Notes* 101, November 10, 2003.

Toder, Eric. "Explaining the TCJA's International Reforms." Tax Policy Center, Urban Institute and Brookings Institution, February 2, 2018.

Tørsløv, Thomas, Ludvig Wier, and Gabriel Zucman. "The Missing Profits of Nations." National Bureau of Economic Research Working Paper no. 24701, 2018.

US Bureau of the Census. *Historical Statistics of the United States, 1789–1945.* US Department of Commerce, Bureau of the Census, 1949.

———. *Historical Statistics of the United States, Colonial Times to 1970.* US Department of Commerce, Bureau of the Census, 1975.

US Bureau of Labor Statistics. National Compensation Survey. Healthcare Benefits: Access, Participation, and Take-up Rates. 2018. Available at www.bls.gov/ncs/ebs/benefits/2017/ownership/civilian/table09a.htm.

US Centers for Disease Control and Prevention. Life Expectancy. 2019. Available at www.cdc.gov/nchs/fastats/life-expectancy.htm.

US Centers for Medicare and Medicaid Services. *National Health Expenditure Accounts.* Washington, DC: Government Printing Office, 2019.

US Congressional Budget Office. "The Distribution of Household Income, 2015." Washington, DC: Government Printing Office, 2018.

US Department of Commerce. Bureau of Economic Analysis. *National Income and Product Accounts of the United States, 1929–2018.* Washington, DC: Government Printing Office, 2019.

US Joint Committee on Tax Evasion and Avoidance. *Hearings before the Joint Committee on Tax Evasion and Avoidance,* 75th Congress, First Session, June 1937.

US Treasury Department, Internal Revenue Service. *Statistics of Income: Individual Income Tax Returns 1960.* Washington, DC: Government Printing Office, 1962. Available at www.irs.gov/pub/irs-soi/60inar.pdf.

———. *Annual Report of the Commissioner of Internal Revenue 1975.* Washington, DC: Government Printing Office, 1975.

———. "Federal Tax Compliance Research: Individual Income Tax Gap Estimates for 1985, 1988, and 1992." IRS Publication 1415 (Rev. 4–96), Washington, DC: Government Printing Office, 1996.

———. *Country-by-Country Report: Tax Jurisdiction Information*. Washington, DC: Government Printing Office, 2018.

———. *Foreign Portfolio Holdings of U.S. Securities*. Washington, DC: Government Printing Office, 2018.

———. *Internal Revenue Service Databook 2018*. Washington, DC: Government Printing Office, 2019.

Ventry, Dennis J. "Tax Shelter Opinions Threatened the Tax System in the 1970s." *Tax Notes* 111, May 22, (2006): 947.

Viard, Alan, and Robert Carroll. *Progressive Consumption Taxation: The X Tax Revisited*. Washington, DC: AEI Press, 2012.

Wang, Ben. "Supplying the Tax Shelter Industry: Contingent Fee Compensation for Accountants Spurs Production." *Southern California Law Review* 76 (2002): 1237–1273.

Wartzman, Rick. *The End of Loyalty: The Rise and Fall of Good Jobs in America*. New York: PublicAffairs, 2017.

Watson, Garrett. "Resisting the Allure of Gross Receipts Taxes: An Assessment of Their Costs and Consequences." Tax Foundation, Fiscal Fact no. 634, February 2019.

Wearden, Graeme, and Larry Elliott. "Google CEO: We're Happy to Pay More Tax." *The Guardian*, January 24, 2018.

Witters, Dan. "U.S. Uninsured Rate Rises to Four-Year High." *Gallup*, January 23, 2019.

Wolff, Edward. *Top Heavy: A Study of Increasing Inequality of Wealth in America*. New York: The Twentieth Century Fund Press, 1995.

———. "Time for a Wealth Tax?" *Boston Review*, February 1, 1996.

Wright, Ronald. *A Short History of Progress*. Toronto: House of Anansi, 2004.

Wright, Thomas, and Gabriel Zucman. "The Exorbitant Tax Privilege." National Bureau of Economic Research Working Paper no. 24983, 2018.

Zucman, Gabriel. "The Missing Wealth of Nations: Are Europe and the U.S. Net Debtors or Net Creditors?" *Quarterly Journal of Economics* 128, no. 3 (2013): 1321–1364.

———. "Taxing Across Borders: Tracking Personal Wealth and Corporate Profits." *Journal of Economic Perspectives* 28, no. 4 (2014): 121–148.

———. *The Hidden Wealth of Nations*. Chicago: University of Chicago Press, 2015.

————. "Global Wealth Inequality." *Annual Review of Economics* 11 (2019): 109–138.

Zwijnenburg, Jorrit, Sophie Bournot, and Federico Giovannelli. "Expert Group on Disparities within a National Accounts framework—Results from a 2015 exercise." OECD Working Paper No. 76, 2017.

LIST OF ILLUSTRATIONS